POSTCARD HISTORY SERIES

Charleston
1900–1915

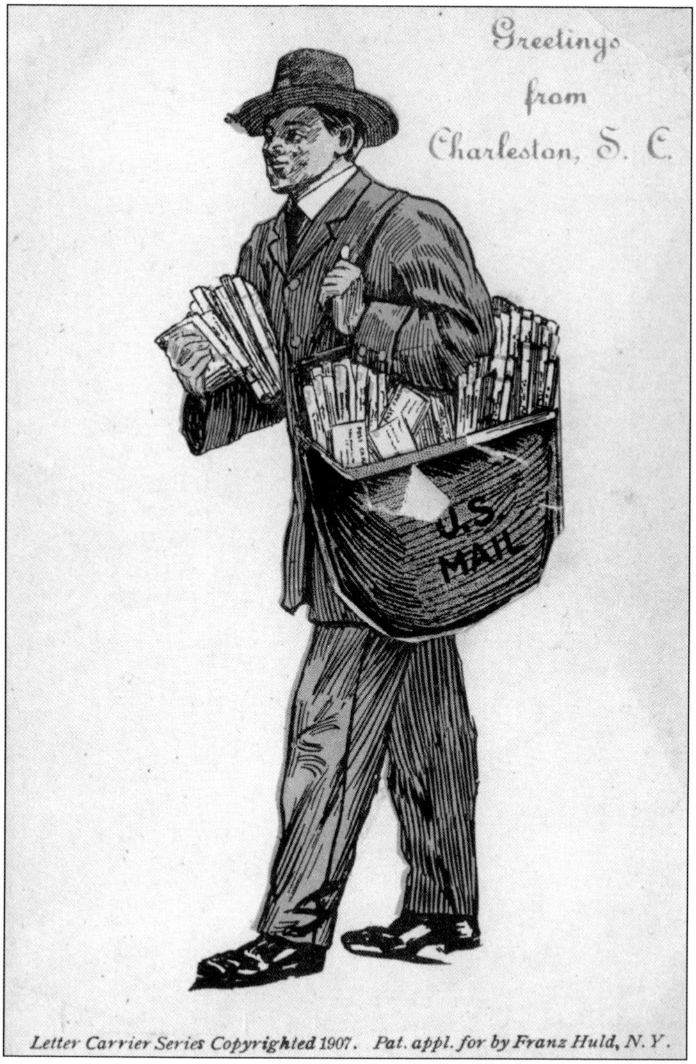

The postman is delivering postcard greetings from what many call America's most historic city. With the personal greeting comes a photograph of Charleston. (Author's collection.)

On the Front Cover: Perhaps the men, and even the ladies, are remembering that fateful April morning some 45 years earlier when Charleston's women and children joined their men on the Battery to watch as the cadets from the South Carolina Military Academy joined others around Charleston's harbor, and on Confederate general P.G.T. Beauregard's command, opened fire on Fort Sumter and began a civil war that would last four years and claim the lives of many South Carolinians, including probably some of those on the Battery that morning. Perhaps they are just some native Charlestonians or out-of-town visitors enjoying a sunny April morning. (Author's collection.)

On the Back Cover: In early Charleston, King Street ran from Beaufain Street to South Battery. Beyond that, it had various names as a road that led to the interior of the colony. As Charles Town grew beyond its walls, its streets extended outward. Even then, wagons carried and brought goods to and from Charleston's merchants. Today, King Street is still the center of downtown Charleston's shopping. (Author's collection.)

POSTCARD HISTORY SERIES

Charleston 1900–1915

Raymond K. Benton Jr.

ARCADIA PUBLISHING

ISBN 978-1-4671-1492-9

Published by Arcadia Publishing
Charleston, South Carolina

Printed in the United States of America

Library of Congress Control Number: 2015941075

For all general information contact Arcadia Publishing at:
Telephone 843-853-2070
Fax 843-853-0044
E-mail sales@arcadiapublishing.com
For customer service and orders:
Toll-Free 1-888-313-2665

Visit us on the Internet at www.arcadiapublishing.com

To my wife of 38 years, Gail M. Benton,
and my two daughters, Lauren and Kristen, I dedicate this book.

Contents

Acknowledgments

Without the start by my father, Raymond K. Benton Sr., and my stepmother, Margit S. Benton, on my family's genealogy, I would never have gotten involved with it and started my collection of 20th-century Charleston postcards as part of that project. Recently, I discovered the Facebook page Charleston History before 1945 and decided to share my images with them. To my surprise, I received a lot of positive feedback, encouraging me to try to get my collection published. I was particularly encouraged by local historian and friend Robert N. Rosen. To all, thanks.

All images come from the author's collection.

INTRODUCTION

I grew up in Charleston, as did my father and grandfather. As a young Charlestonian, I walked the streets and rode the city buses, oblivious to the beauty of the city in which I had the good fortune to have been born. I barely noticed the comings and goings of buildings. Even as a history major at the College of Charleston, I concentrated on European history and not that of my home.

Then, several years ago, I took over working on the genealogy of my father's family, who had moved to Charleston from the Walterboro area of Colleton in 1900. Having acquired a lot of information, including the fact that my grandfather had been born in Charleston in 1900, I decided I needed photographs, other than family ones, to go with the collected family data. I wanted images of their Charleston.

I decided on early 1900s postcards and began collecting both black-and-white and hand-colored images. Over time, I acquired over 300 images. Of the images collected, some were real photographs and some were more stylized, with power lines removed and so forth. Some were used and postmarked, which dated them. Others were unused and therefore harder to date.

In 1906, the *News and Courier* reprinted the following from the *Chicago Record-Herald*: "The picture postcard has proved to be not only a joy to the millions, but a source of profit to the postoffice department. The cards are easy to handle and do not increase the expenses of postoffice [*sic*] administration in proportion to the revenue they bring in . . . Probably hundreds of thousands of persons in America alone, and certainly millions, if all the world is included, are picture postcard collectors." The cost of mailing a postcard was 1¢ to any state, Canada, or Mexico.

Putting together the postcard images I was able to collect from those saved by others in the past through their collecting and the text that make up this book invoked many memories, most of which I had not thought of for years. I read about the girls of Charleston going to the Memminger Normal and High School from Courtenay, Craft, and Bennett Schools. At one time or another, I attended all three of those schools, having graduated from Courtenay in 1958. As for Memminger itself, I read of its efforts to build a school library and can remember going to Memminger and checking out books at a library, some of which were shelved and some of which were just stacked on the floor. I can recall the squeaky floors of the old museum and the old police station. I walked through both more times than I can remember. I loved the old museum and its exhibits, like its mummy, and used to often visit with my father, a police detective. I walked through the back of the old St. John Hotel many times going from somewhere to somewhere else. On the other hand, their Colonial Lake, King Street, Hampton Park, White Point Garden, and Battery looked a lot like mine, except that the cannons along the Battery have been moved to the fringes of White Point Garden to make way for progress.

Some buildings that I remember needed to be replaced, like the old St. John Hotel and the old police station, while there are some, like the orphan house, that I wish could have been saved. I could picture it, remodeled, as a dormitory for the College of Charleston.

As Charleston has moved through the decades, efforts by organizations such as the Preservation Society of Charleston, formerly the Society for the Preservation of Old Dwellings, founded in 1920, have tried to save what was Charleston for what is Charleston. They began by saving the Joseph Manigault House, which had been built in 1803, from giving way to the progress of becoming a gas station or something else, as the orphan house progressed into a Sears Roebuck. The Sears Roebuck did have an escalator, though. I believe it was Charleston's first. Thanks to foresight and effort, the Manigault House is still there for me, my children, my grandchildren, and you to see and enjoy.

As you look through the images in *Charleston: 1900–1915*, it may invoke memories like mine, or if you did not grow up in what is widely viewed as America's most historic city, let this book introduce you to the Charleston that was, the Charleston I have discovered.

One

Greetings

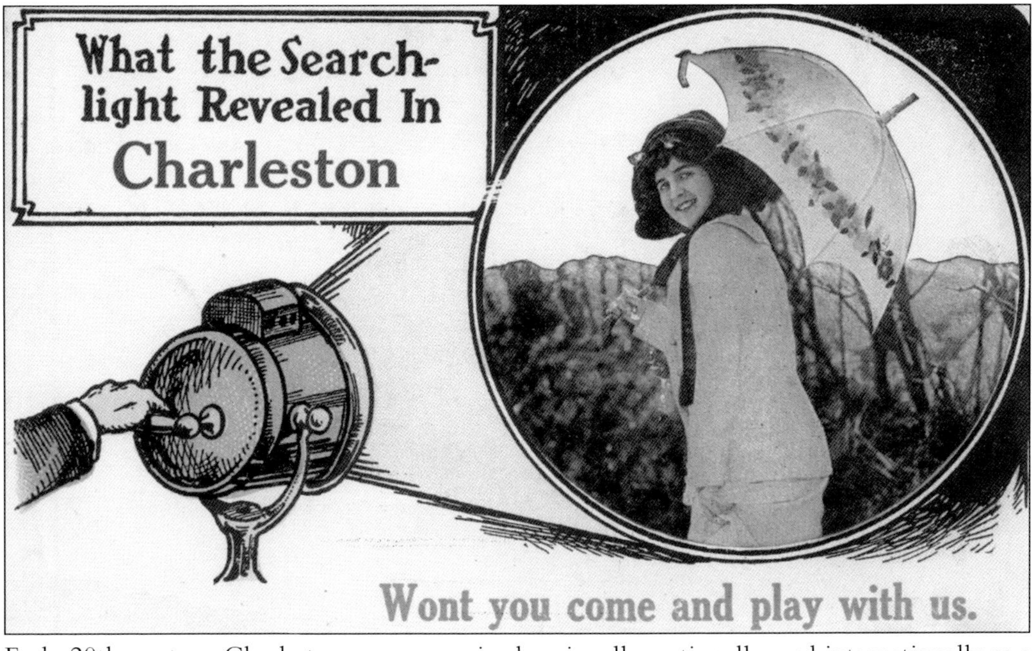

Early 20th-century Charleston was recognized regionally, nationally, and internationally as a place to do business or go for fun. Charleston's harbor and ports were among the best in the nation. With a large naval shipyard, its harbor had to be kept dredged and deep. Ships from up and down the seaboard, as well as from around the world, loaded and unloaded at Charleston's port. The port shipped products such as South Carolina cotton, rice, and tobacco and received goods like bananas and finished goods. Additionally, it was a cruise ship port that brought people to visit Charleston's historic sites, one of its three beaches, or its beautiful gardens or come to attend a business conference or convention.

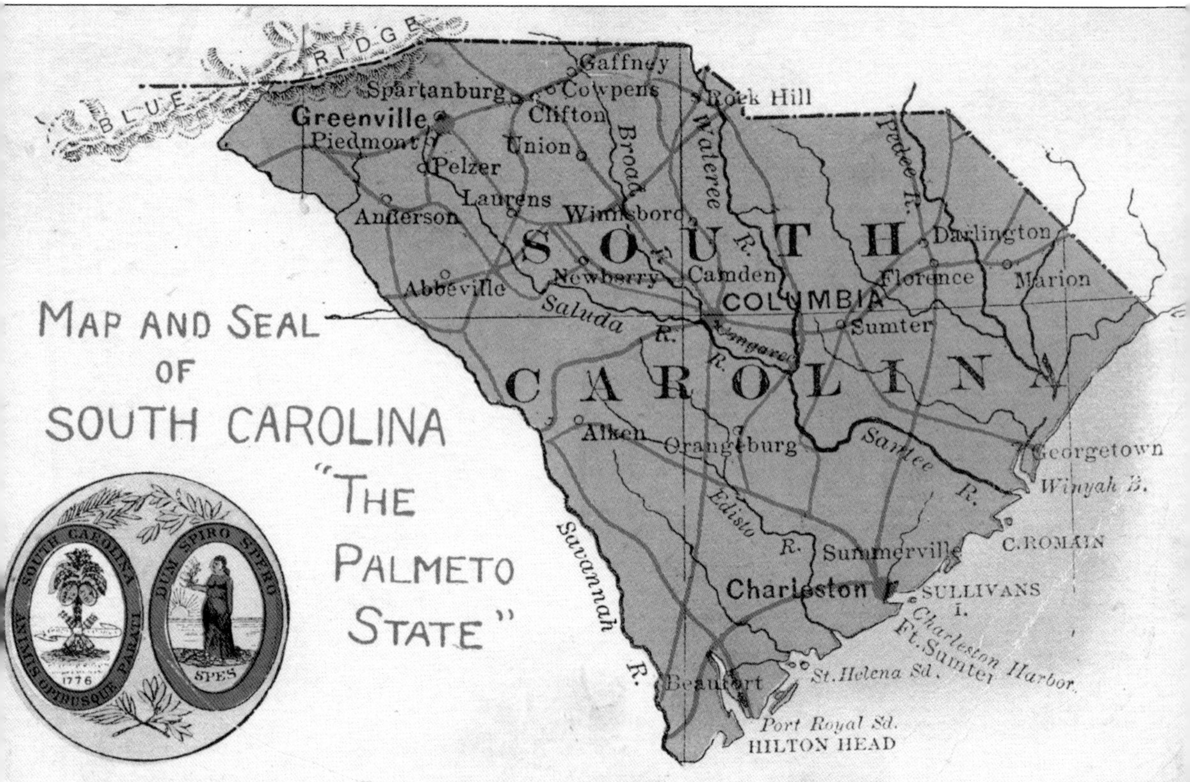

In 1663, King Charles II of Great Britain gave the lands of Carolina to the Lords Proprietors and in 1670 the colony's first permanent settlement was made on the Ashley River. A decade later, the settlement of Charles Town was moved to its present location, and in 1783, Charles Town, with the revolution won, changed its name to Charleston. Five years later, South Carolina became the eighth state to ratify the Constitution of the United States, and in 1860 it became the first state to secede from the union. At the Civil War's end, Charleston was less than 50 years removed from the postmark on this postcard.

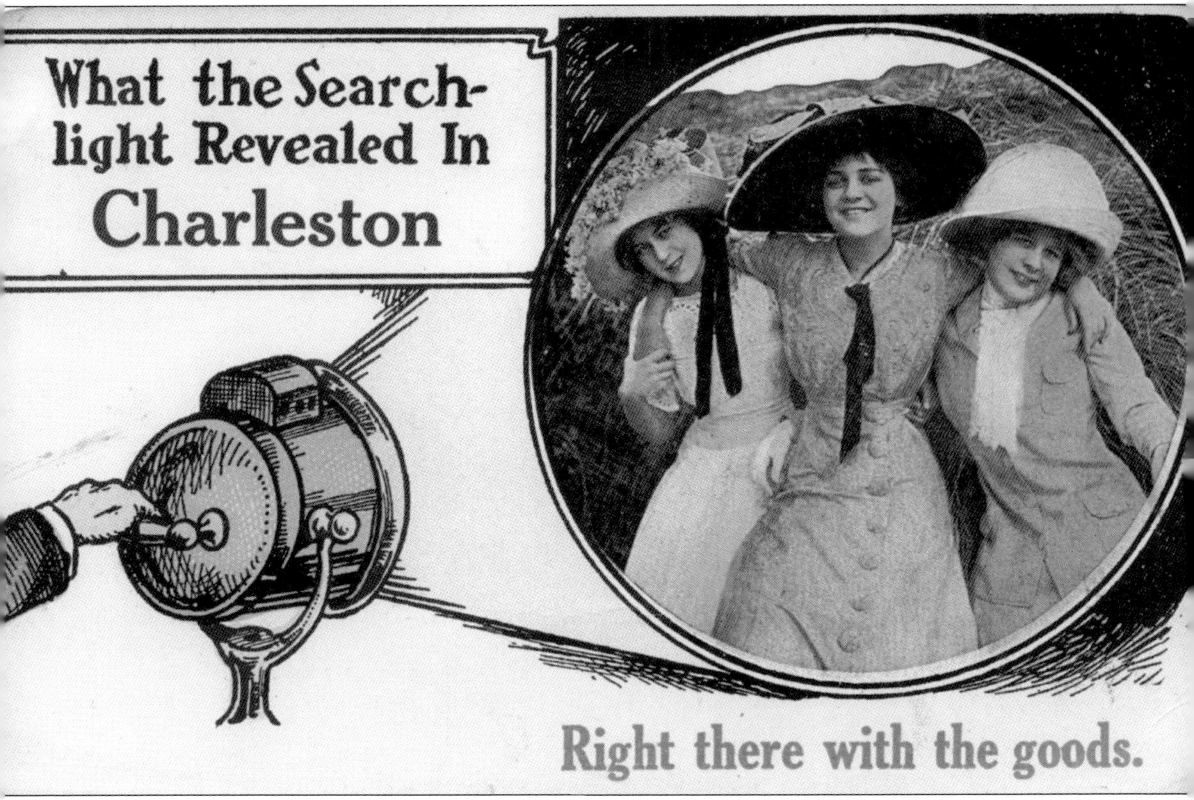

This greeting may have been sent by a store or business in Charleston to lady shoppers to let them know about the store or business. On the back, a business might have written a short note to tell the addressee of what new goods it or Charleston had to offer.

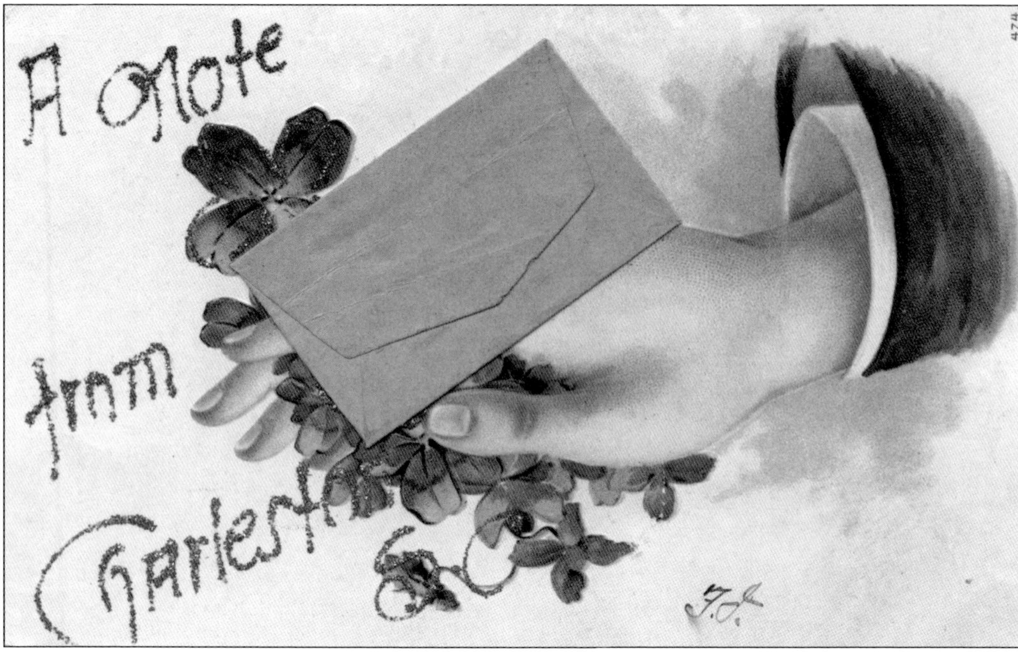

One of these types of feminine greeting cards may have been sent from one of the ladies visiting Charleston from a sister Southern state or even California, New York, Ohio, or Montana, among the other states attending the 10th annual convention of the United Daughters of the Confederacy, held at the Hibernian Hall in 1903. It might even have been sent from a lady in Charleston to friends or relatives in Philadelphia to let them know the Liberty Bell had arrived safely in Charleston for the South Carolina Inter-State and West Indian Exposition. Its train arrived the morning of January 9, 1902, as thousands awaited. It was welcomed with a 13-gun salute from the Lafayette Artillery.

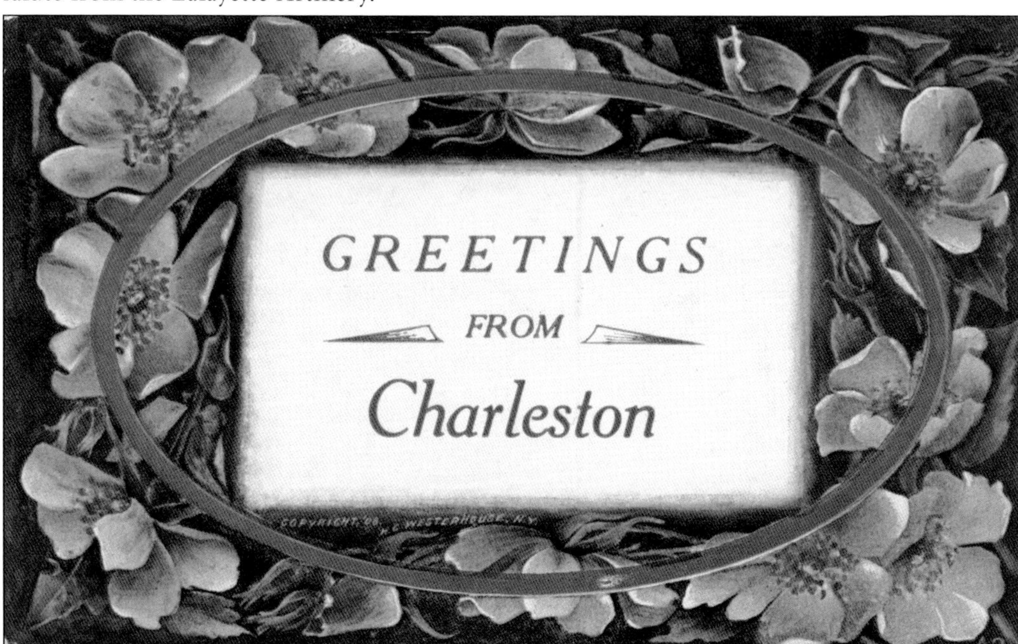

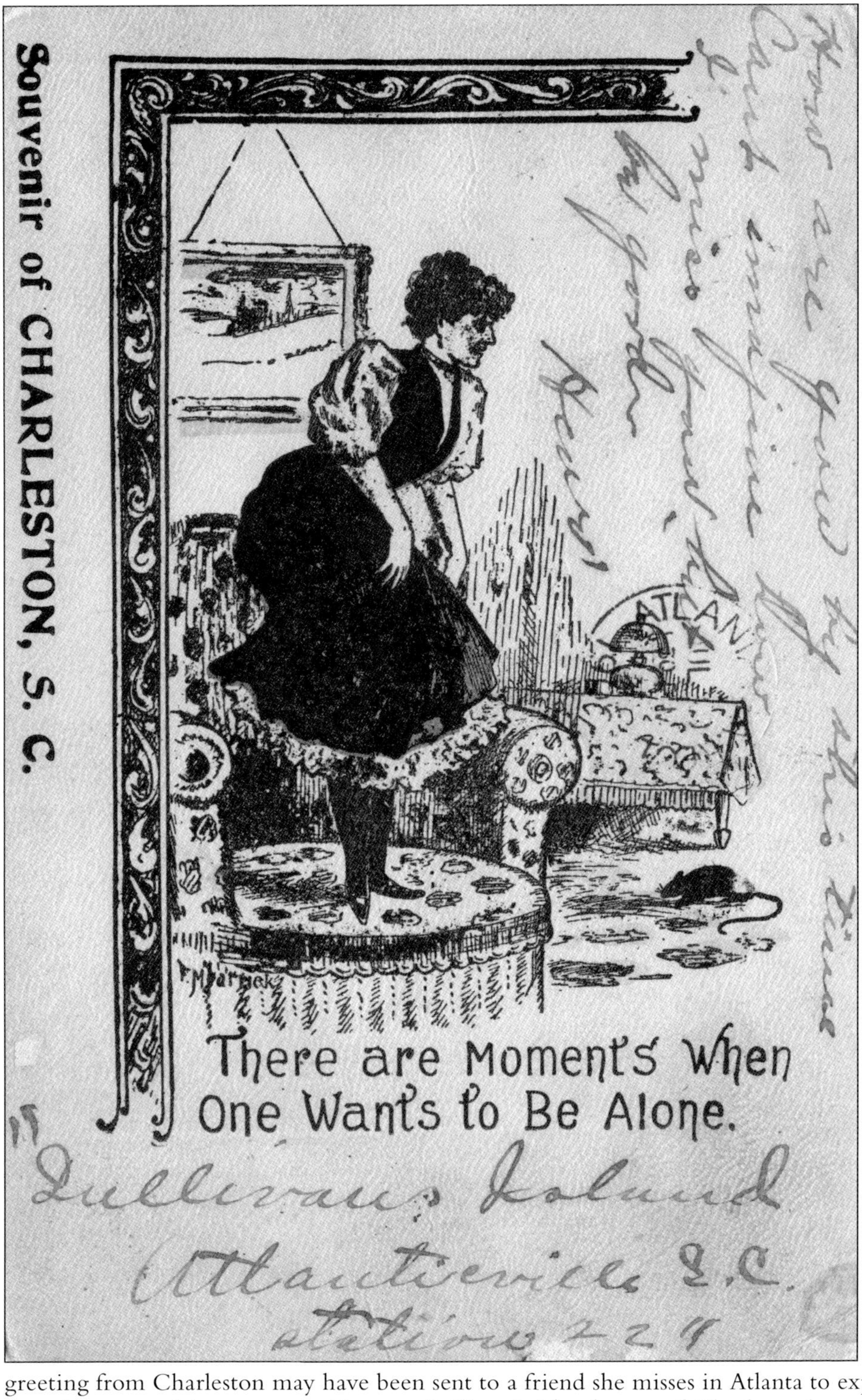

This greeting from Charleston may have been sent to a friend she misses in Atlanta to explain both her absence and her return address at Sullivan's Island, one of Charleston's popular beach getaways.

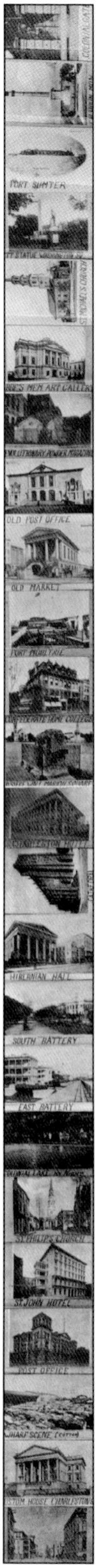

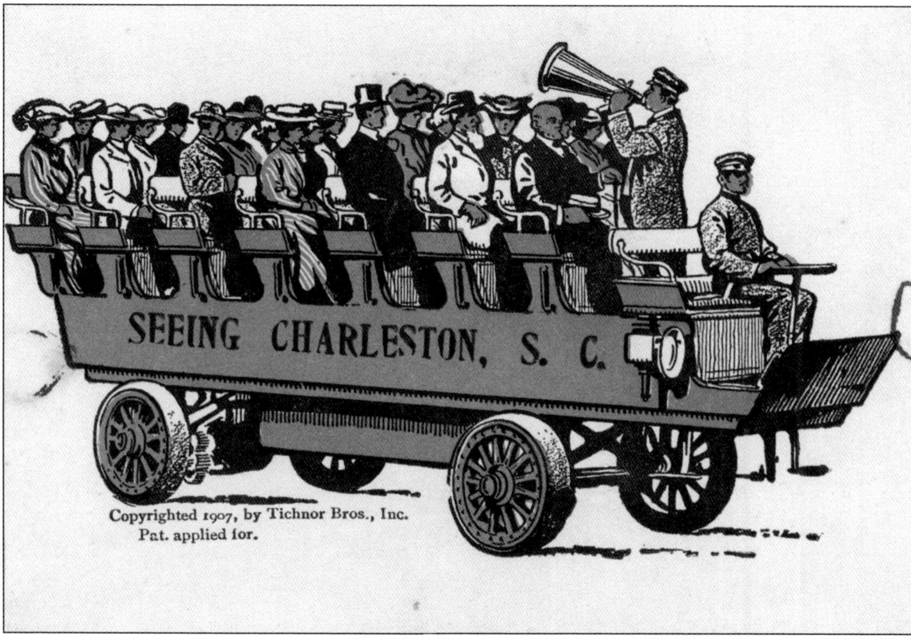

The Motor Jitney Company began operating four yellow on black, eight-passenger jitney buses on July 5, 1915, charging 5¢ per ride. The company planned on a fleet of eight that would run as yet undecided regular routes. While jitney was slang for a nickel, a jitney was defined as a small bus that carried passengers on a regular route for that amount. Within the bifold card is an accordion-like dropout with small black-and-white images of some 24 Charleston sights that one might see riding the *Seeing Charleston* jitney.

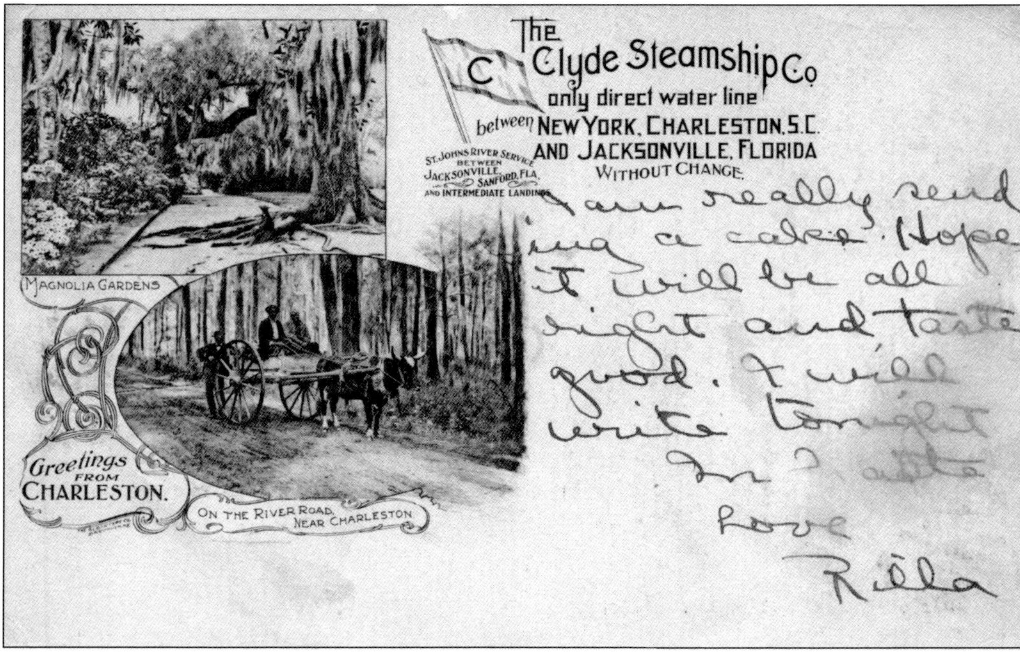

The Clyde Steamship Co. ran a regular route between the three cities noted. According to the message, the sender is sending a cake to the addressee. One cannot help but wonder if this pastry was a famous Lady Baltimore cake. The Woman's Exchange of Charleston sent them everywhere, after Owen Wister of *The Virginian* fame made them famous in his novel *Lady Baltimore*.

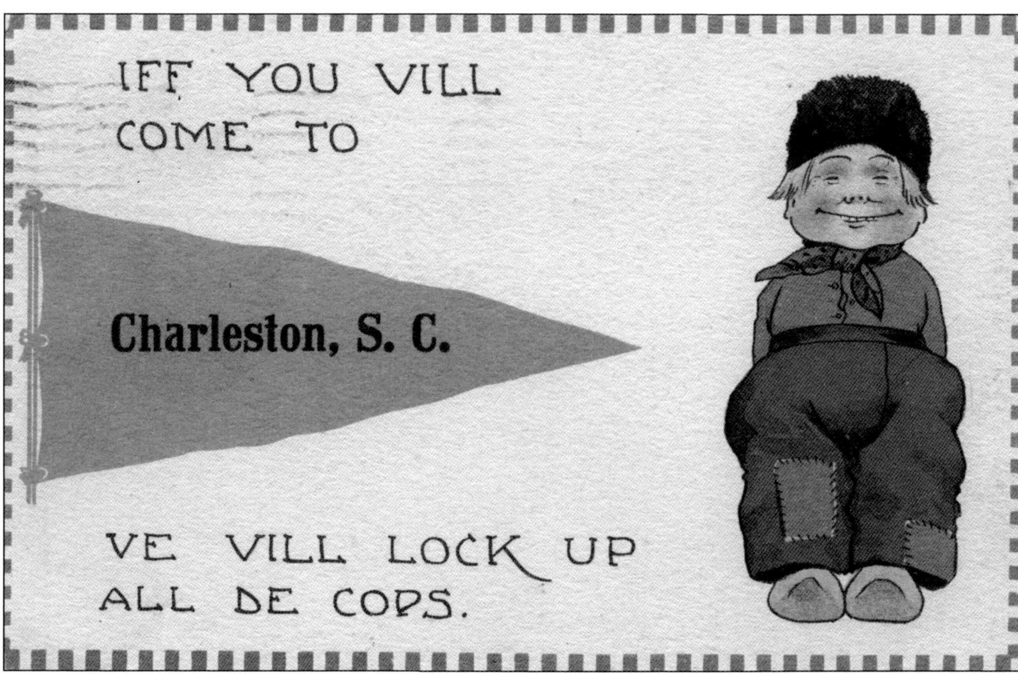

The German Rifle Club sponsored an annual schuetzenfest, a target-shooting festival. The club began in Charleston in 1855, the oldest club of its kind in the United States. It celebrated its golden jubilee in 1905.

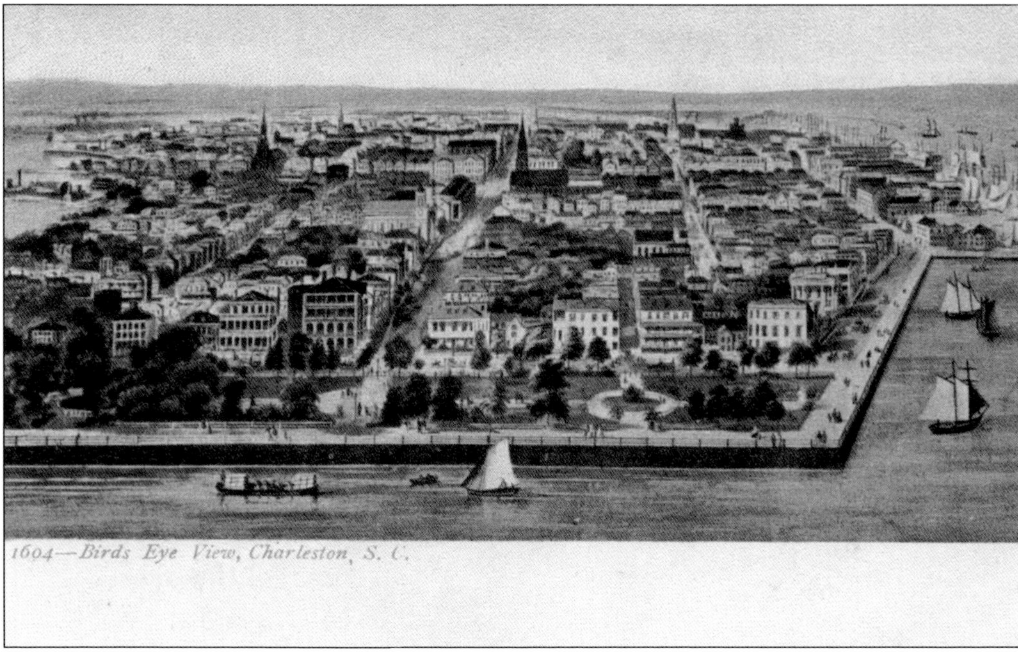

Originally, Charles Town was settled on the banks of the Ashley River in April 1670, when the first of three ships, the *Carolina*, the *Albemarle*, and the *Port Royal*, landed. On the three ships were almost 150 settlers, including William Sayle, who was to be the colony's first governor. In 1680, Charles Town was moved to a more defensible location, where the Ashley and Cooper Rivers meet at Oyster Point. There, it grew and prospered. By 1775, it had an estimated population of 12,000. In 1783, after the American Revolution, Charles Town became Charleston.

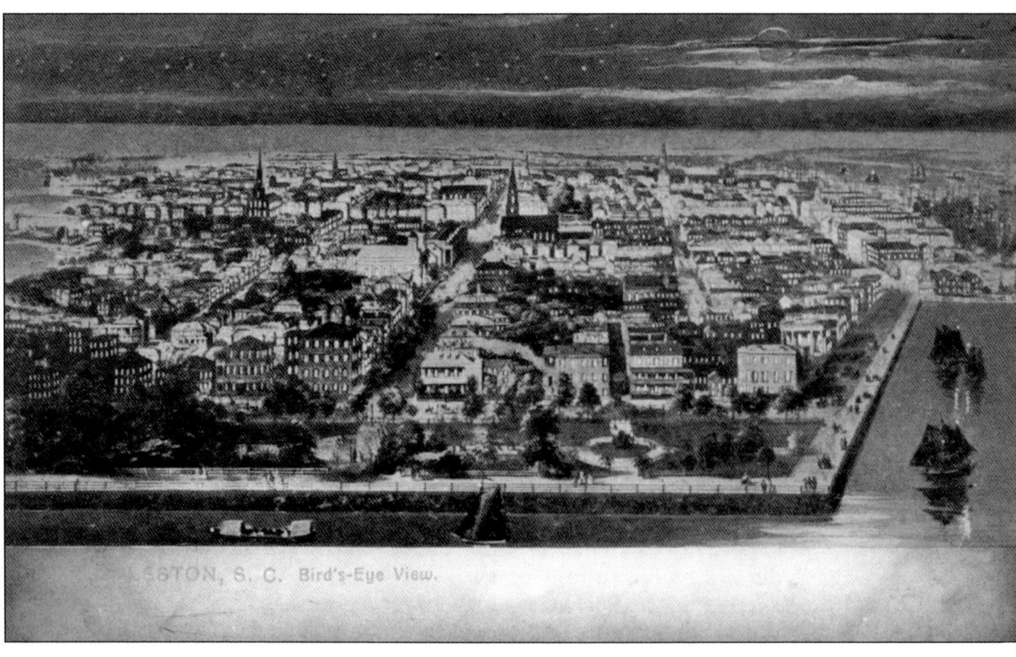

Two

CHURCHES

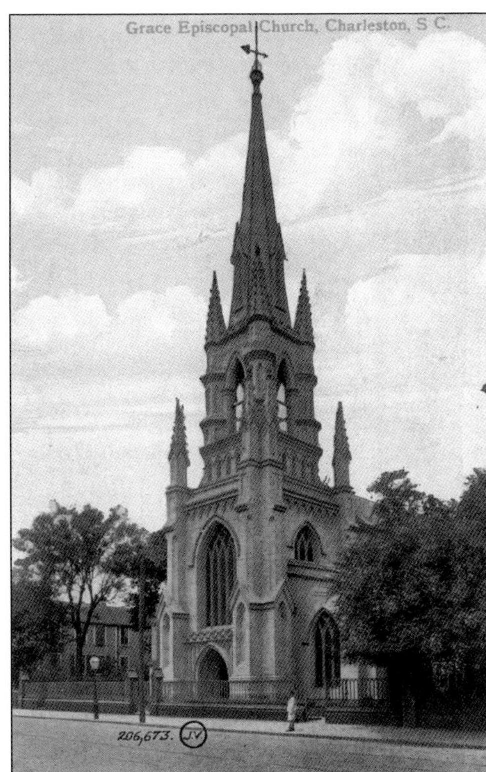

Grace Episcopal Church, located at 98 Wentworth Street, was Charleston's fifth Episcopal church but the first in the center part of the pre–Civil War city. On Sunday, January 31, 1847, the congregation began services in the College of Charleston's chapel. The construction of this building began in June 1847, and it was consecrated in 1848 by Bishop Christopher Gadsden.

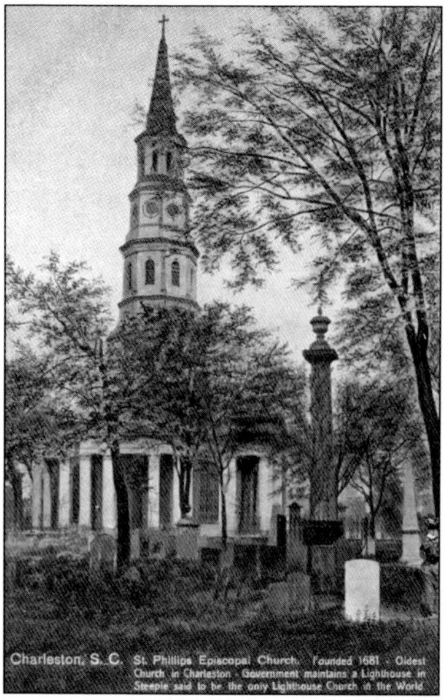

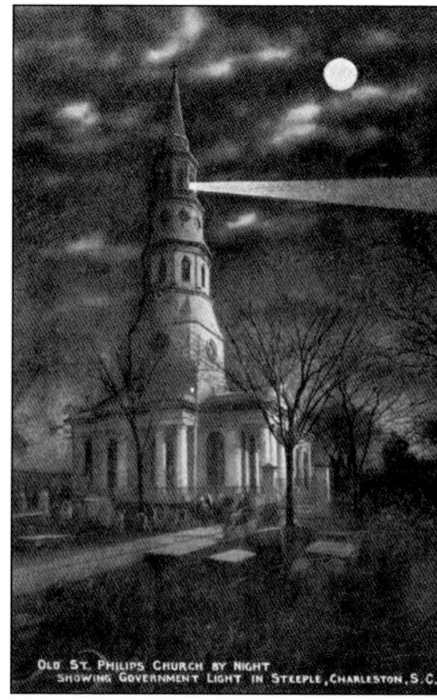

St. Philip's Episcopal Church, established in 1681, erected a wooden building where St. Michael's is today. Damaged by the hurricane of 1710, a new St. Philip's Church was begun on then-new Church Street. Completed in 1723, it was lost to fire in 1835. The present building was begun and completed within two years, excepting the steeple, which was added a decade later. From it, a range lighthouse operated for 22 years, ending in 1915. Among those in St. Philip's two cemeteries are Edward Rutledge (signer to the Declaration of Independence), Charles Pinckney (signer of the Constitution), Gen. James Gadsden (for whom the Gadsden Purchase is named), DuBose Heyward (author of *Porgy*), Alicia Rhett (actress who portrayed India Wilkes in *Gone with the Wind*), and John C. Calhoun. The cemetery for native Charlestonians surrounds the church, while the other for strangers is across Church Street. Calhoun, born in Abbeville, was buried in the strangers' cemetery. He was removed to the friendly side and buried in an unmarked grave for his protection, during the Civil War. On November 13, 1884, Calhoun was reburied across the street, again, where he still rests.

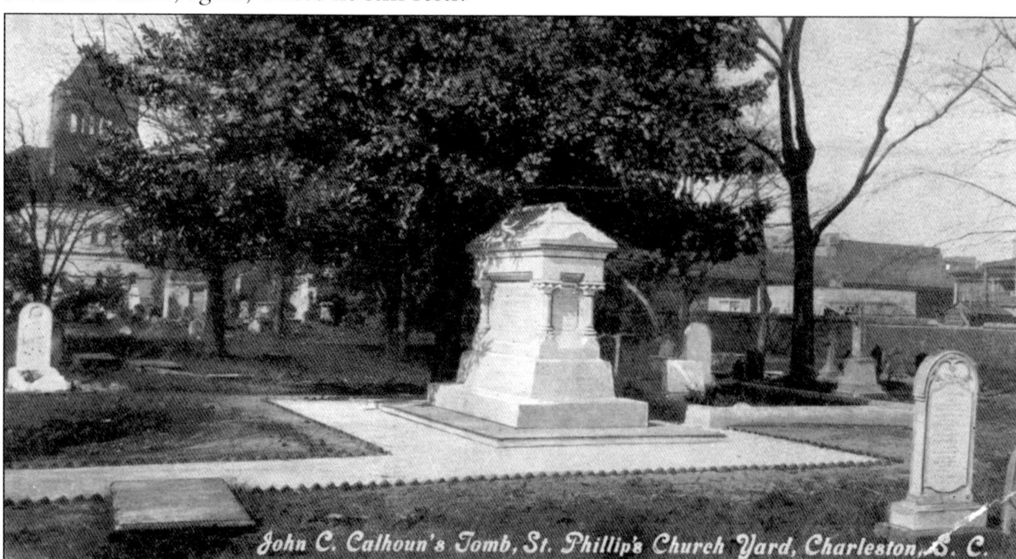

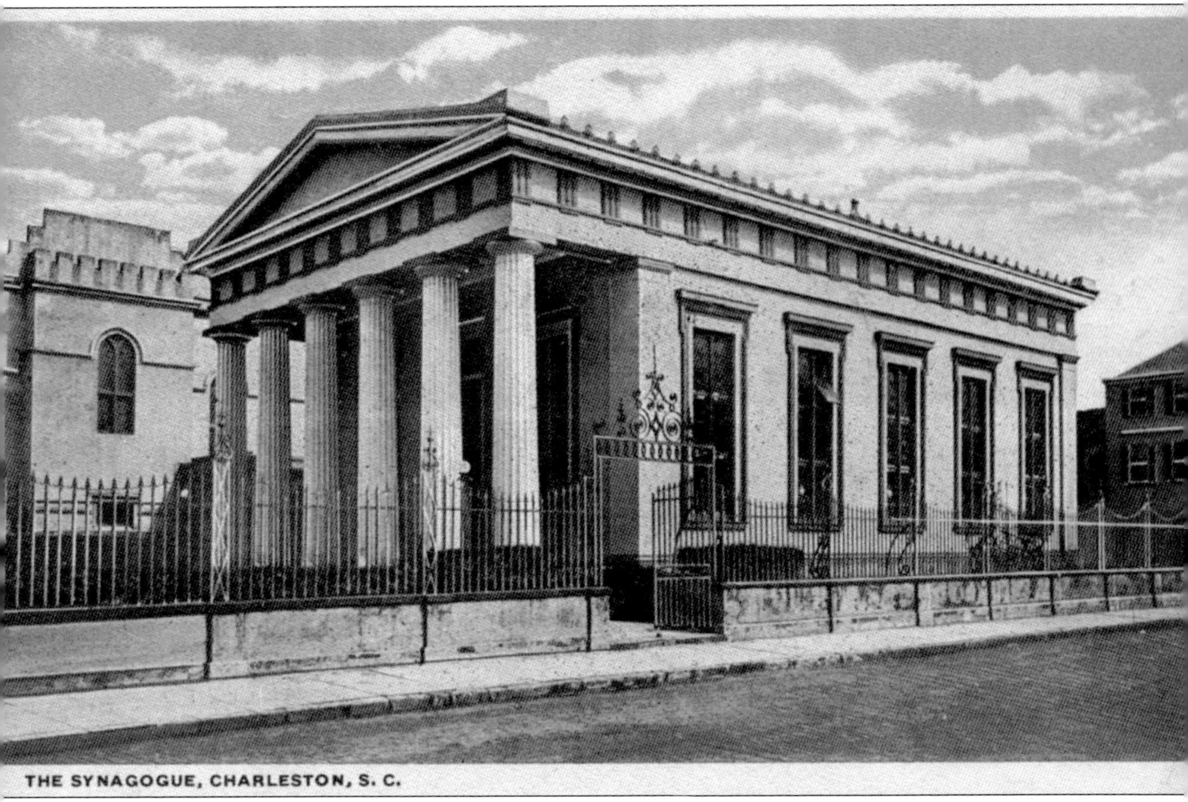

Kahal Kadosh Beth Elohim's Synagogue, 90 Hasell Street, is the oldest continuously operating synagogue in the country. Built in 1840, it replaced the one dedicated in 1794 and destroyed by fire in 1838. It was also the first synagogue to install an organ. Those who did not approve of the organ formed Shearith Israel on Wentworth Street. The organ was removed to Columbia only to be destroyed by Sherman.

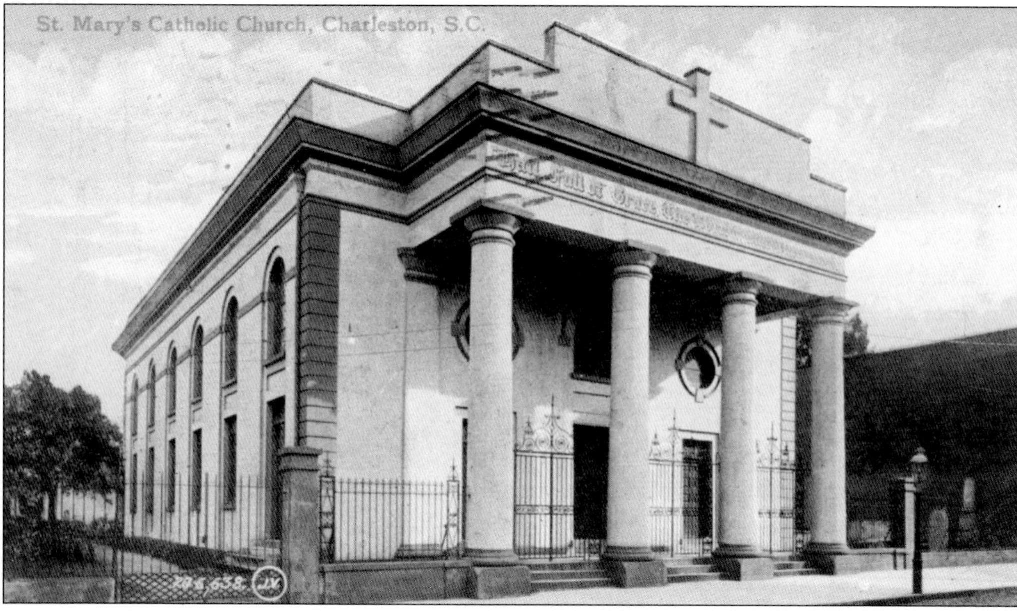

St. Mary of the Annunciation is located at 89 Hasell Street. Established on August 24, 1789, it was the first Roman Catholic church in South Carolina. Its first brick structure was built in 1801, burned down in 1838, and replaced by this one a year later. On September 14, 1905, during the Festival of the Exaltation of the Holy Cross, a piece of the true cross was, for the first time, viewed and venerated in Charleston.

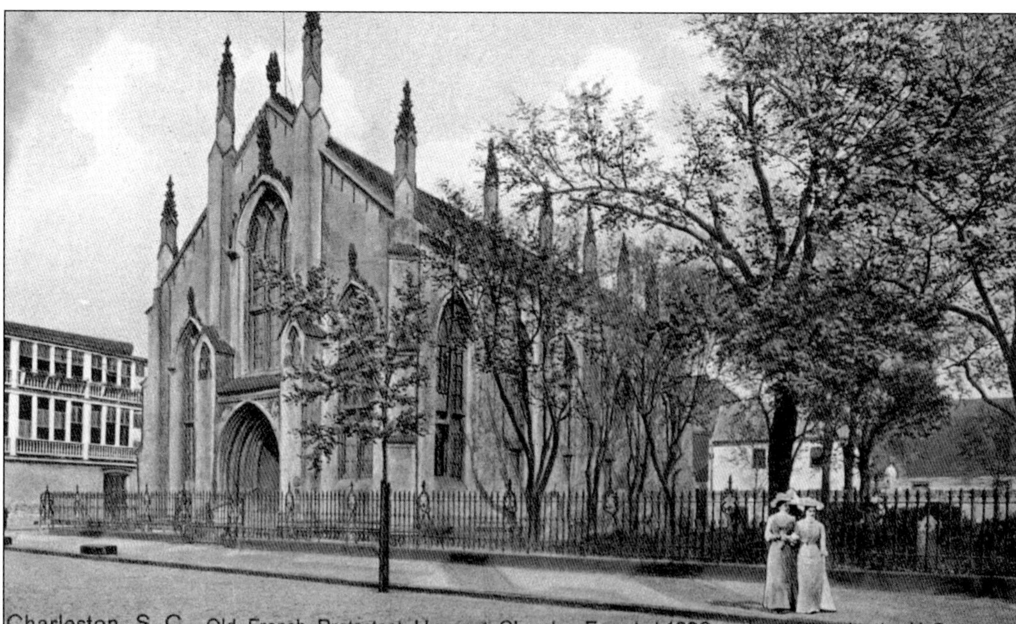

The Old French Huguenot or French Protestant Church, located at 136 Church Street, is not the first such church to occupy its location. All of its predecessors were destroyed by fire. This Gothic-style building was completed in 1845, and the church celebrated its 225th anniversary in it in 1912. Alexander Hamilton, Francis Marion, and Martha Washington all have memorial tablets within the church.

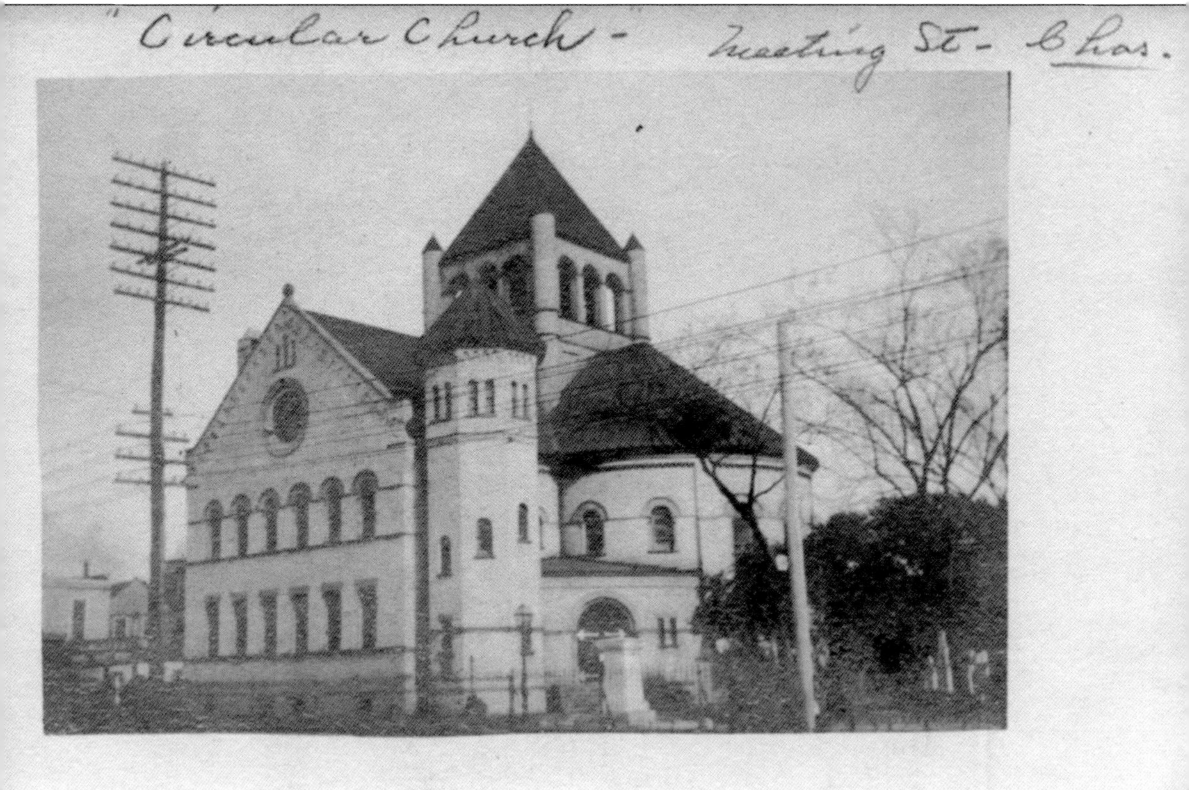

The present Circular Congregational Church was formally dedicated on January 18, 1892, and is the third to occupy this site. This church replaced its predecessor, which burned down in the fires of 1861. The church, originally dating from 1681, is located on Meeting Street at the site of the city's first meetinghouse, which gave name to the street. It has the city's oldest burial site. One monument is dated 1695.

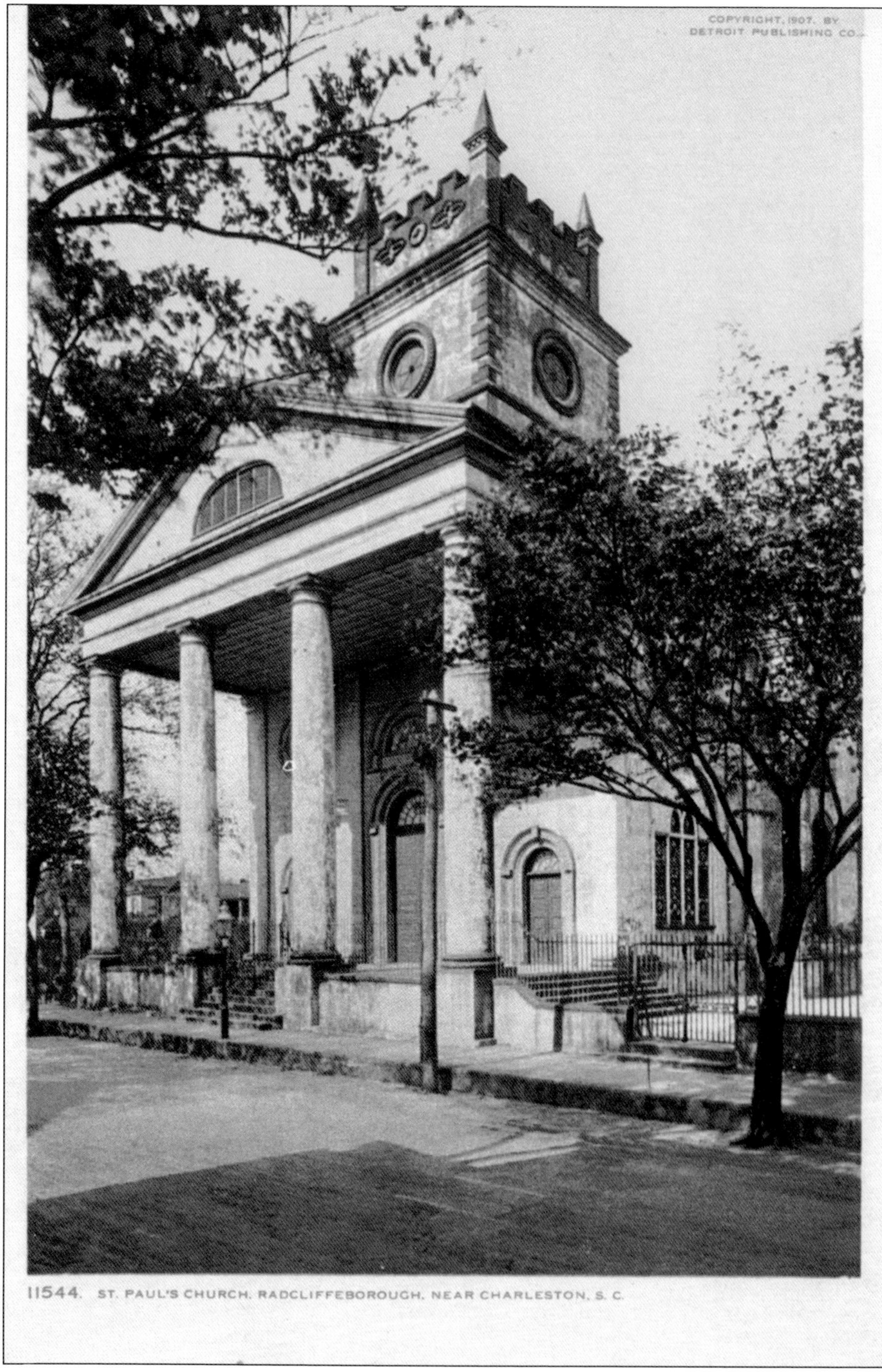

St. Paul's Church Radcliffeborough, now known as the Cathedral Church of St. Paul and St. Luke, is located at 126 Coming Street. Its cornerstone was laid in 1811 and was consecrated five years later. During the Civil War, to avoid injury from Union shelling, both St. Philip's and St. Michael's congregations with their rectors held services at St. Paul's. St. Paul's and St. Luke's, which had formerly been located on Charlotte Street, combined congregations in 1949.

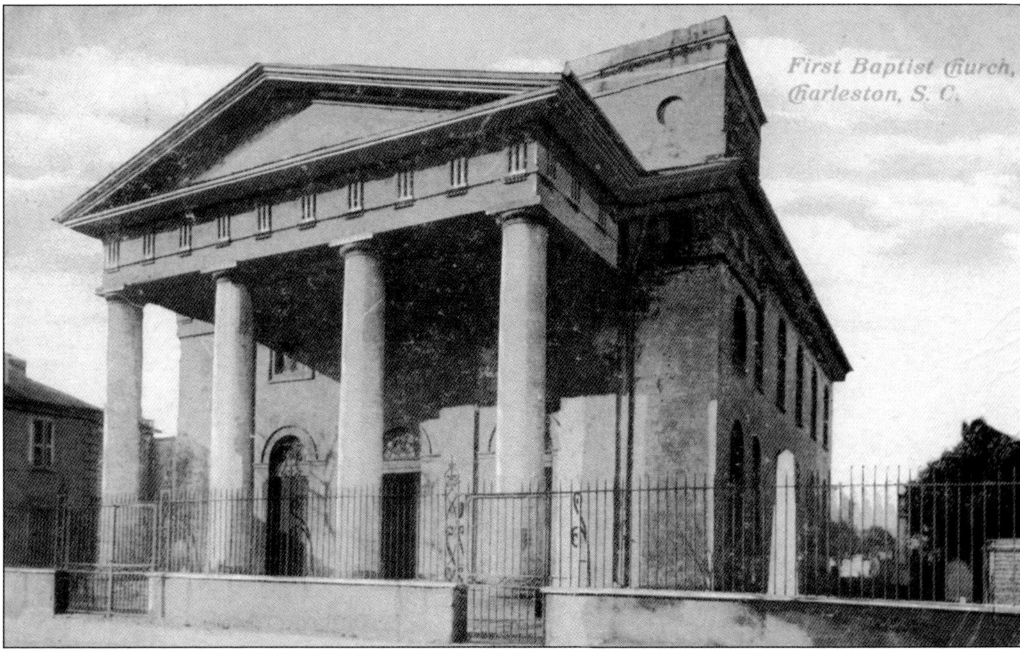

First Baptist Church, the oldest Baptist church in the South, is located at 61 Church Street. The building, designed by Charleston architect Robert Mills, who designed the Fireproof Building and the Washington Monument, began when a small congregation of 28 led by William Screven relocated from Kittery, Maine, in 1696. It was established on September 25, 1682. On October 11, 1908, First Baptist Church officially celebrated its 225th anniversary.

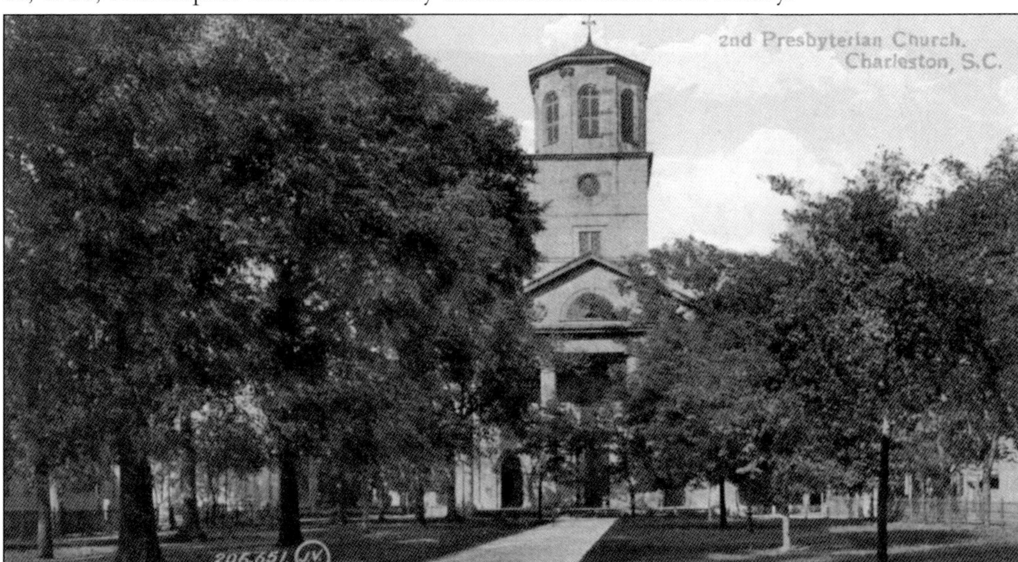

The Second Presbyterian Church of the City and Suburbs of Charleston is located at 342 Meeting Street, at Meeting at Charlotte Streets, on land donated by the Wragg family. The public green between the church and Meeting Street is known as Wragg Square. The church was founded in 1809 and funded by a series of legislature-approved public lotteries, according to the November 13, 1810, *Charleston Courier.*

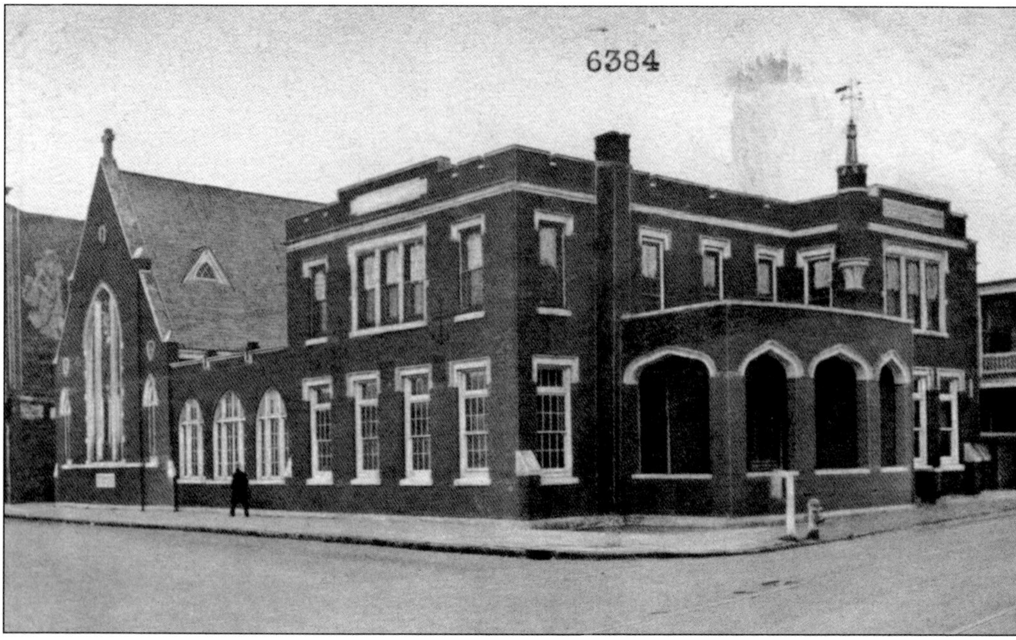

The Church of the Redeemer and Harriot Pinckney Home for Seamen was on the corner of Market and East Bay Streets. In 1853, Harriot Pinckney, daughter of Gen. Charles Cotesworth Pinckney, bequeathed to the Rev. Charles Cotesworth Pinckney, among others, in trust, the land of her father for a Protestant Episcopal church. Today, the church is closed, and the structures are part of the commercial buildings in the market area.

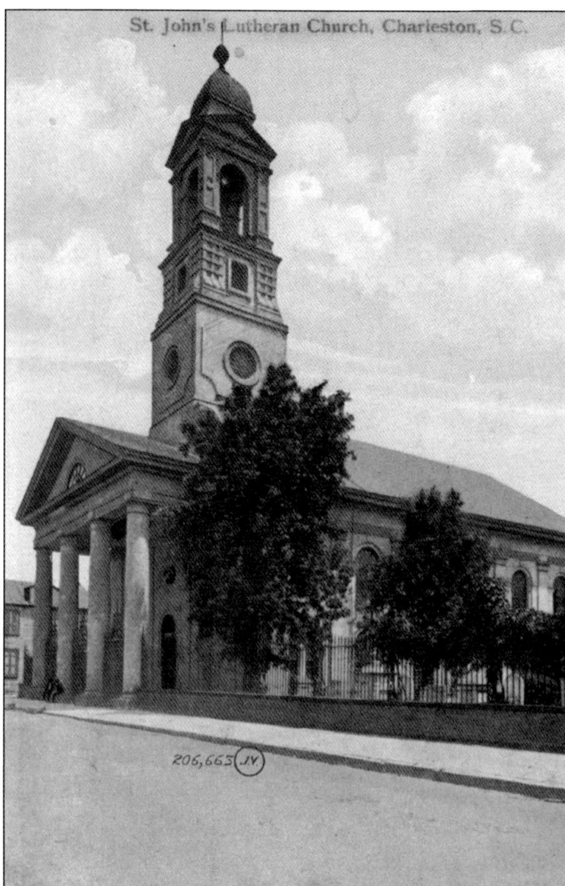

St. John's Lutheran Church is located at 5 Clifford Street. An article in the March 25, 1918, *Evening Post* describes the church celebrating its centennial and Dr. John F. Ficken's historical address. The church's congregation, Charleston's oldest Lutheran, began with pilgrims from Strasburg, Germany, in 1734 and their first building in 1759. This church was built between 1816 and 1818, with its bell-shaped steeple added some 50 years later.

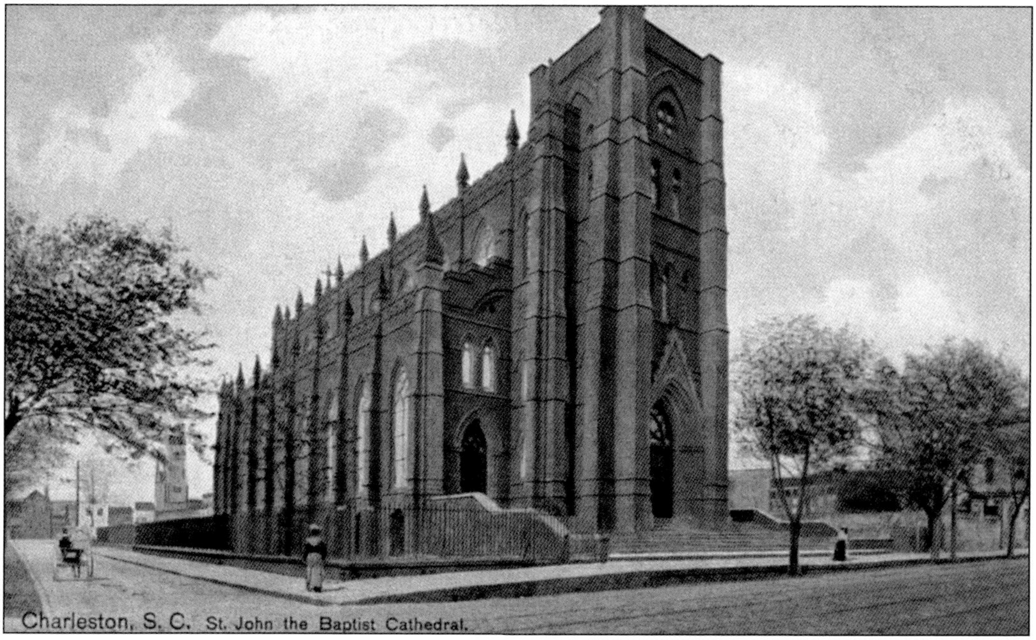

The St. John the Baptist Cathedral, at 120 Broad Street, is the second such structure built on this lot, which was purchased in 1821. The first, the Cathedral of St. John and St. Finbar, was destroyed in Charleston's great fire of December 11, 1861. The Civil War, postwar economics, the cyclone of 1885, and the earthquake of 1886 all delayed the rebuilding efforts. The cornerstone to this German Gothic–style brownstone building was finally laid on January 12, 1890, and its doors opened on April 14, 1907. St. Finbar's name was dropped from the name of the cathedral because Bishop Northop declared that he was not a saint under the Roman calendar. The interior has vaulted ceilings, 14 stained-glass windows that depict 14 events in the life of Christ from birth to resurrection, and a white marble altar. Representatives from all the Catholic parishes made up the committee that oversaw the construction of St. John the Baptist Cathedral because the church represented all the Catholics of Charleston.

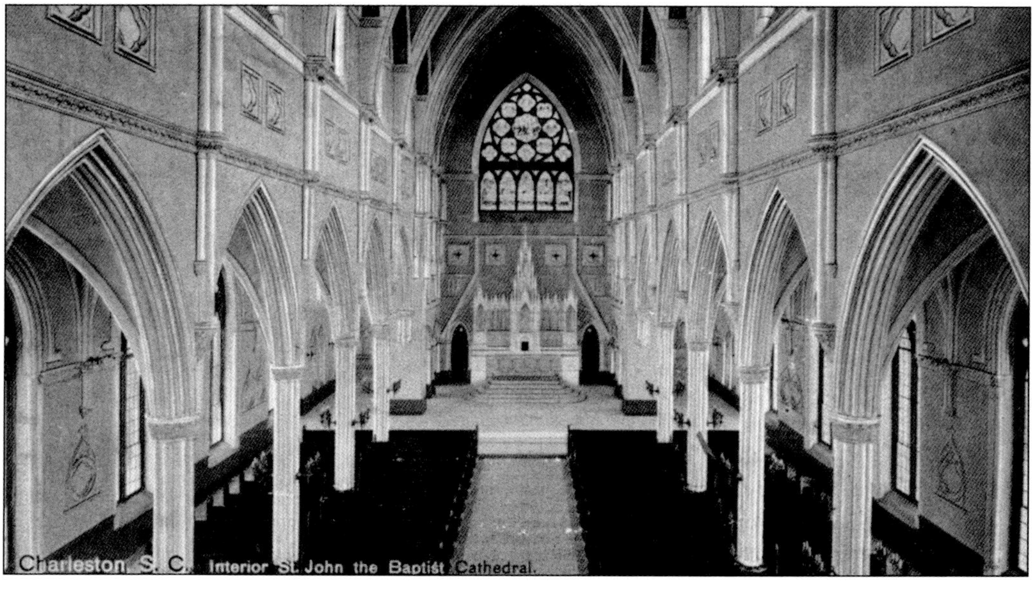

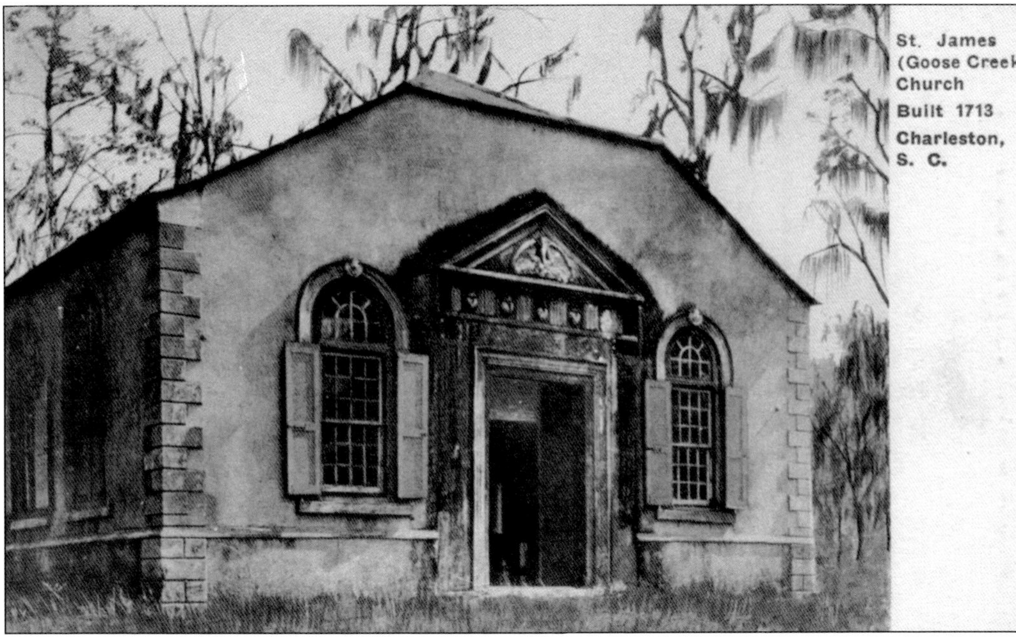

While St. James Church was begun by planters from Barbados in 1713, its vestry was not incorporated until 1778. The church is a small one-room rectangular-shaped stucco structure with a jerkinhead roof. It has arched windows with shutters and cherub busts adorning the arches' peaks. In 1905, a group from Charleston came up and placed a tablet in the church to the memory of Rev. Samuel Thomas, who ministered to the people of the Goose Creek area from 1702 to 1705. According to the tablet, he was the "first missionary sent to South Carolina, by the Society of the Propagation of the Gospel in Foreign Parts." During the Revolutionary War, it is said that the king's coat of arms over the church's pulpit saved it from British troops.

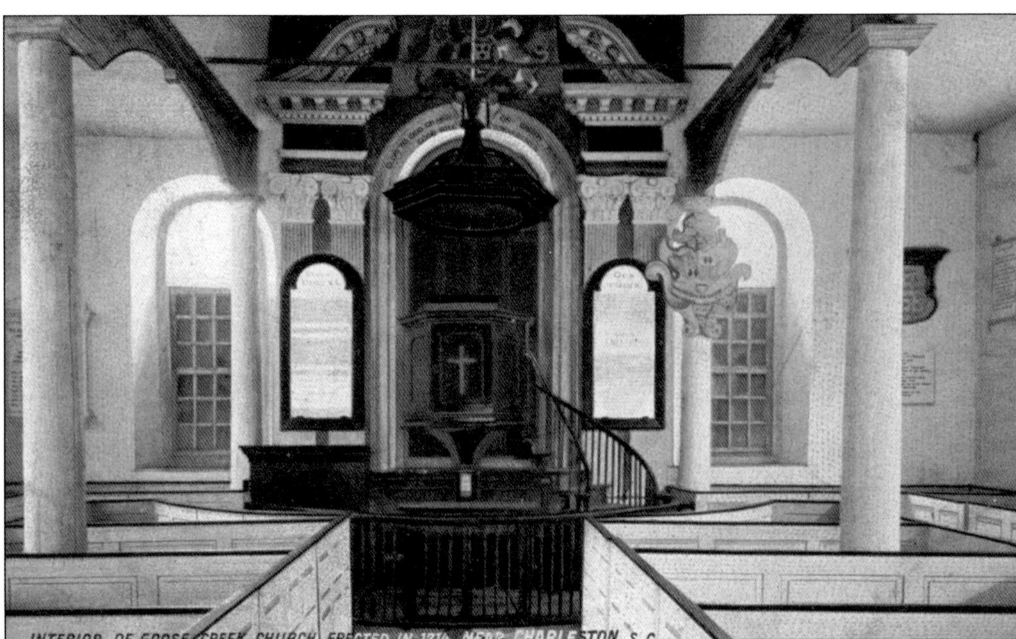

St. Matthew's German Lutheran Church is located on King Street across from Marion Square. On September 13, 1908, most of the German crew of the kaiser's SMS *Freya*, led by their band, marched through Charleston's streets to services here. The church was constructed shortly after the Civil War and dedicated in 1872. Its steeple, at 297 feet, became the biggest attraction on King Street in 1965, when a fire made it come tumbling down, filling the street.

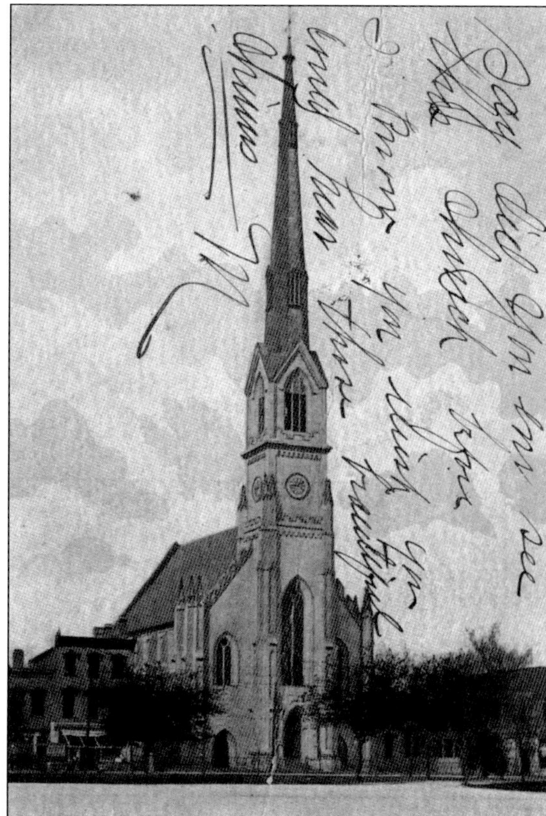

Charleston, S. C. St. Mathews German Ev. Lutheran Church

Old St. Andrews Church, built about 1706, is located at 2604 Ashley River Road. Rev. John Grimke-Drayton, owner of Magnolia Gardens, headed the Anglican church for 40 years, serving both whites and slaves. The church closed during the Civil War years but reopened in 1876. It closed again upon the death of Grimke-Drayton, its rector, in 1891 and remained closed until 1948, when it reopened.

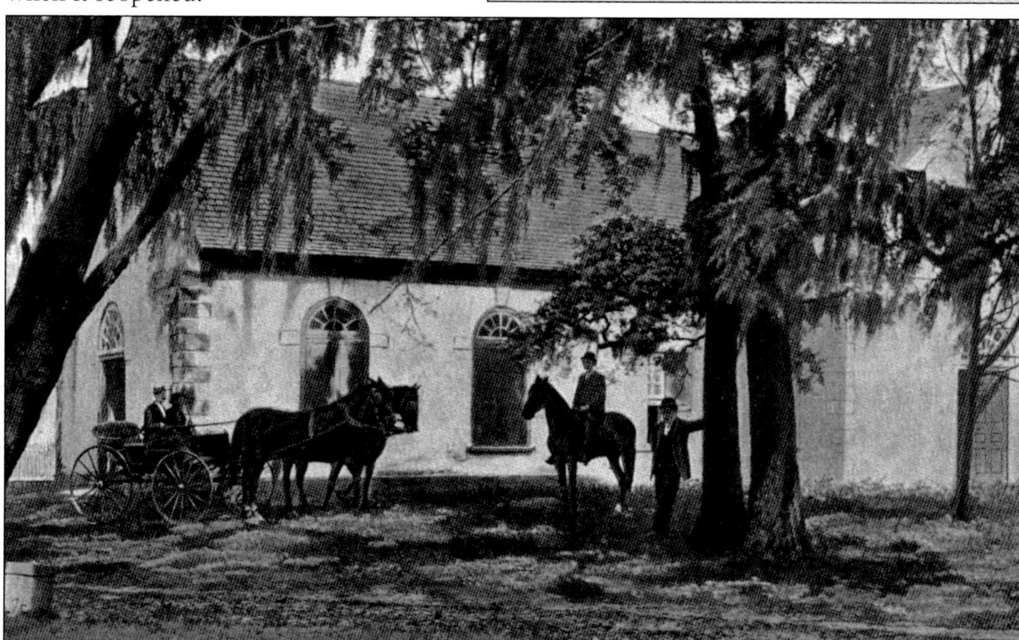

Old St. Andrews Parish Church - Built 1706 near Charleston, S.C.

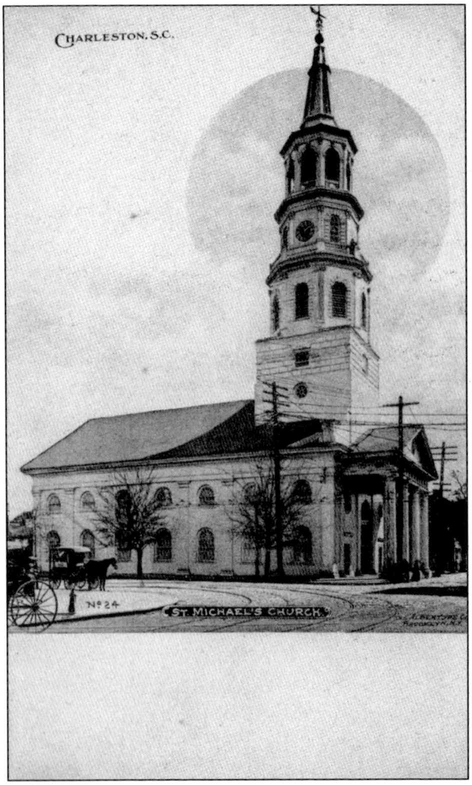

St. Michael's Episcopal Church was built where the original St. Philip's had been, on the corner of Broad and Meeting Streets, representing church law or the law of God on the Four Corners of Law. In 1751, Charleston had two parishes—St. Michael's and St. Philip's, with the dividing line down the middle of Broad Street, and St. Michael's was built over the next decade. Both John Rutledge, a US Supreme Court justice, governor of South Carolina, member of the Continental Congress, and signer of the Constitution, and Charles Cotesworth Pinckney, a Revolutionary War officer who fought with Washington and signed the Constitution, are interred in St. Michael's Churchyard. John's brother, Edward Rutledge, a signer of the Declaration of Independence, and Pinckney's cousin Charles, also a signer of the Constitution, are buried nearby at St. Philip's.

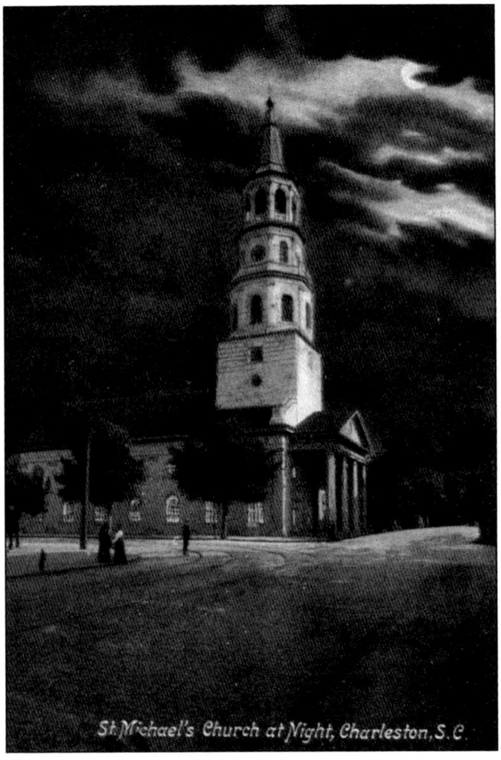

Three

STREET SCENES

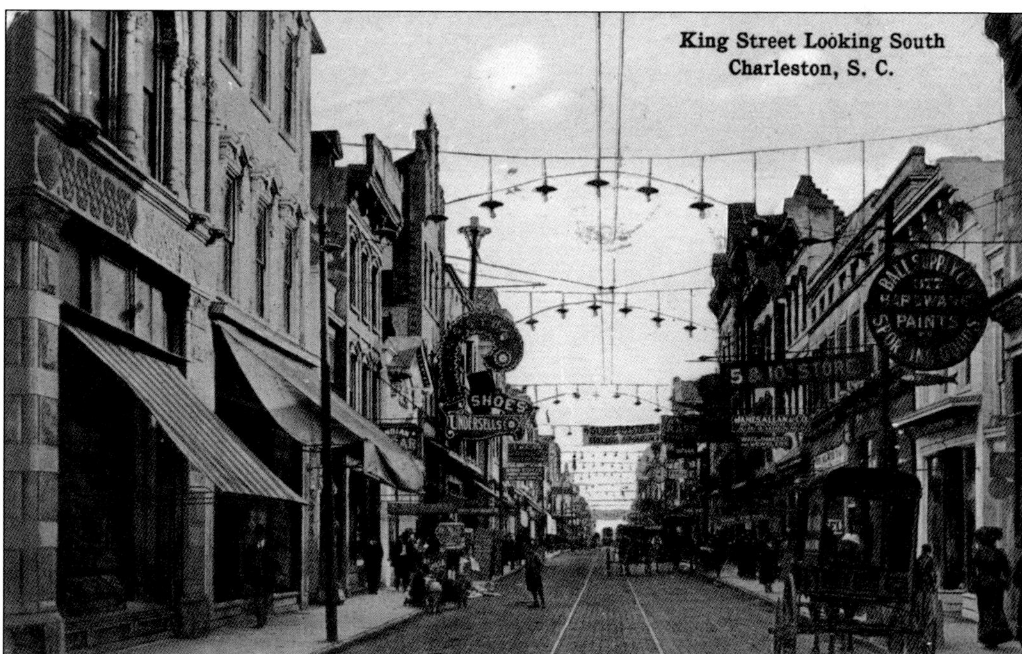

Considering that Charles Town was a royal colony, the name King Street seems both appropriate and obvious. It evolved into and still is downtown Charleston's shopping center. Notice the store signs down the street that are there to attract strolling shoppers: hardware and paints, 5 & 10, shoes, and dozens more. At this time, King Street was serviced by the trolley system for the convenience of potential shoppers, as well as accommodating automobiles and both horse-drawn wagons and carriages, and was designed to be lighted for nighttime shopping.

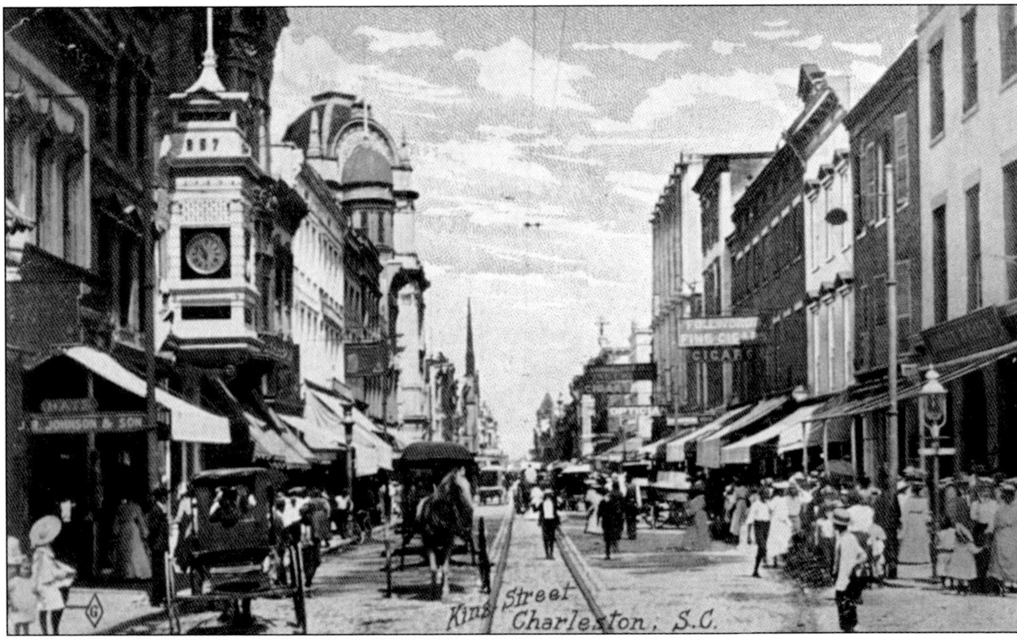

Perhaps this group was on King Street for the Saturday night culmination of Charleston's Gala Week or fall festival. This festival went on for years. It was fair-like in that tents were pitched on Calhoun Street and Marion Square. There, one could see sideshows with things like the "world's smallest horse" and the "fattest" whatever or buy trinkets or sweets or nickel bags of confetti. Young ladies and gentlemen would buy paper pom-poms to waive in their opposite's faces. On Saturday nights, there would be confetti fights and tosses up and down King Street. By church time Sunday morning, everything would be back to normal, after several inches of confetti, hundreds of bushels, had been swept and the tents taken down.

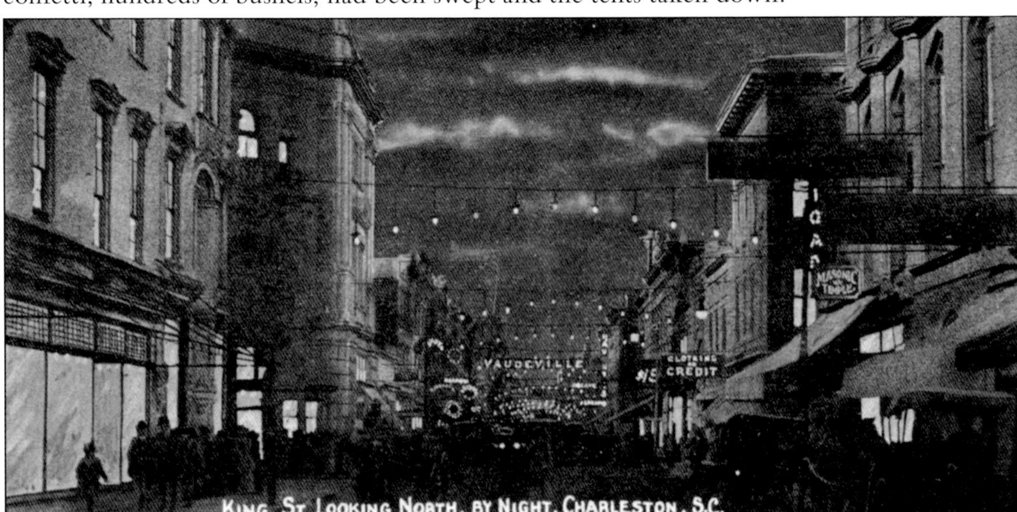

Down the street in this Charleston's night scene, the banner spanning the street reads "Vaudeville." The Victoria Theater opened at 68 Society Street, between King and Meeting Streets, on March 27, 1911. About 3,000 people paid from 10¢ to 30¢ to visit the theater on opening night. The Victoria became the Victory Theater at the end of World War I, and then it became history in 1945.

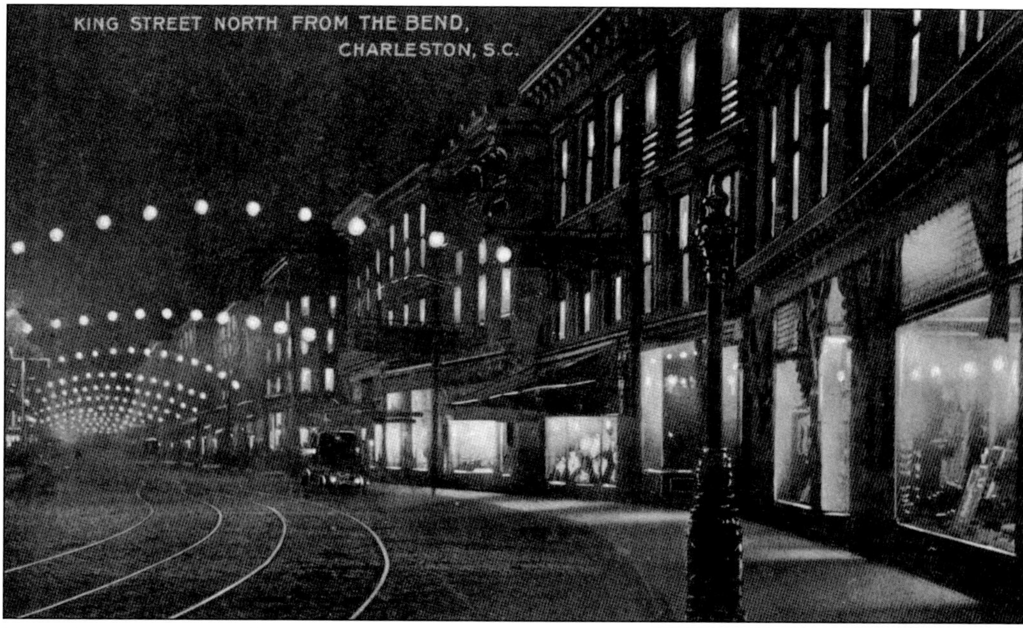

King Street seems eerily empty and ghostlike. A lone car ventures under the arches of lights that seem to be leading it down the bricked King Street toward the Battery area. The car drives past the well-lit windows wrapped in fog, making what should be colorful displays look like a series of monochromatic photographs.

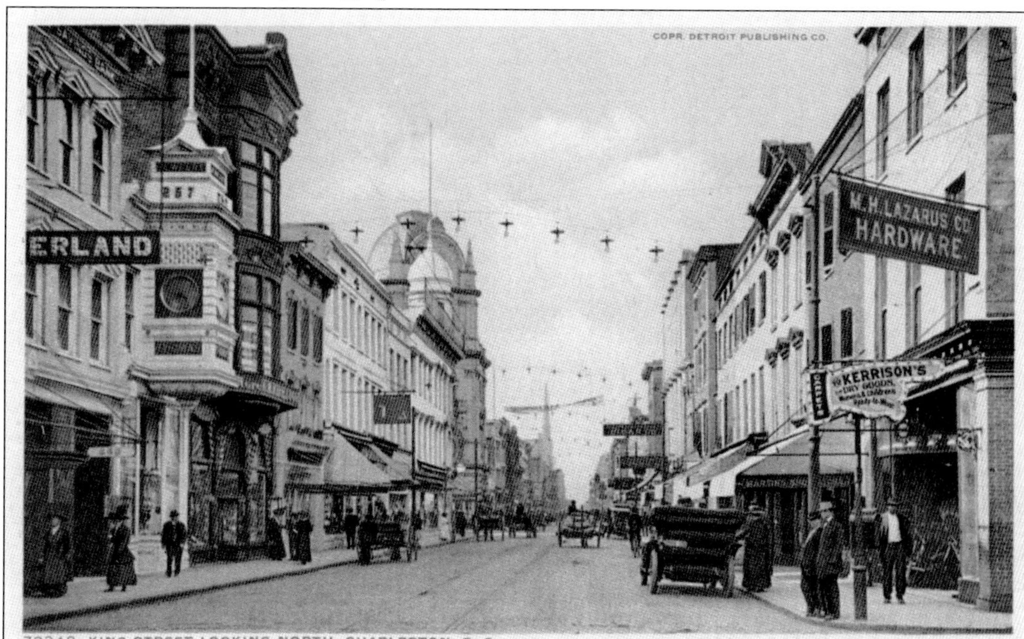

King Street is where the past meets the future in the present. Here, men and women wear yesterday's fashions while shopping for tomorrow's new look. Here is where the horse-drawn carriage meets the gas-driven horseless carriage under the streetlights that run on the same electricity that runs the street's other means of transportation, the trolley. Their Charleston shows some of their fathers' and hints at the Charleston of their children.

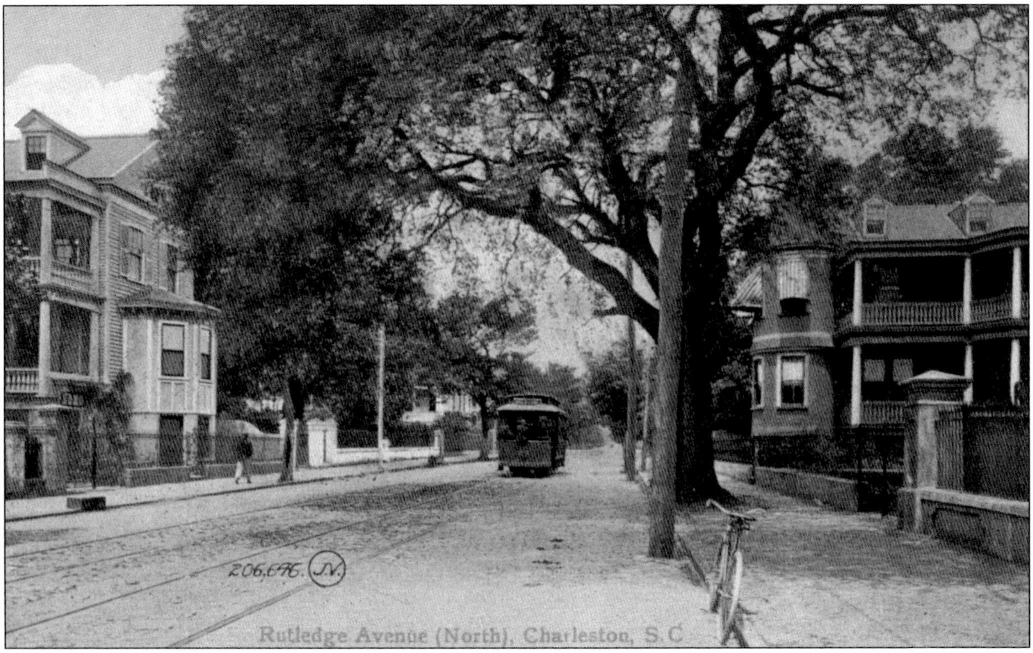

Rutledge Avenue was named after John Rutledge. Rutledge had been governor of South Carolina during the Revolutionary War as well as a delegate to both the First Continental Congress and the Constitutional Convention. Additionally, he served on both South Carolina's and the United States' supreme courts. Here, the bricked street looks to be a small-town street on a lazy day.

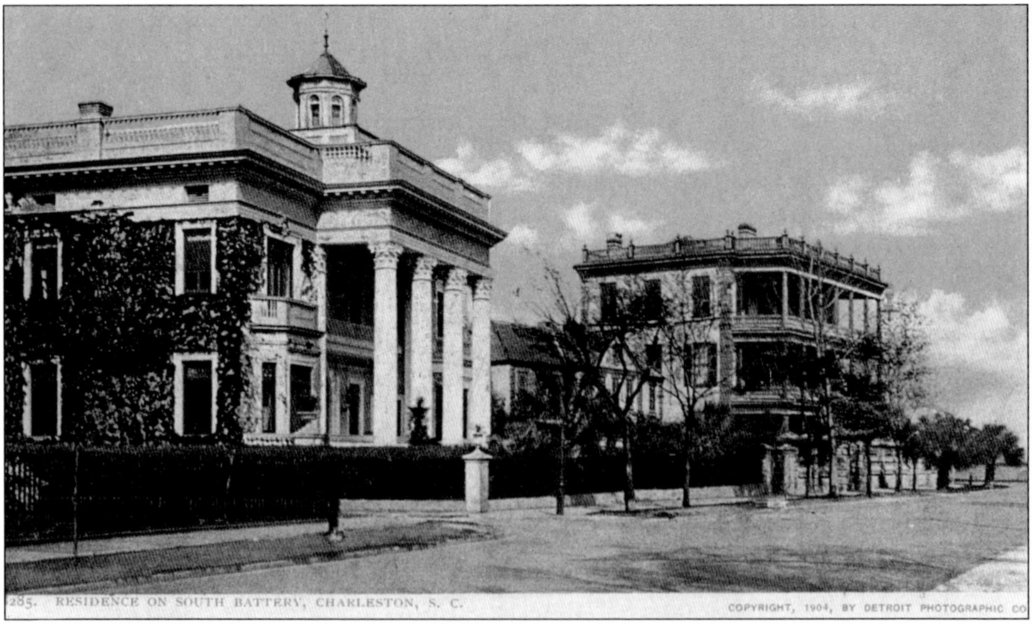

The columned house at 4 South Battery, once known as the "White House of South Carolina," is the Villa Margherita. It was built about 1892 by Andrew Simonds as a wedding present for his bride, Daisy Breaux O'Donovan, of Louisiana. Among Daisy's and the villa's guests were Presidents Cleveland, Taft, and Theodore Roosevelt, as well as author Sinclair Lewis. Today, the Villa Margherita is a private residence, as it began.

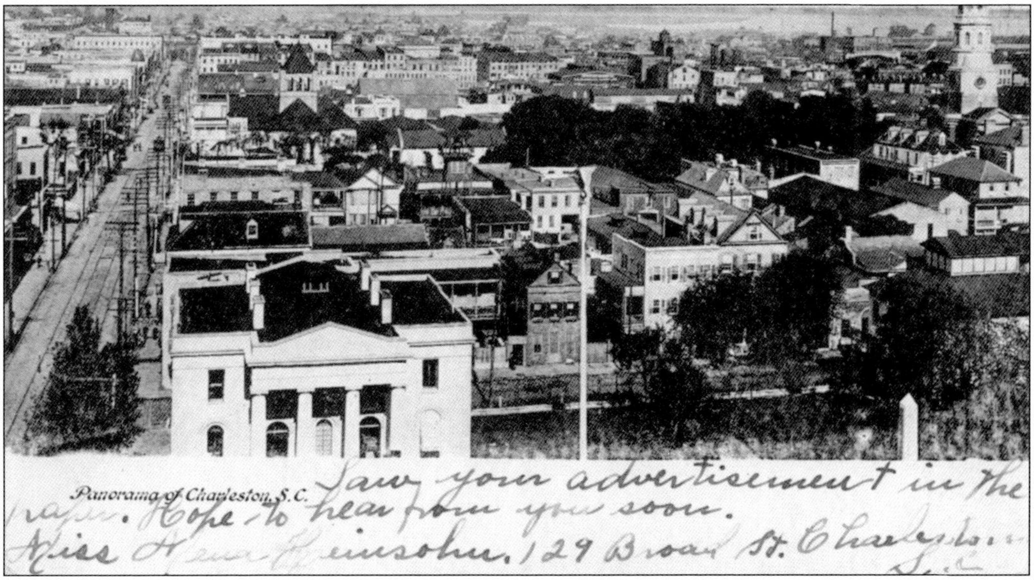

On October 28, 1909, Buffalo Bill Cody and Pawnee Bill were in Charleston for their Wild West Show. Along with them was Carter Couteurier, a ticket collector at one of the sideshows. He had been born in Charleston and fired one of the first shots that April morning in 1861. That night, Colonel Cody told Couteurier that Charleston was charming, and he wished he had been born here, too. Couteurier reminded his friend that he had been on the Union's side.

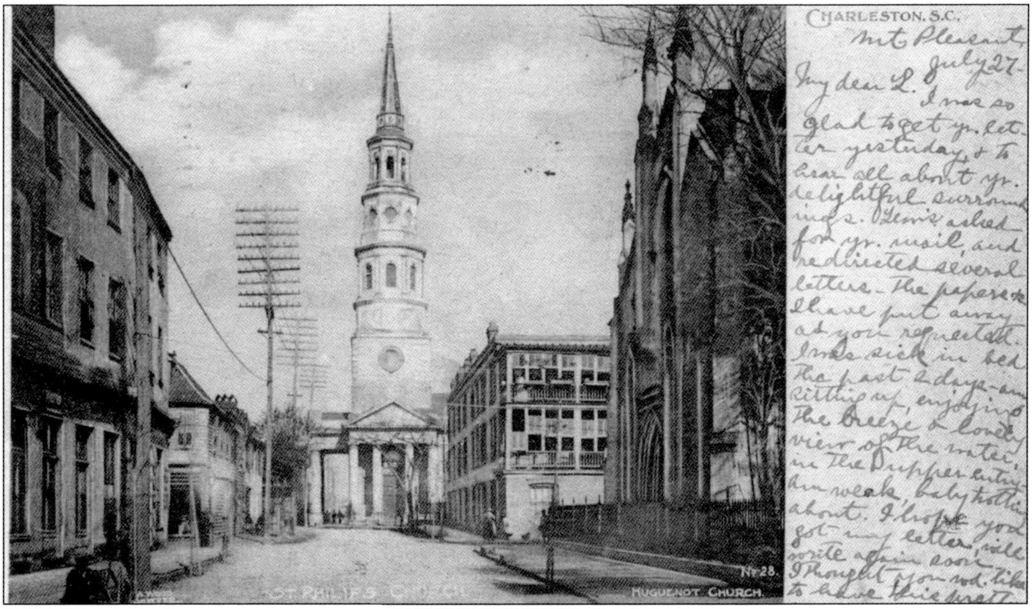

Church Street is pictured here with an old sawyer plying his trade to the left, in front of the former Planter's Hotel, and the Huguenot church on the right, with power lines running down the left side toward St. Philip's Church. St. Philip's was originally sited at Broad and Meeting Streets, the present location of St. Michael's Episcopal Church. As a result of the hurricane of 1710, the church was relocated to its present site. After coping with hurricanes, fires, and disease, the new church finally succumbed to fire in 1835. It was rebuilt only to have its steeple used as a target for Union cannons.

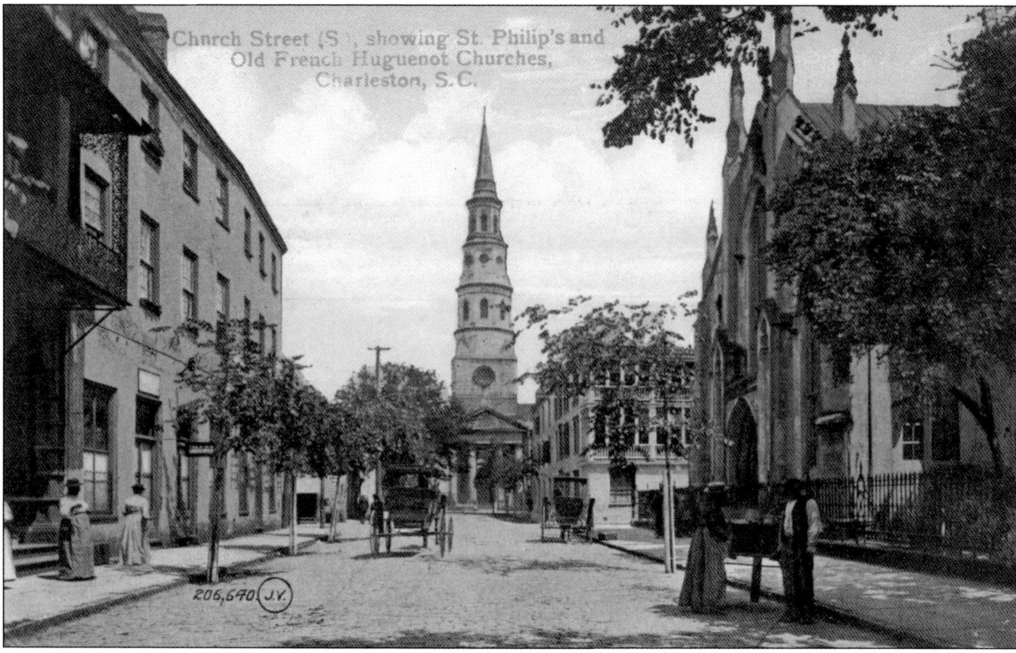

This view shows multiple carriages on what appears to be a bricked Church Street. St. Philip's Church is at the end, while the French Huguenot Church is to the right. To the left, where the ladies are about their business, is what was previously the old Planter's Hotel, but is now the Dock Street Theatre.

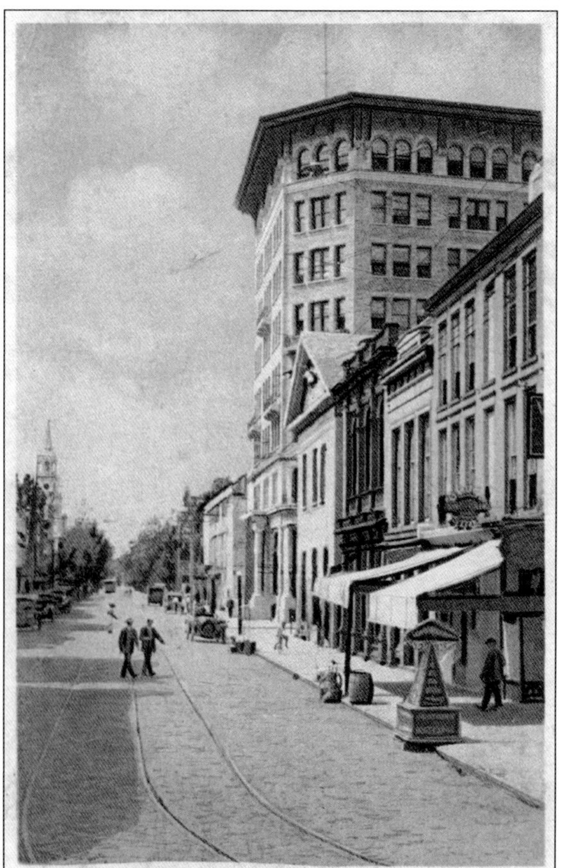

This is the view down Broad Street from the Exchange Building. The People's National Bank moved $3.25 million in money and assets across Broad Street to its new facilities in the new eight-story People's Building, on the corner of Broad and State Streets. The monies and assets were moved by gentlemen just crossing the street carrying paper bags that could have been their lunches.

Four

BUILDINGS

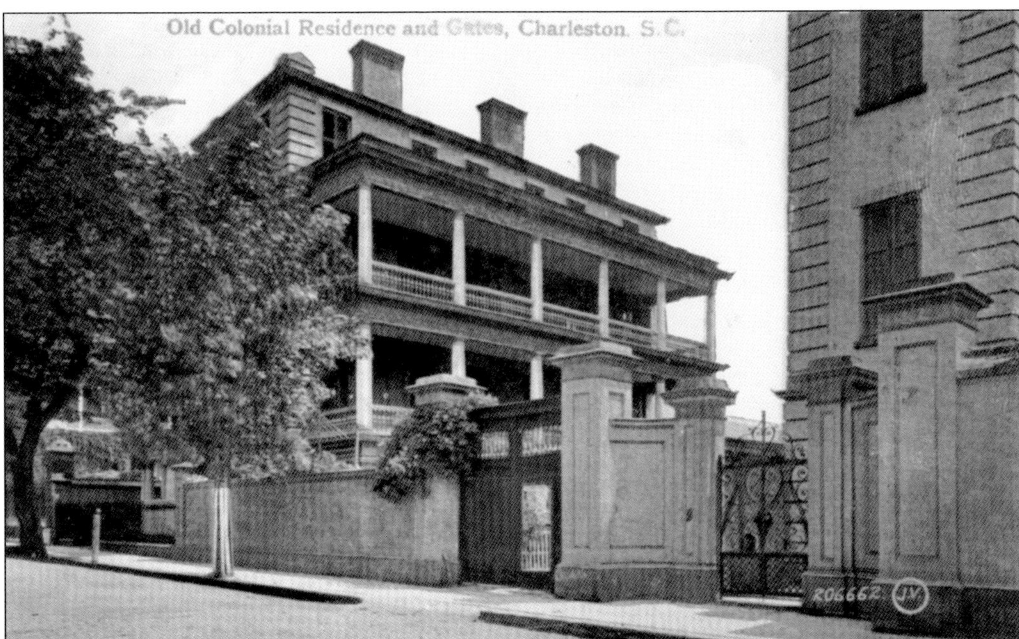

Many of the older houses of Charleston, like this one, seem to front on one of many quaint streets, but the street doors of these colonial houses do not open into the houses. Instead, the door opens onto the house's lower piazza. The piazza faced the owner's private gardens, which were usually behind a wall, as here. The privacy walls and the street doors allowed the house's owners to use the piazza and open windows to catch the breezes without being viewed or disturbed by passersby.

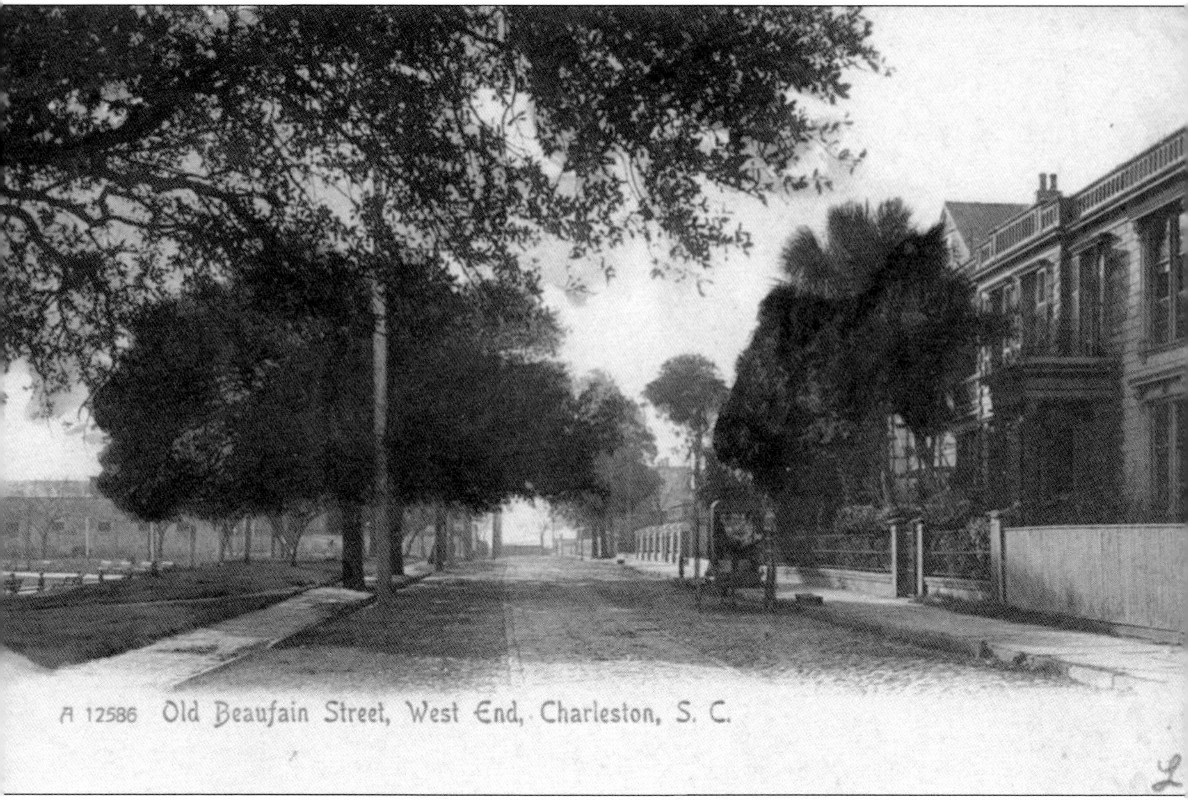

About 1831, John J. Audubon painted his great blue heron, probably while in Charleston. Some 80 years later, on July 24, 1911, the residents of this quiet cobblestoned street had their afternoon disturbed. A great blue heron appeared across the street from their homes on Colonial Lake. The great bird, chased by a group of young boys who were trying to capture it, tried to escape. It headed toward the Beaufain Street houses and crashed into a dwelling. It never recovered from its injury. According to the *Evening Post* of July 25, 1911, the bird was to be mounted for the Charleston Museum. It is still part of the museum's bird exhibit.

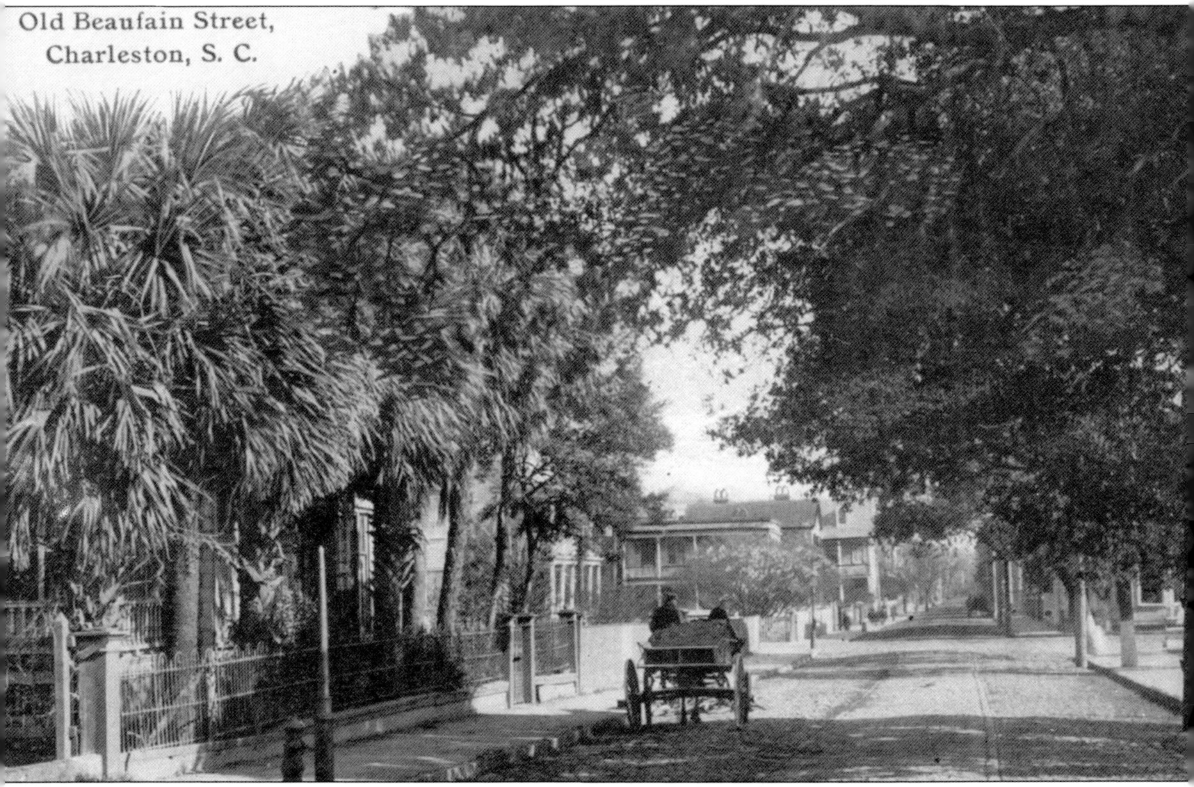

The September 23, 1906, *News and Courier* contains a cute story, "A Deal in Cabbages," about a vegetable huckster who guided his almost-empty wagon down a street, like Beaufain Street, until being stopped by a lady and asked if he had anything left. The salesman confessed to having one nice cabbage left. He had just sold the lady the 10¢ cabbage for 5¢ when another lady approached asking the same question. The huckster, to his first customer's surprise, said he had one cabbage left, and it was 10¢. The second customer agreed to buy the cabbage and offered her dime. Shocking the first customer, he took the cabbage from her arms and handed it to the second buyer, taking the proffered dime. The second customer left with the cabbage, as its first owner protested. The huckster handed the first owner the dime, telling her he had made her a nice profit on her cabbage. Before leaving aboard his now-empty wagon, he told the still-confused first customer that making profits like that is how people become rich.

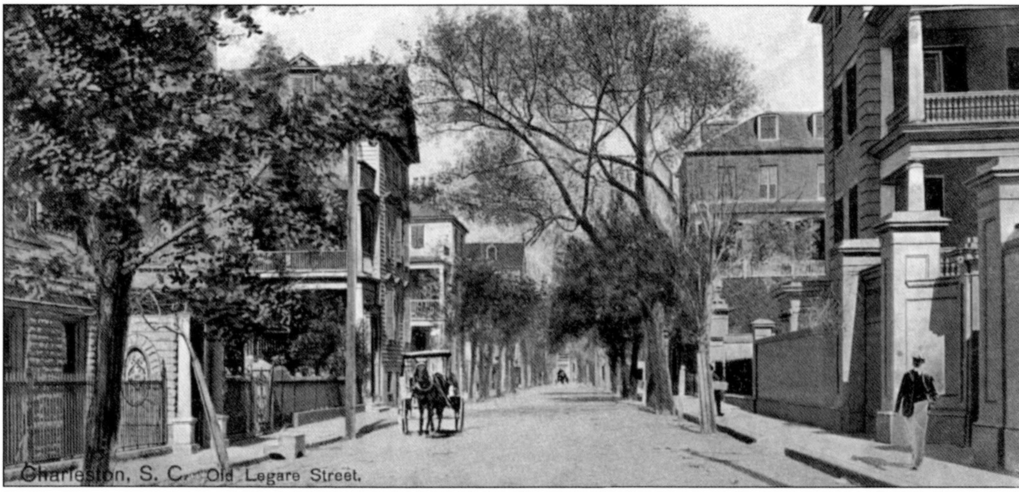

Legare Street was named after Charleston silversmith Solomon Legare, a wealthy French Huguenot. The houses on the street show the French Huguenot features of gables and multileveled piazzas, as do others on Charleston's Huguenot-named streets, such as Beaufain Street. Just past the gentleman on the right's head, one will see the pillar to the gate to the house's garden. There is a large dot to the left of the head that is another usual feature of some older Charleston houses, the placing of the home's doorbell on the gate to the garden, instead of on at the door that entered onto the lower piazza, allowing those sitting on the piazza to see who was calling. The *Evening Post* of April 11, 1902, quotes a visitor from Kentucky's impression of Charleston: "It is a historical fact it was settled by the French Huguenots and they have truly left their impression upon it. The architecture of the old French school is predominantly in evidence in the tall houses with their gable fronts flush to the streets, their picturesque piazzas running from front to rear with entrance by a front door. A most interesting feature to a stranger is the bell being placed at the gate instead of the door."

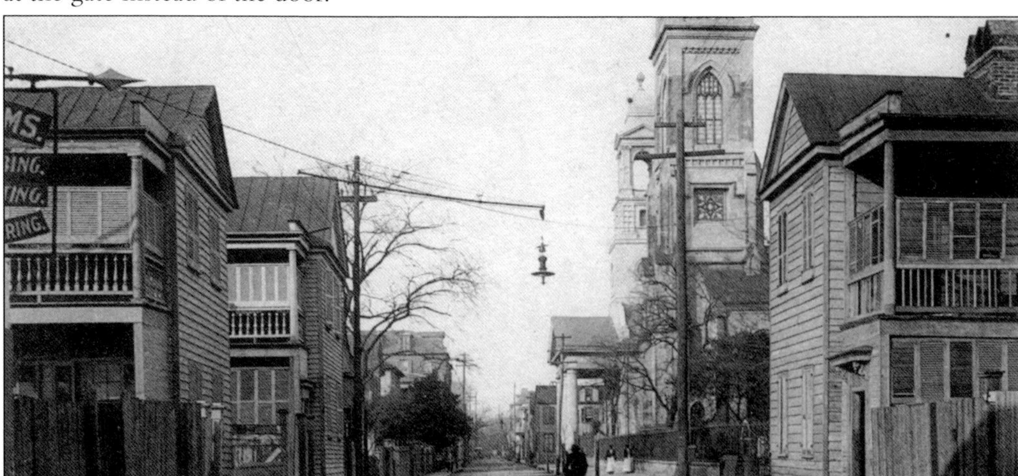

President-elect Taft, a Unitarian, worshiped at this Unitarian church on January 24, 1909, while visiting Charleston. The church, located at 4 Archdale Street, stands where the two aproned ladies are visiting. Its graveyard is left more natural and overgrown than those of most churches. Annabel Lee of Edgar Allan Poe fame is said to haunt the graveyard.

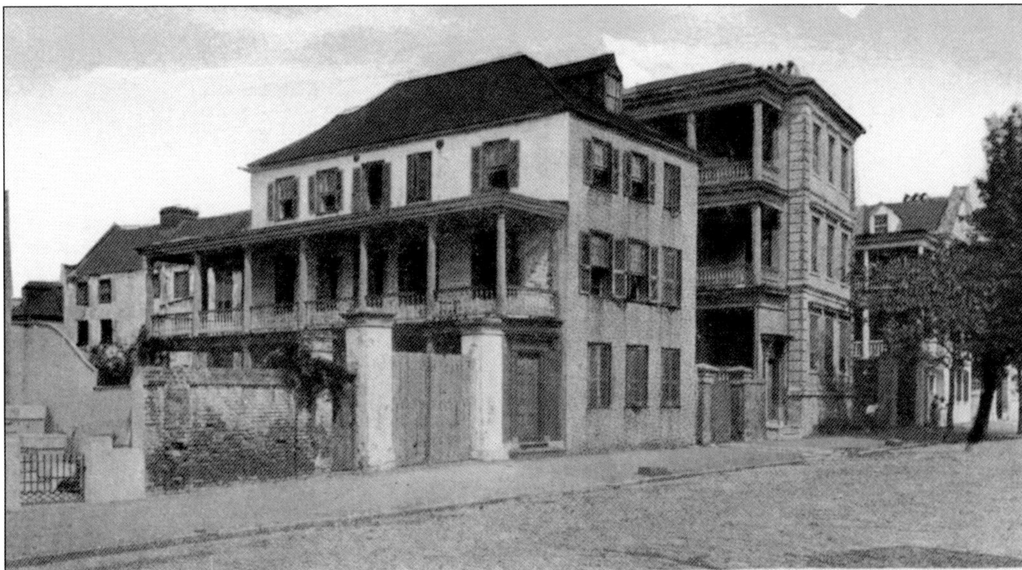

1420 OLD COLONIAL HOUSE, SHOWING SLAVE QUARTERS IN REAR, CHARLESTON, S. C.

The residence at 43 East Bay Street is referred to as the George Sommers House. It is located on part of what was referred to a lot No. 1 of the Grand Modell near the city wall. The house may date from around the Revolutionary War, as the *City Gazette* of November 12, 1791, references it.

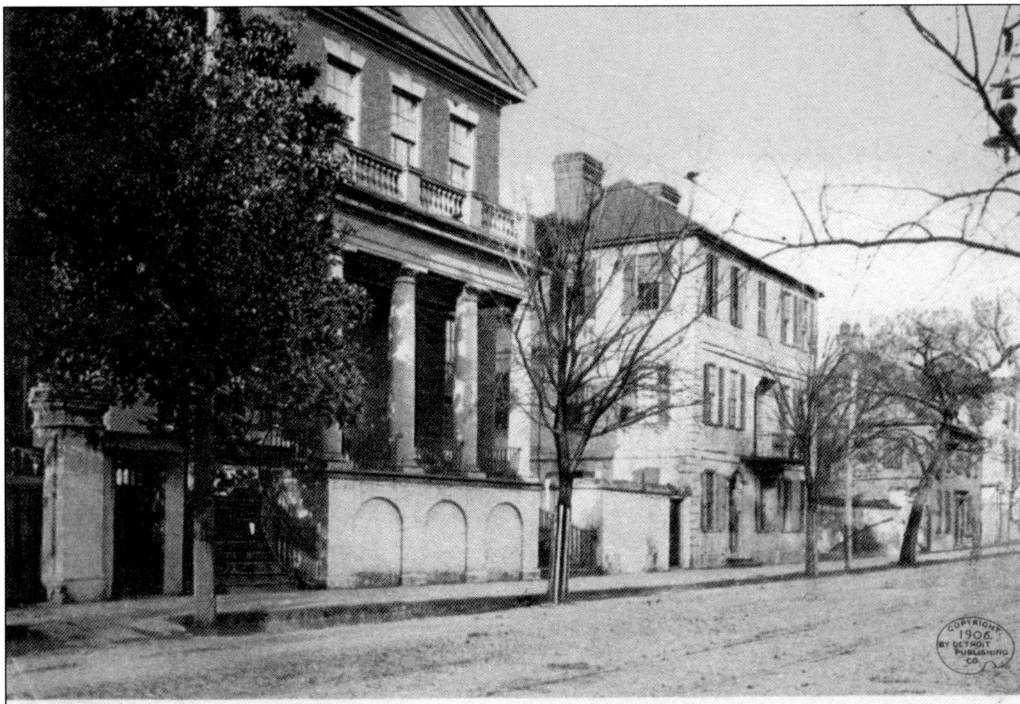

0555. A BIT OF WEST BROAD STREET, CHARLESTON, S. C.

This house is at 114 Broad Street. The building was begun about 1790 and completed years later by Colonel Pinckney. For a brief period in 1863, it was used by Confederate general P.G.T. Beauregard as his headquarters and as such hosted Confederate president Jefferson Davis.

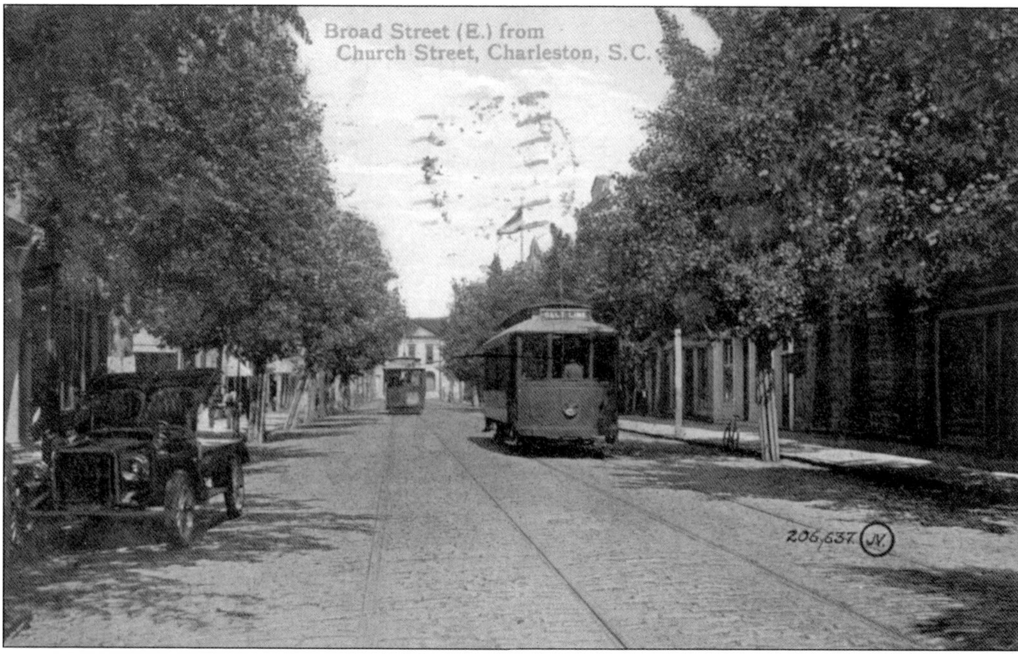

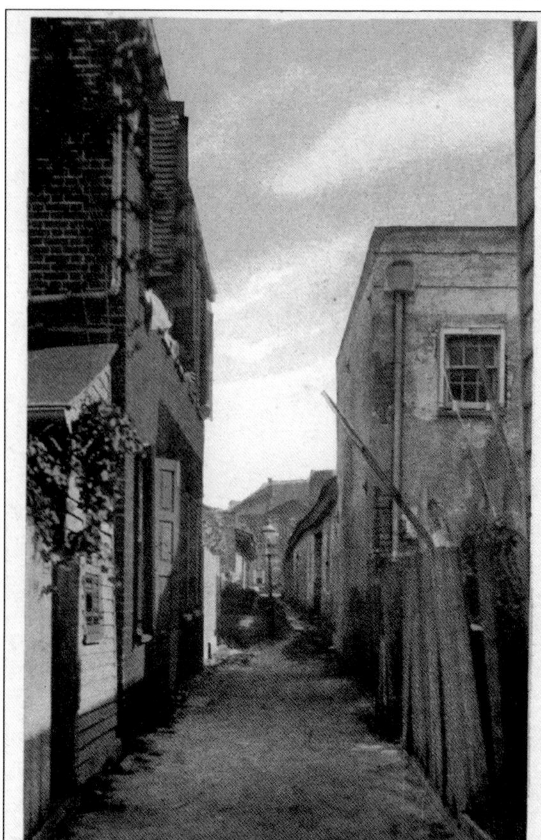
1424 LONGITUDE LANE, CHARLESTON, S. C.

Trolley cars were used throughout the city for transportation. The trolley routes even extended to the new Navy Yard, north of the city. On March 19, 1909, Dr. Booker T. Washington took the trolley to the Navy Yard and joined the list of distinguished visitors to tour the dry docks as well as other parts of it. Later that evening, after a probable return trolley ride to the city, he was introduced by then-mayor Hon. R.G. Rhett at Charleston's Emanuel A.M.E. Church, where he discussed the education of Charleston's black population and their potential as skilled labor.

This street runs between Church and East Bay Streets. A small black cannon was discovered 1853 when excavating the lane. The Longitude Lane residents half buried it, barrel down, in the middle of the narrow end of the street to make it impossible for wagons taking cotton to the press at the other end to use the cut-through. In 1933, the city confiscated the cannon. The residents tried to get it back but lost in court in what has been called the Battle of Longitude Lane. A stone post is now found where the cannon was.

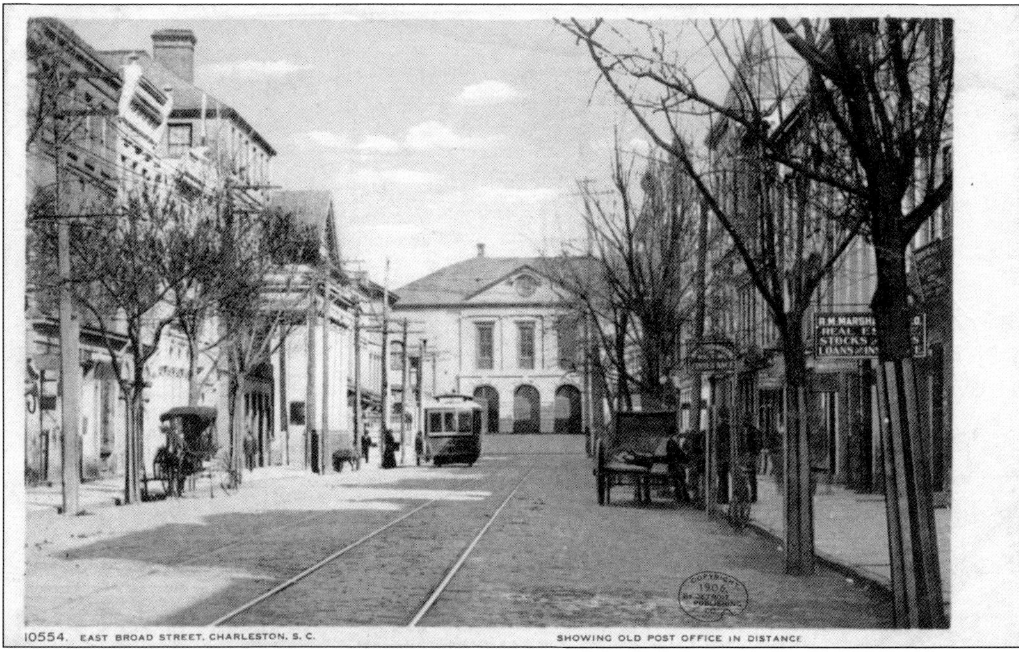

Broad Street appears bricked. At the end is the present Exchange Building, or the old post office, where Broad and East Bay Streets meet. An electric trolley goes both up and down the street. To the left is a horse-drawn carriage, while to the right are a horse-drawn wagon and a bicycle.

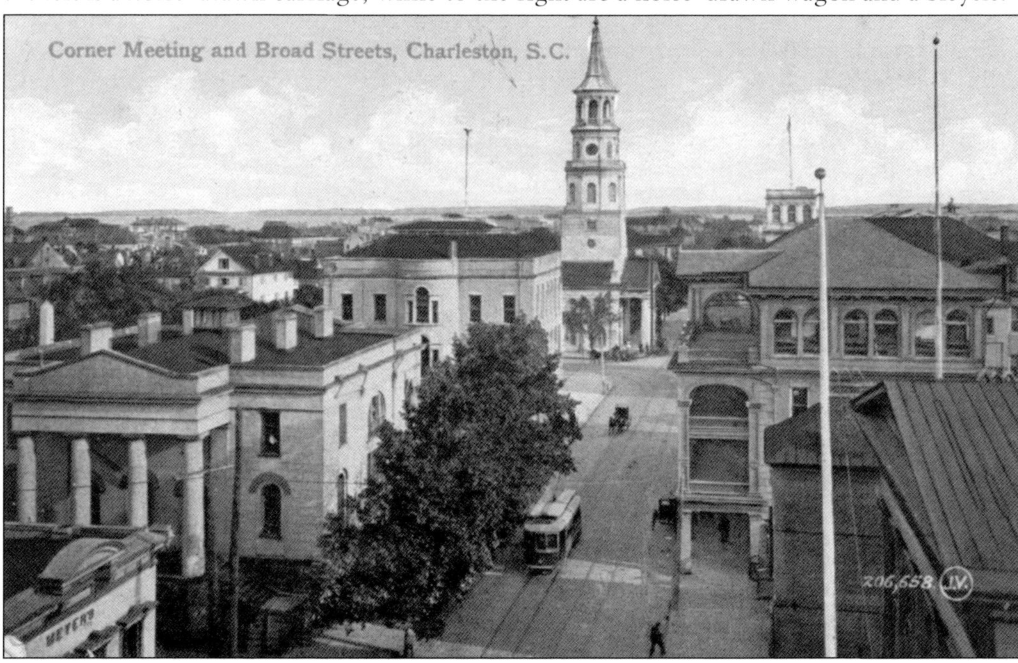

This view looks down Meeting Street, probably from the Hotel St. John, which opened in 1902. To the left, the columned building is the Fireproof Building, currently the home of the South Carolina Historical Society, and just beyond that is Charleston City Hall. Across Broad Street is St. Michael's Church. To the right is the Commercial Club, where the current Charleston County Office Building is located. Note the horse-drawn carriages and the electric trolley.

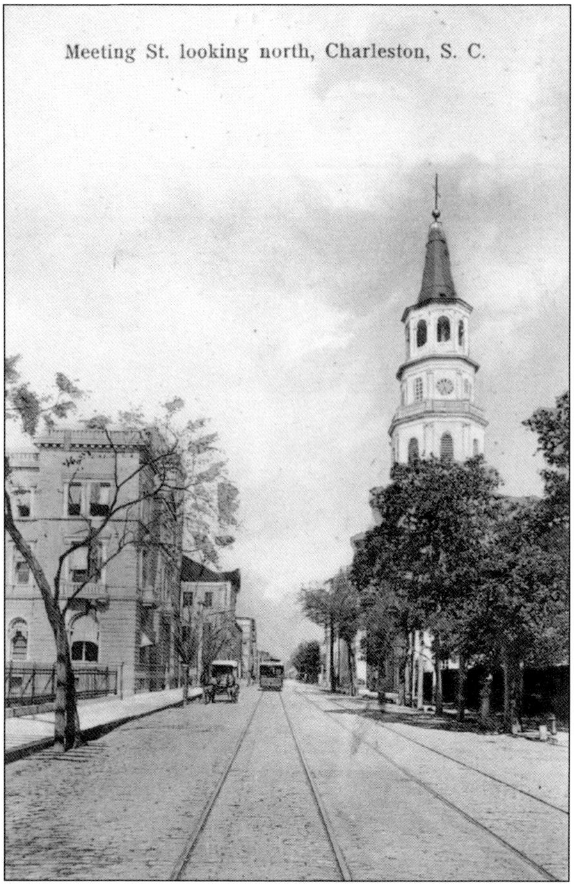

Notice what looks like a bricked Meeting Street with St. Michael's steeple rising above the trees to the right and the post office to the left. On the bricked street is a parked automobile and coming down its tracks is the trolley.

Pictured here is Meeting Street with the trolley coming up it. Rising above the street is St. Michael's steeple. To the right is the South Carolina Society Hall. It was completed about 1804; the portico was added in 1825. Mel Gibson's *The Patriot* was filmed in Charleston, and in a night scene King George III is hanged in effigy from the portico.

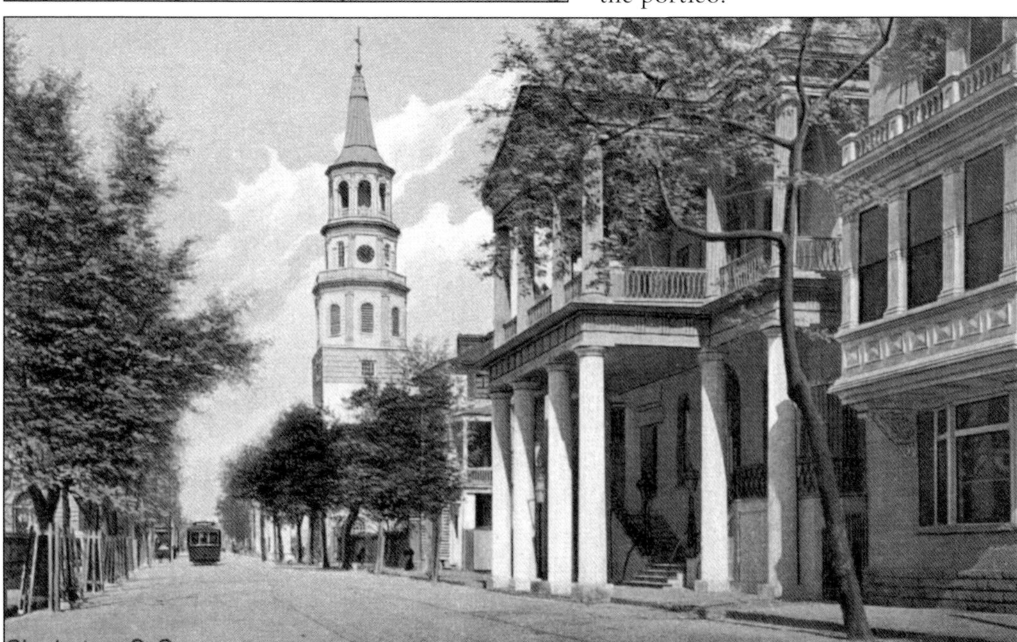

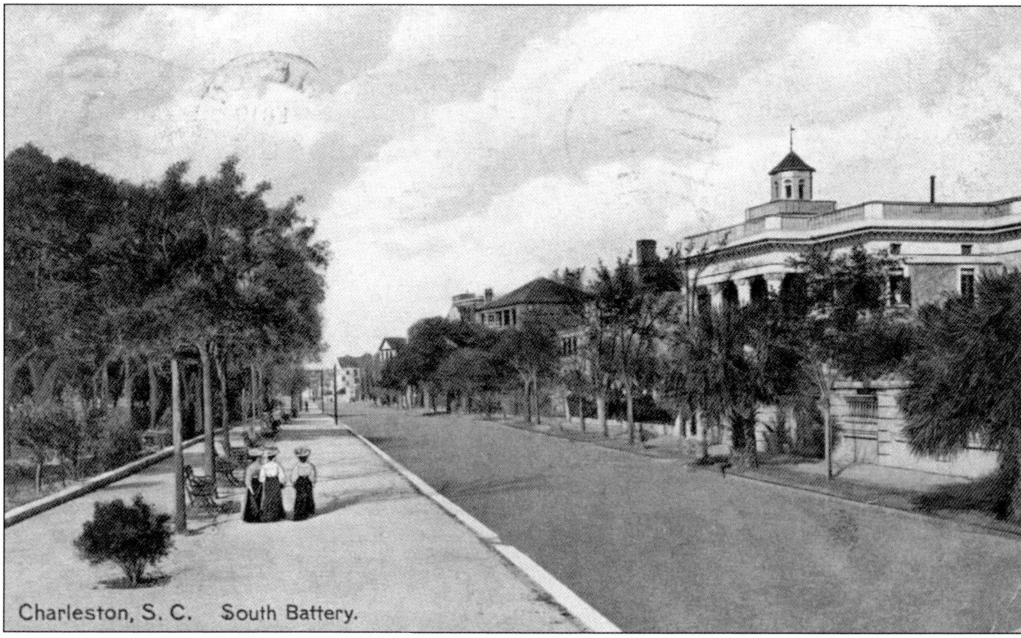

These three women are strolling along the fringe of White Point Garden. The columned house to the right is the Villa Margherita. Perhaps on their stroll they saw the monument noting the hangings of the "Gentleman Pirate" Stede Bonnet and pirate Richard Worley, as well as members of their crews, or the fountain donated by the Daughters of the Confederacy near the bandstand.

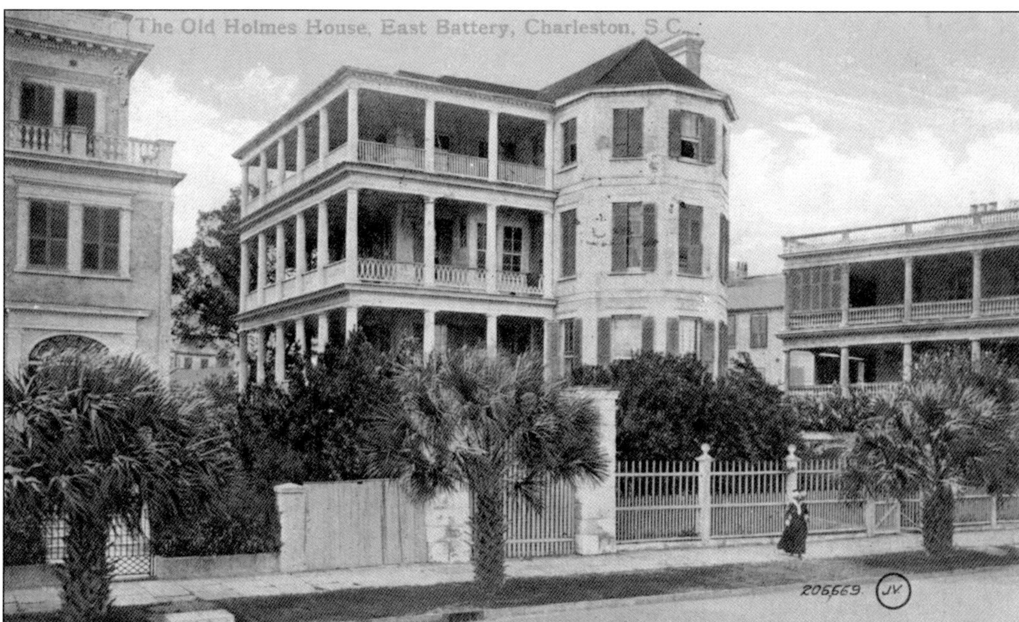

The picturesque palmetto tree–lined East Battery is the perfect background for the well-dressed lady in front of the Holmes Mansion. By the palmetto tree to the left is a horse block for use when dismounting a carriage or horse. The Holmes Mansion survived the earthquake of 1886 but was so damaged by the hurricane of 1911 it had to be demolished.

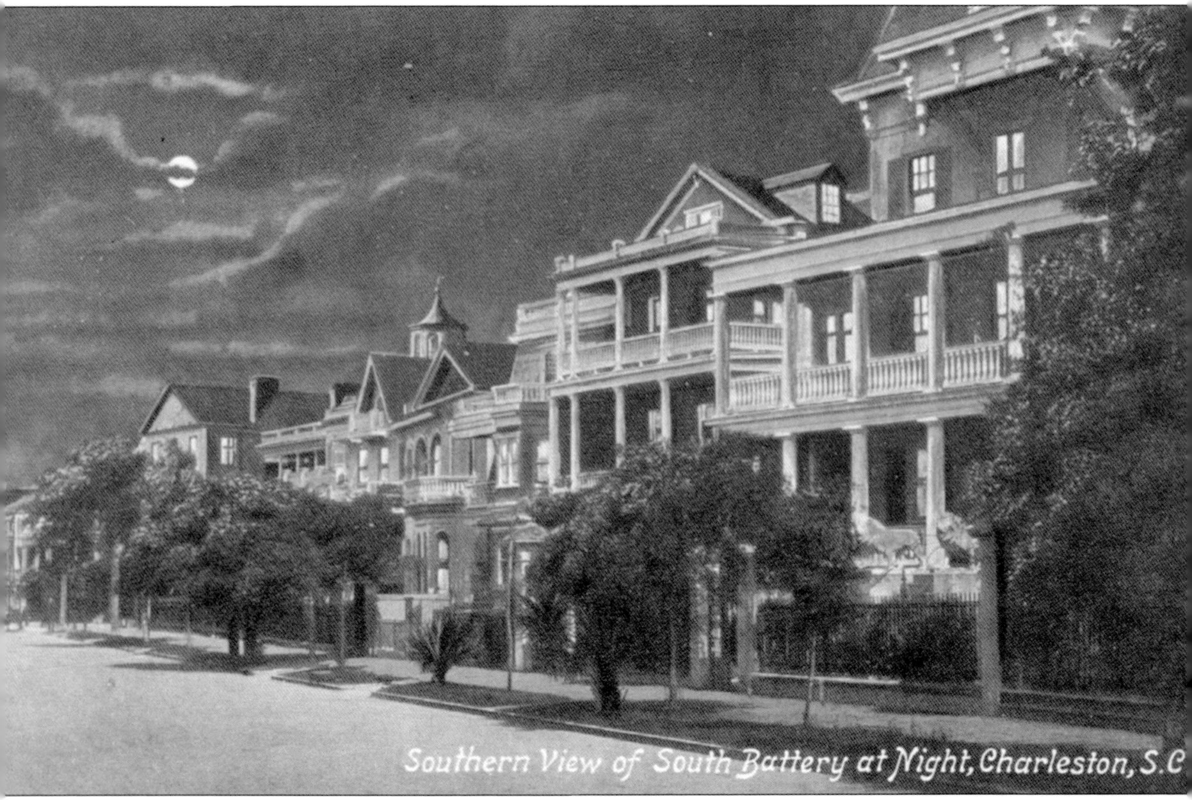

The residents of the Battery area, as well as strollers, were treated to natural fireworks displays a few days and nights in August 1912. On the night of August 10, a larger than ordinary shooting star was reported with a comet-like tail. The fireworks were so plentiful, the residents here would only have had to sit on their piazzas to catch a cool evening breeze and gaze skyward.

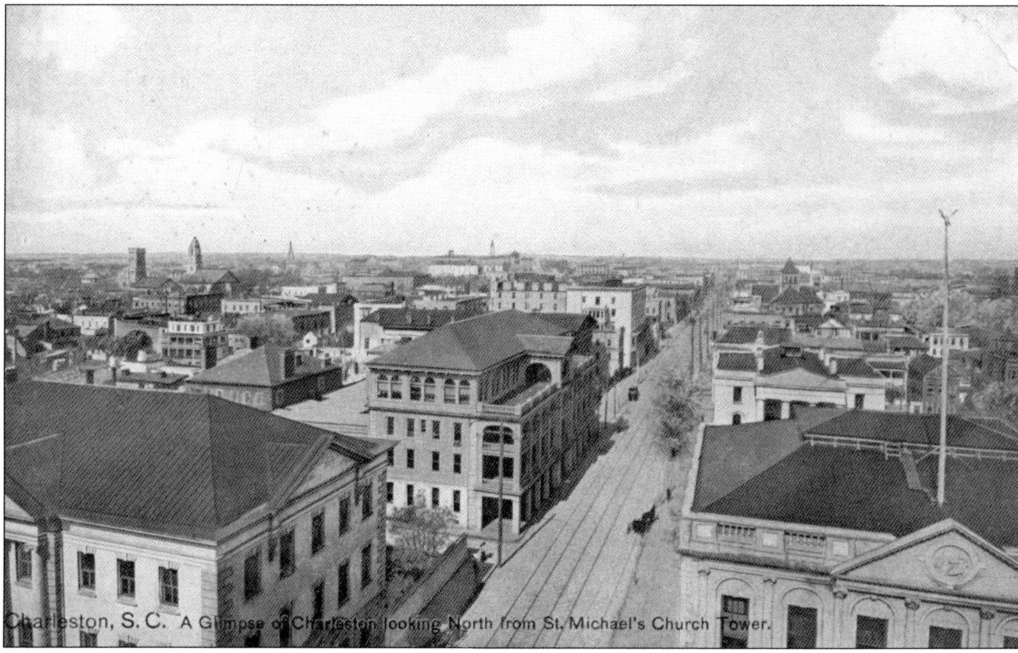

These views down Meeting Street show different perspectives. One is street-level. To the right is Charleston City Hall, while on the left is the county courthouse. Beyond the courthouse is the Commercial Club. Beyond city hall are the fence and gate that protect and open to Washington Square Park and its statues and memorials. Beyond the park is the Robert Mills–designed Fireproof Building. Note all the electrical wires needed for electric lights and the trolley system. The other is a bird's-eye view from the steeple of St. Michael's and shows the county courthouse to the left and city hall to the right, as well as rooftop views of the Commercial Club to the left and the Fireproof Building to the right and the rooftops of Charleston in the direction toward Marion Square, as well as the trolley tracks.

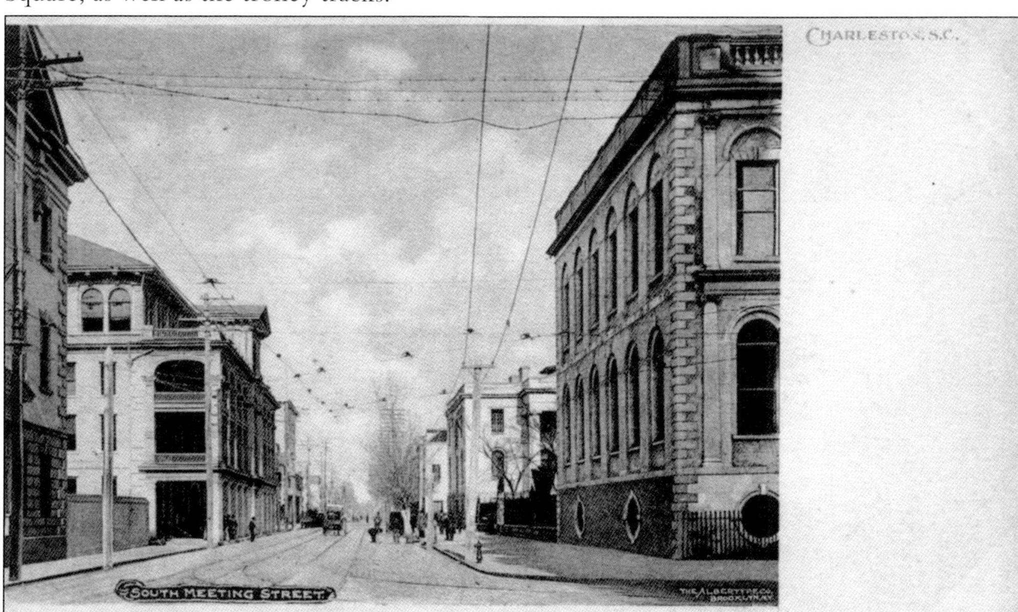

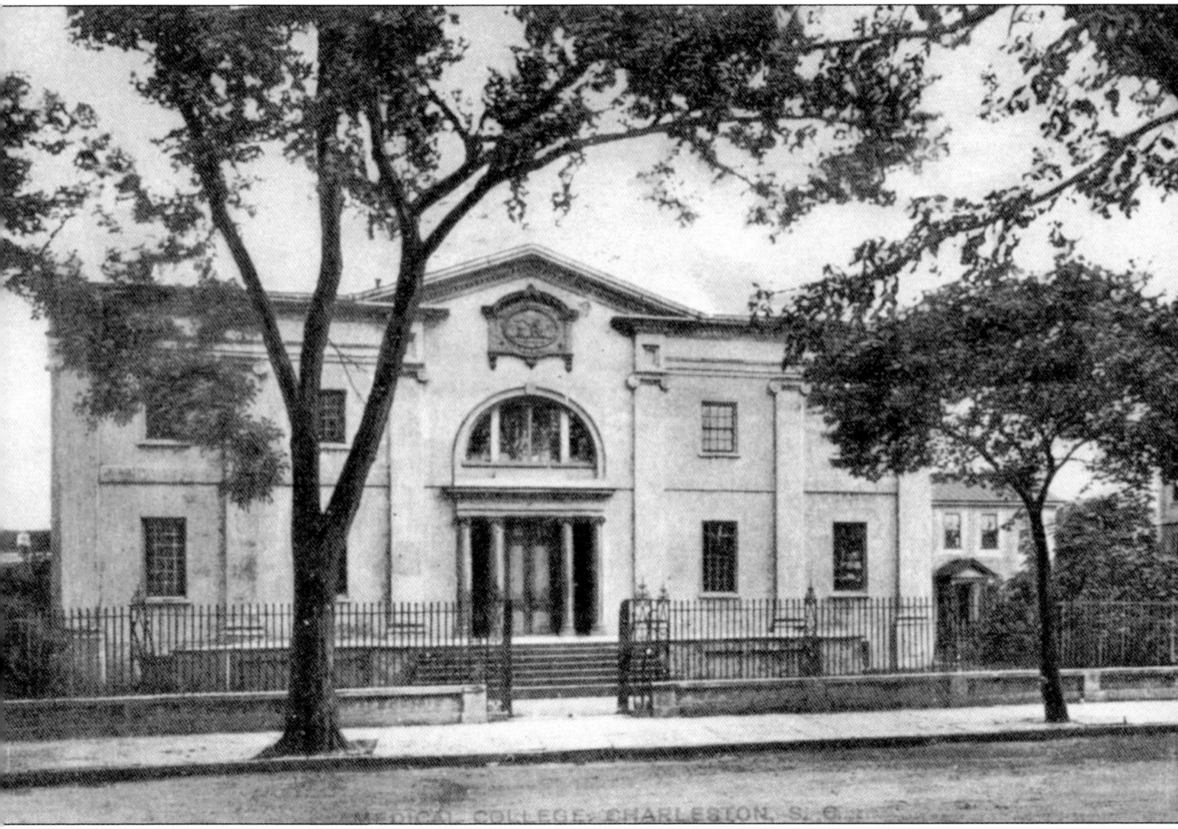

With its medical society and medical library, Charleston had a medical reputation before its medical college was chartered in 1823. It was the 10th such school in the country. The privately owned school opened on Queen Street in Charleston in 1824, and except for the years of the Civil War, it has stayed open continuously. In 1913, it became a state school.

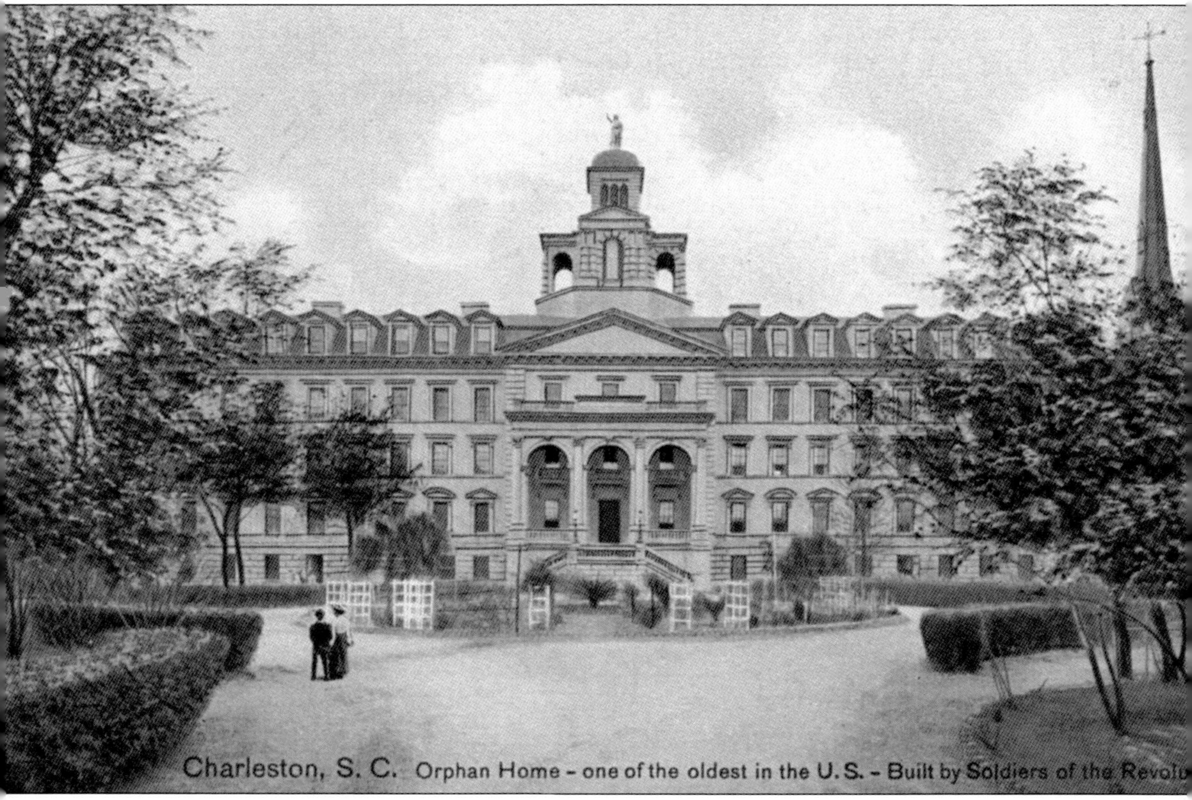

The Charleston Orphan House was founded in 1790 for orphans from the Revolutionary War, opening with 22. George Washington visited the next year and laid its cornerstone. The building was remodeled in the 1850s; it faced St. Philip's Street and was bounded by what was called Boundary Street, now Calhoun Street. In 1858, it celebrated its 69th anniversary and housed 333 children. While it had grown, the orphan house had lost seven from the previous year—six were given to relatives, 10 were bound out to various professions (blacksmith, printer, druggist, merchant, saddler, and milliner), and one became a domestic. The structure was razed in 1956 to make room for a Sears Roebuck; the children had been moved to a facility five years earlier. The property is now part of the College of Charleston campus.

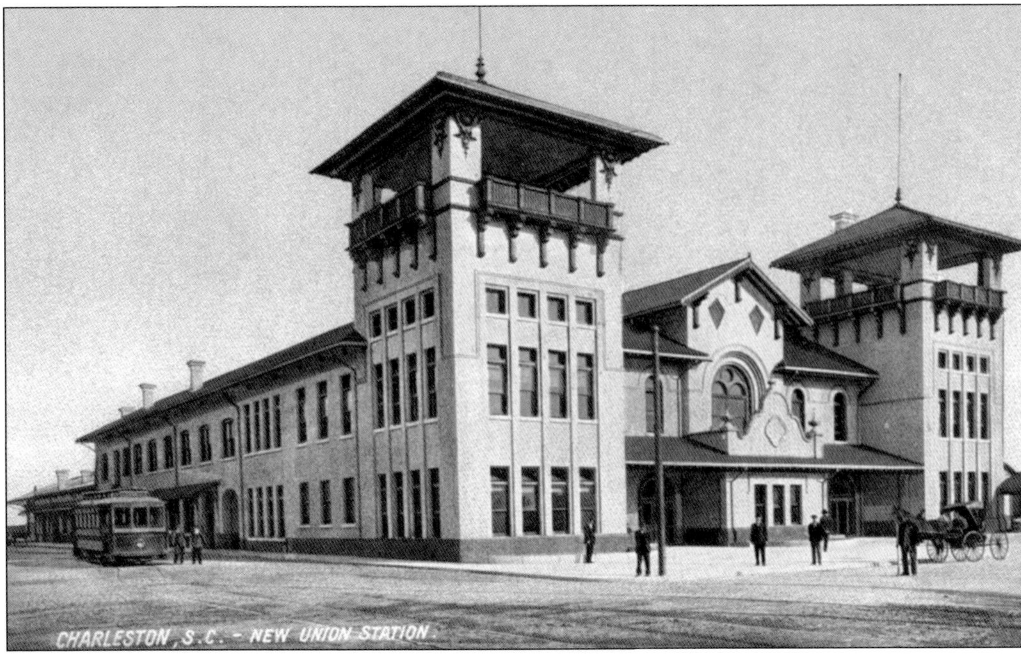

Union Station opened at 12:05 p.m. on November 10, 1907, with the arrival of Southern Railways No. 12 from Columbia. Its passengers were the first to unload at Charleston's new station. Adding to their number were a number of young local guys who decided to jump on the slow-moving train. The Columbus Street station was destroyed by fire on January 11, 1947.

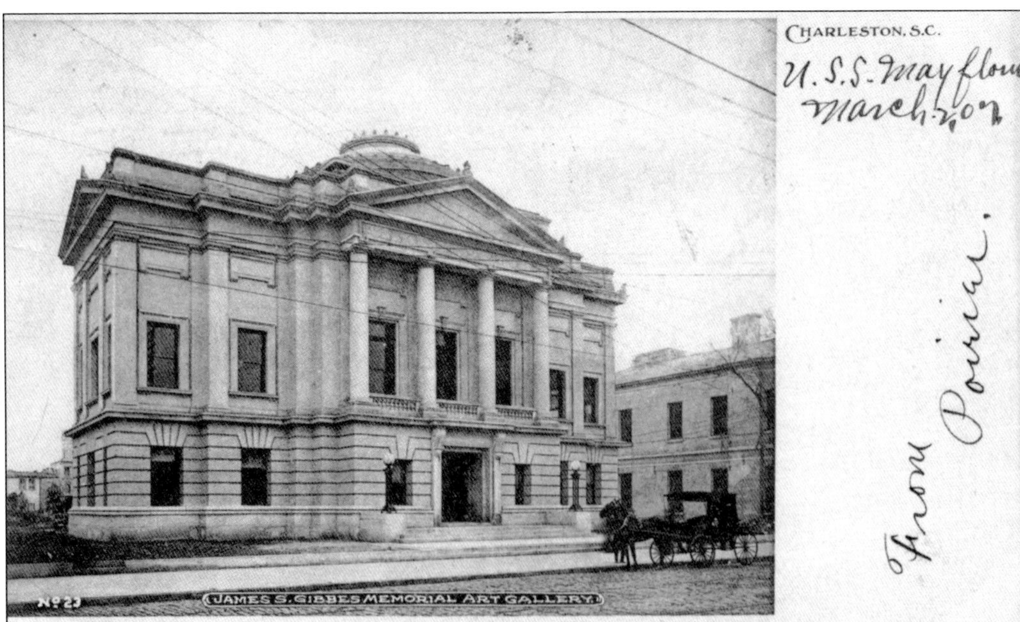

The James S. Gibbes Memorial Art Gallery is located at 135 Meeting Street. Gibbes left $100,000 to be used to buy or construct a building to exhibit paintings. The cornerstone was laid with full Masonic rites on December 8, 1903, and the gallery opened in 1905 with a collection borrowed from Charlestonians, as well as other sources. Today, it houses some 10,000 works of art.

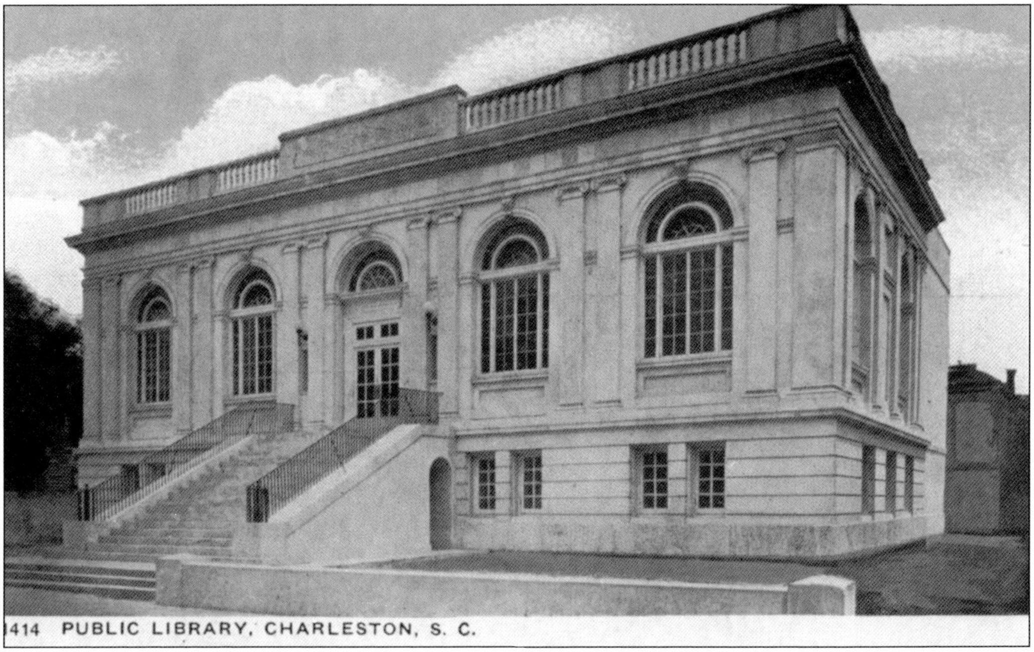

The Charleston Library Society was organized in 1748. Some of the material collected became the beginnings of the Charleston Museum. The society opened the doors to this Italian Renaissance–style fireproof building and its over 60,000-item collection at 164 King Street on July 20, 1914. Today, it has many historical volumes and newspapers available for research and is still open to its subscription members as a regular library.

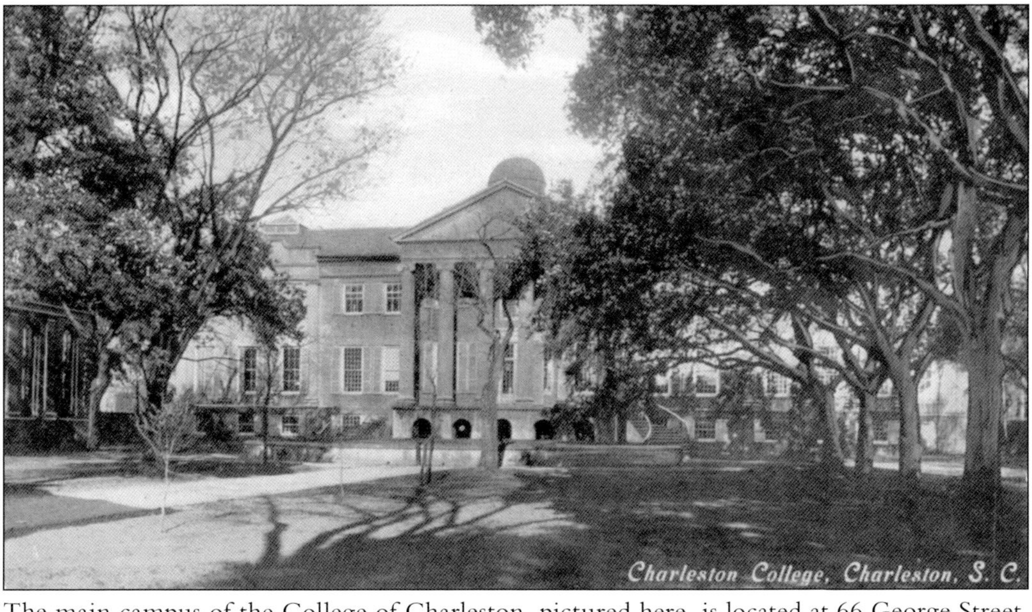

The main campus of the College of Charleston, pictured here, is located at 66 George Street. It was founded in 1770 and chartered 15 years later. It is the oldest college in the state of South Carolina and one of the oldest in the United States. Originally a municipal college, it is now a part of the state system. The building to the left was the school's library. Currently, the college has over 10,000 undergraduate students enrolled and a newer, much bigger library.

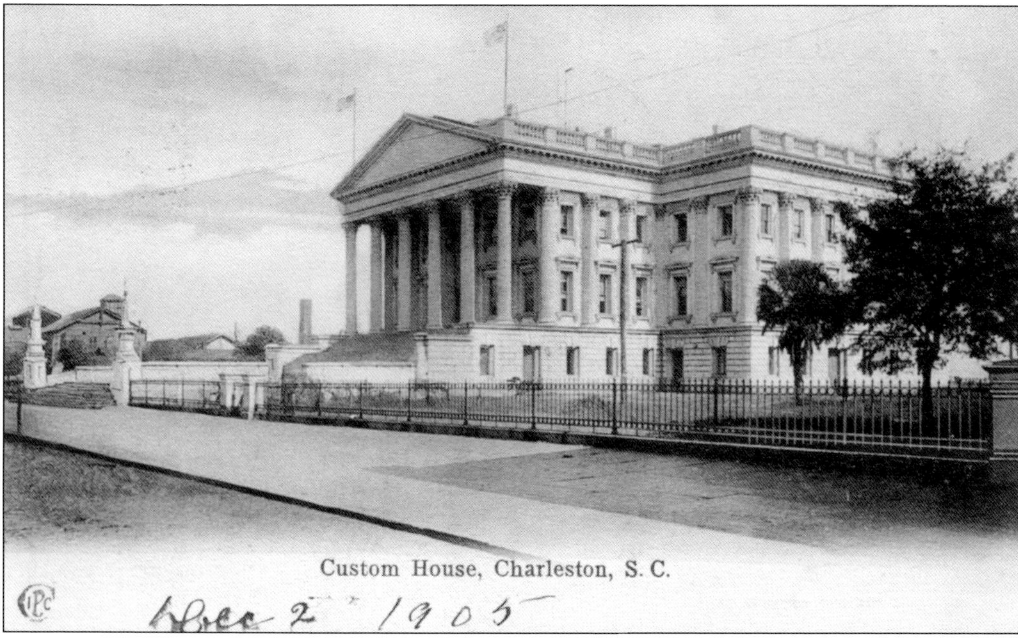

On East Bay Street near the end of the market sheds, land was purchased in 1849 for a new custom house. Construction began four years later, but due to building and political issues and the Civil War, it was stopped, restarted, and not completed until 1879. Electric lights and modern plumbing were added in 1910. The rear of the US Custom House overlooks the Cooper River.

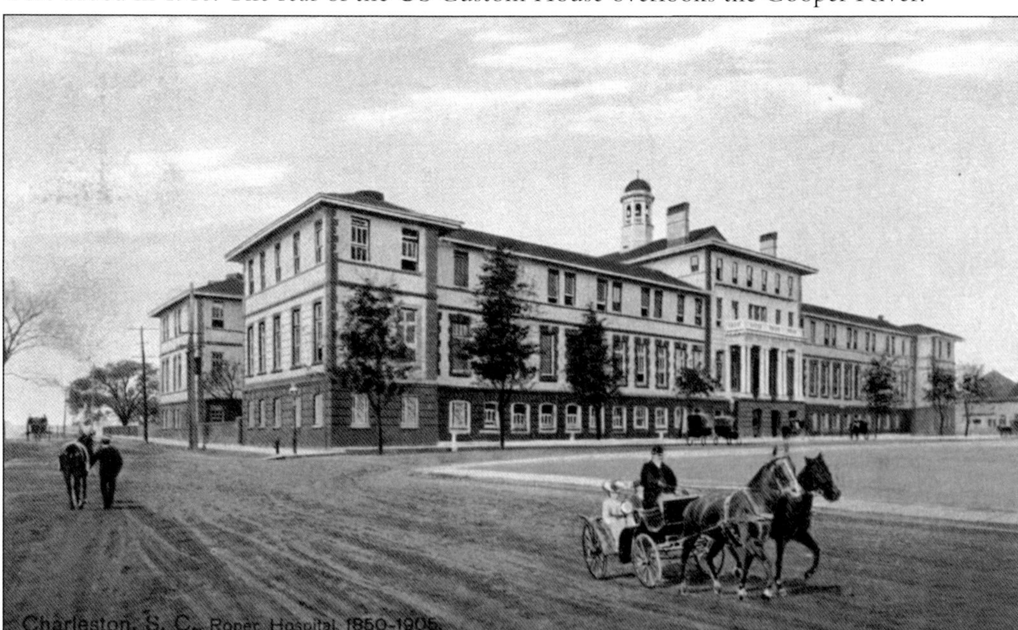

Roper Hospital began with the founding of the Medical Society of South Carolina in 1789 and the 1852 donation of $30,000 to it by Thomas Roper to build a hospital. The first Roper Hospital opened on Queen Street near Logan Street in 1856, only to be destroyed by the earthquake of 1886. A new Roper Hospital opened on Calhoun and Lucas (now Barre) Streets on February 9, 1906. While it was under construction, the hospital operated out of Thomson Auditorium.

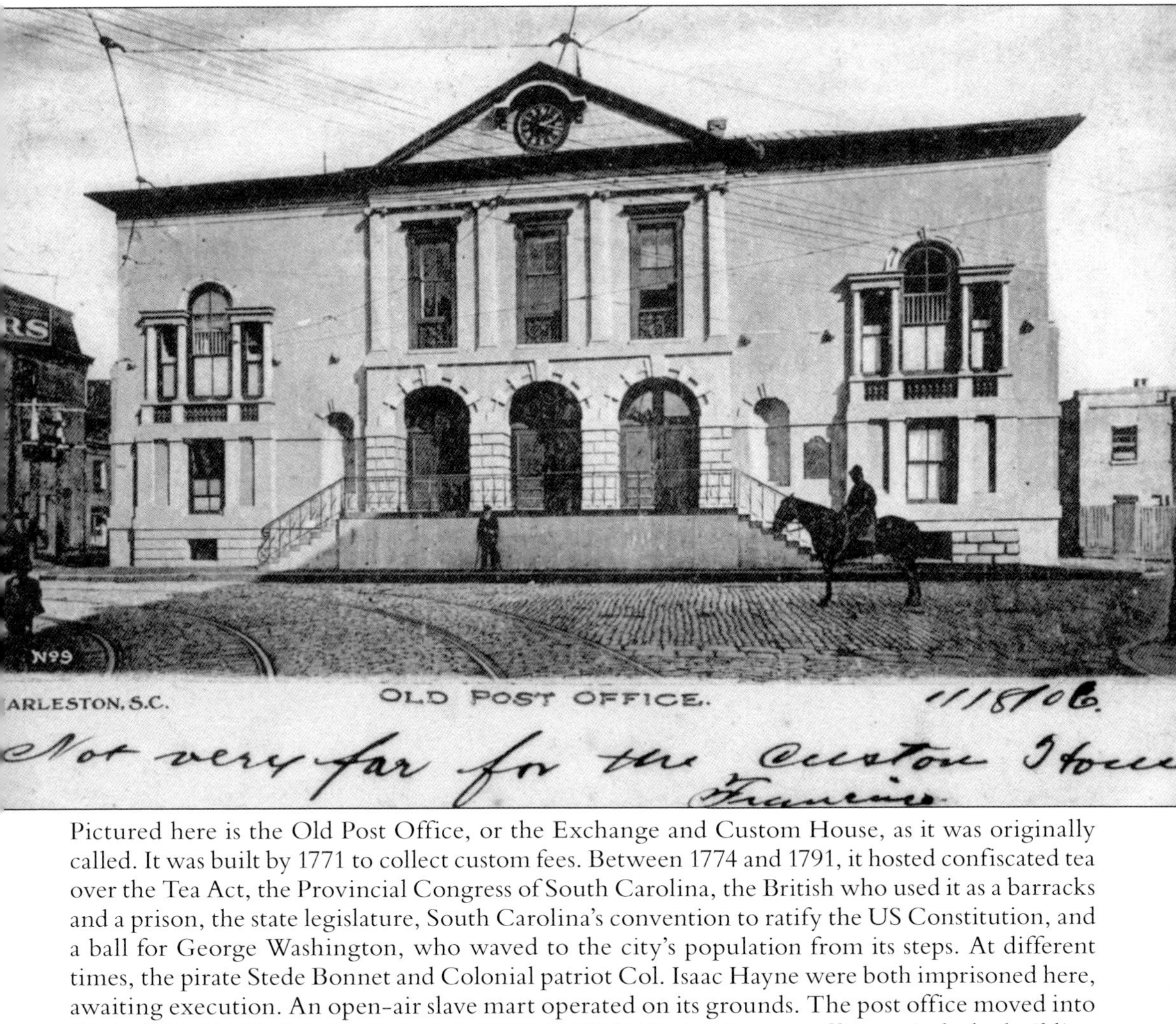

Pictured here is the Old Post Office, or the Exchange and Custom House, as it was originally called. It was built by 1771 to collect custom fees. Between 1774 and 1791, it hosted confiscated tea over the Tea Act, the Provincial Congress of South Carolina, the British who used it as a barracks and a prison, the state legislature, South Carolina's convention to ratify the US Constitution, and a ball for George Washington, who waved to the city's population from its steps. At different times, the pirate Stede Bonnet and Colonial patriot Col. Isaac Hayne were both imprisoned here, awaiting execution. An open-air slave mart operated on its grounds. The post office moved into the building in 1815 and operated there until 1896. During its post office period, the building survived, with repairs, both Union bombardment and the earthquake of 1886. In 1913, title was transferred to the Rebecca Motte Chapter of the Daughters of the American Revolution, which opened it as a museum in 1981.

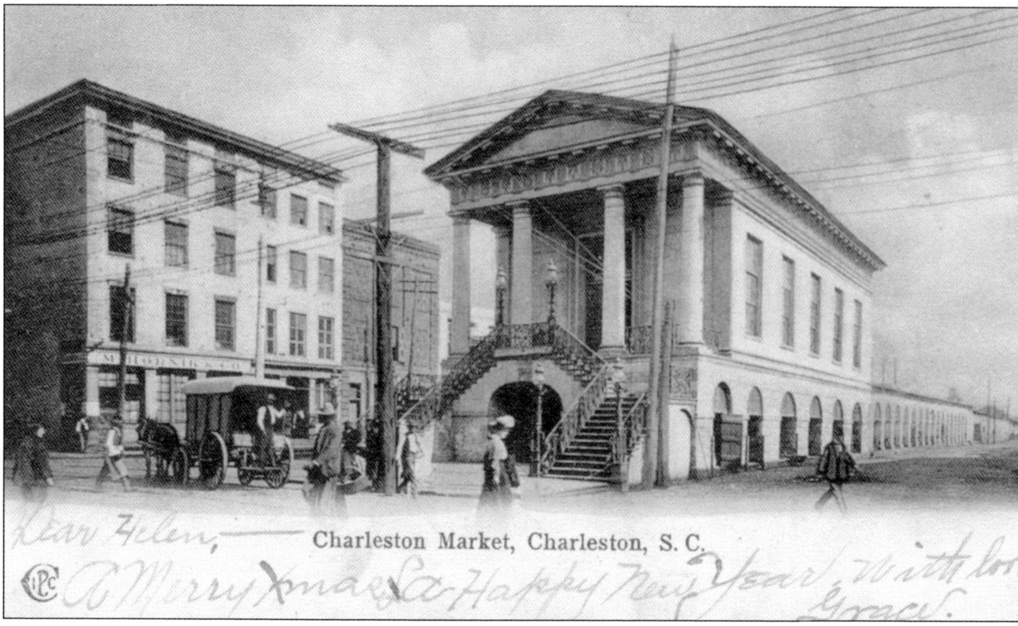

The Market Hall site was originally the site of a Masonic hall that burned down in 1838. The present hall was finished in 1841, as a copy of the Temple of Athena Nike in Athens. In 1899, the United Daughters of the Confederacy took control of it, and today the group runs the Confederate Museum in it. To finance the beginnings of their tenure, the ladies of the UDC used different means, from flower sales and dances to bridge tournaments.

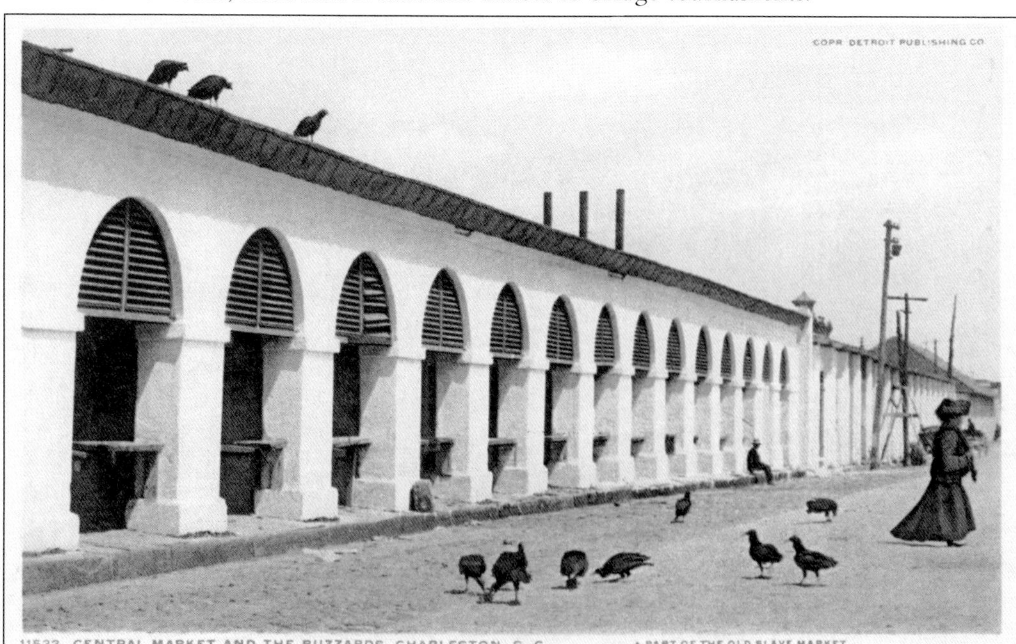

The market sheds, never a slave mart, housed fruit, vegetable, and meat vendors. The scraps from freshly cut meats were thrown into the street daily. As a result, black vultures by the dozens, being scavengers, became commonplace on the market sheds' roofs and in Market Street, eating the scraps. They were considered beneficial and protected by law, with fines for killing them.

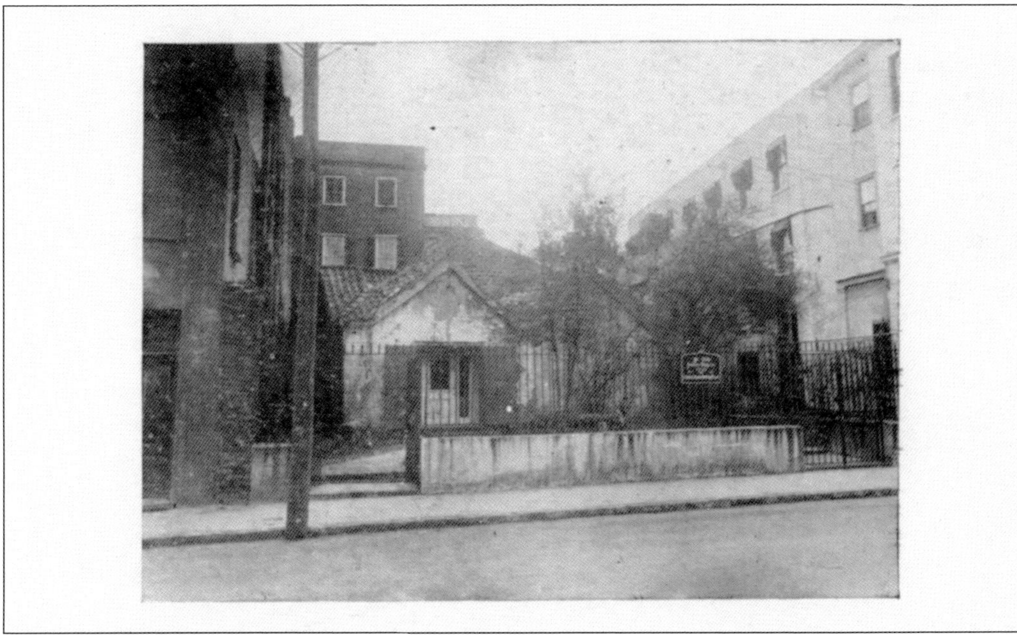

Charleston's Old Powder Magazine, South Carolina's oldest public building, is located at 79 Cumberland Street, a cobblestone street. It was built by settlers about 1713. It has two rooms with 32-inch-thick walls for housing both an arsenal with its gunpowder and a garrison to protect it. It was built at a time when Charles Town might be attacked from the sea by French, Spanish, or even pirate ships. Blackbeard's ships appeared in the city's harbor in May 1718. Charles Town also feared the possibility of Indian problems or slave revolts such as the Stono Rebellion of 1739 or the Denmark Vesey–led uprising of 1822. The building was bought in 1902 by the National Society of the Colonial Dames of America in the State of South Carolina, which opened it as a museum.

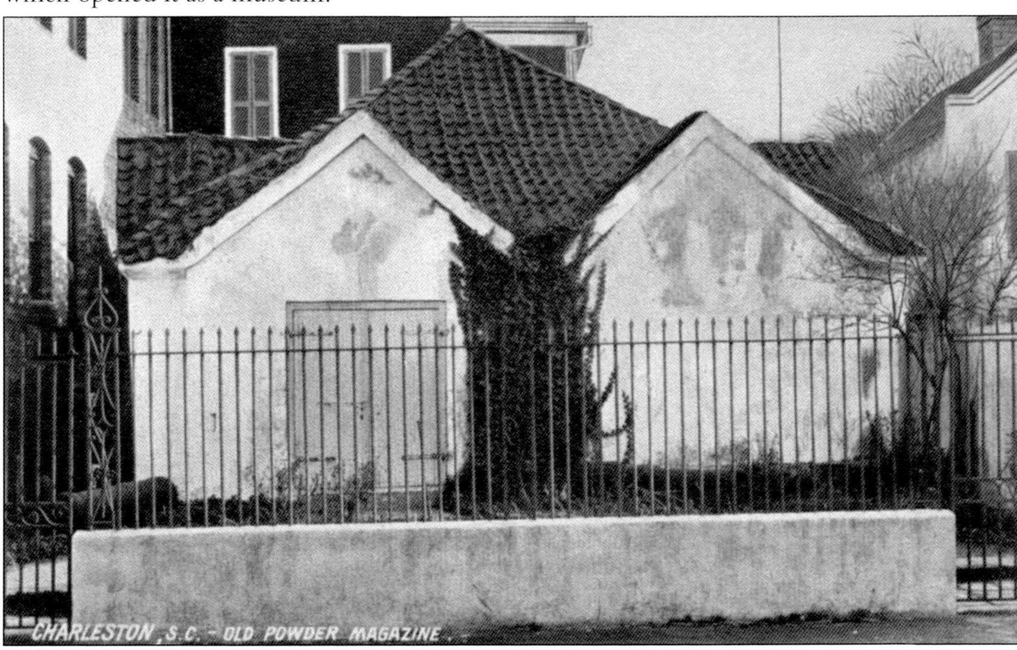

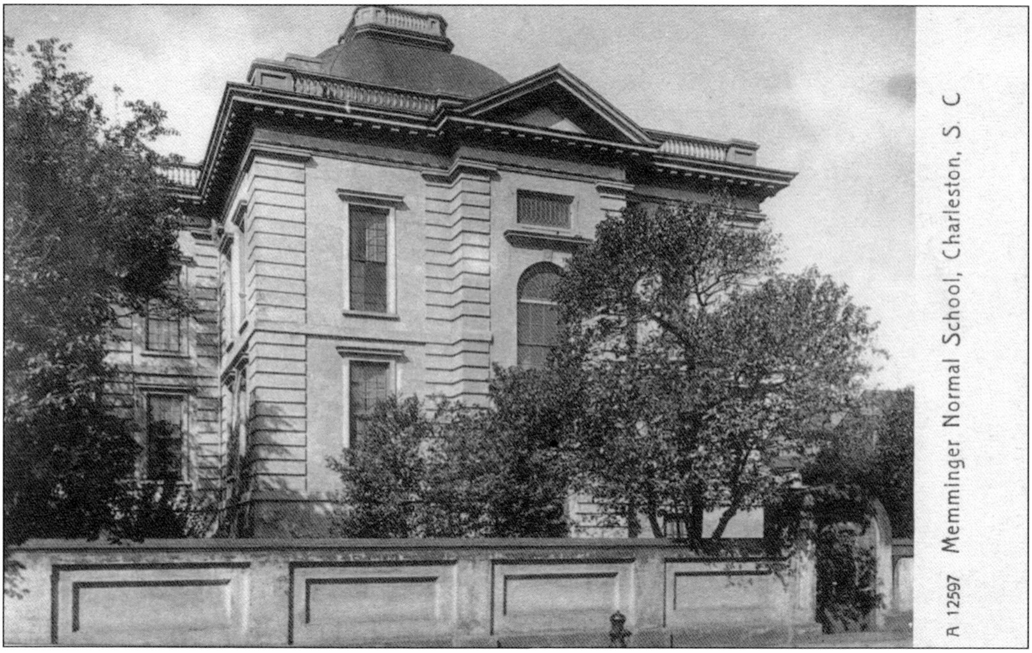

Memminger Normal School was established before the Civil War to educate young women who wanted to become teachers. It started with local teachers working, without pay, a day a week to try to train the initial class of young ladies. On December 20, 1907, the school celebrated its 50th anniversary. By then, it was both a normal school and a high school for girls, accepting girls from Courtenay, Craft, and Bennett Schools. Its library began with a donated set of the *Encyclopaedia Britannica* and continued growing with a school tradition called Library Day. The last day of school before the Christmas break, the girls were to bring any books, reference or novels, they had or could have donated from neighbors, school supporters, or alumni. By 1907, the school had a library of some 2,500 volumes of art, history, science, and fiction.

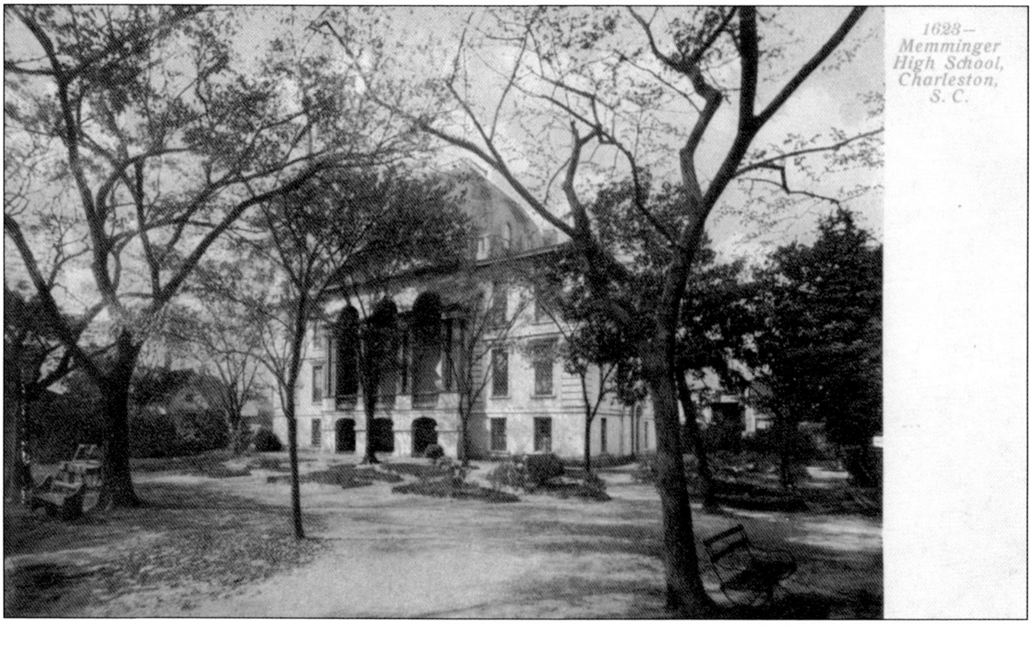

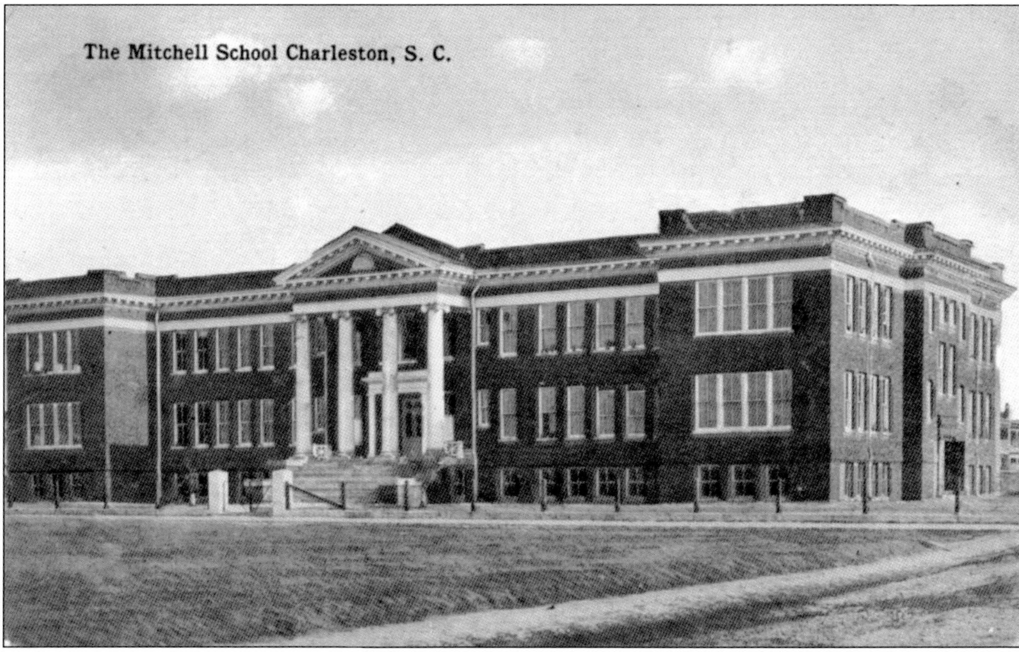

The Julian Mitchell School was located on Rutledge Avenue and opened as a public grammar school on September 27, 1909, with a staff of single women as its first teachers, likely from Memminger Normal School. It appears to be about the same today, but it has been rebuilt and is now called the Mitchell Math and Science Elementary School. It is listed at 2 Perry Street, which faces Rutledge Avenue, with its playground between the two, while on Ashley Avenue and Bee Street stood Porter Military Academy, a private school founded shortly after the Civil War, which occupied an entire block with its parade grounds. It taught classics such as French, Latin, and Greek as well as history, science, and English. In 1964, it merged with the Gaud School for Boys, founded in 1908, to form the existing Porter-Gaud School.

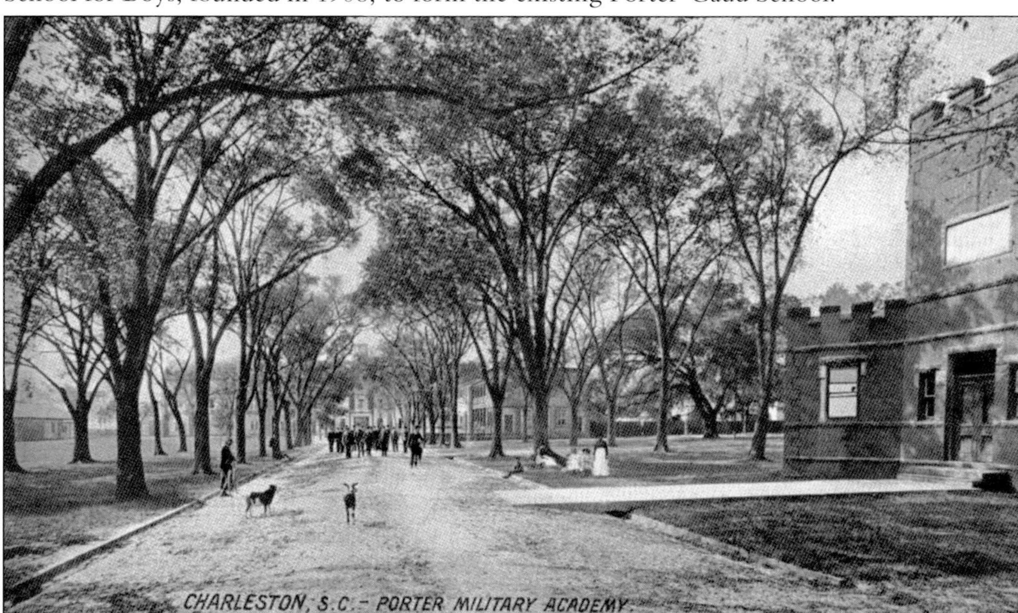

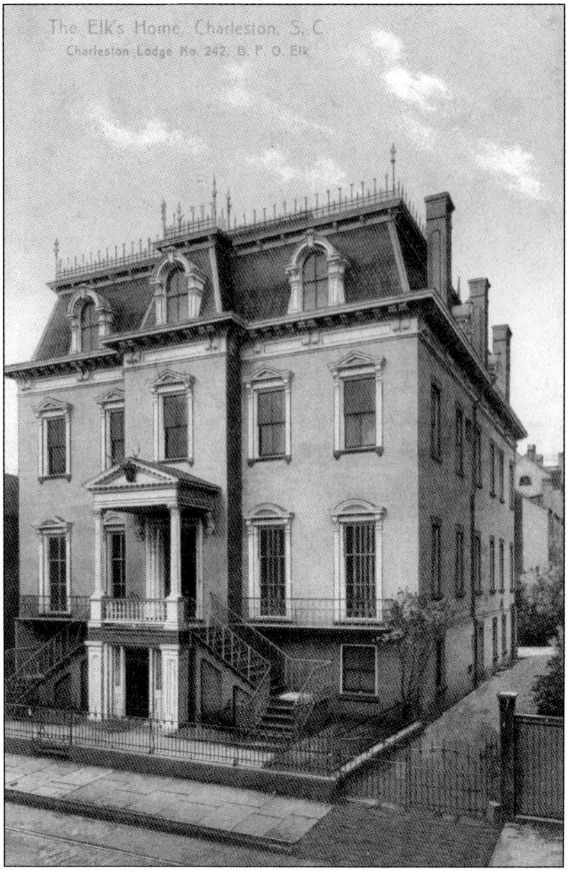

The property located at 54 Wentworth Street was built about 1885, but on March 24, 1909, it was dedicated by the Charleston Lodge No. 242, Benevolent and Protective Order of Elks. The three-story clubhouse had two parlors on the first floor, with one and a dining room reserved for ladies. The second floor had bedrooms for rent to members, and the third was a lodge meeting room.

This City of Charleston Police Station, built at a cost of $70,000, was located at the corner of St. Philip and Vanderhorst Streets and opened for operation on April 30, 1908. The station provided the chief with a bedroom, and a lounging area with a reading room was available for the officers. The police department has moved, and this station was razed.

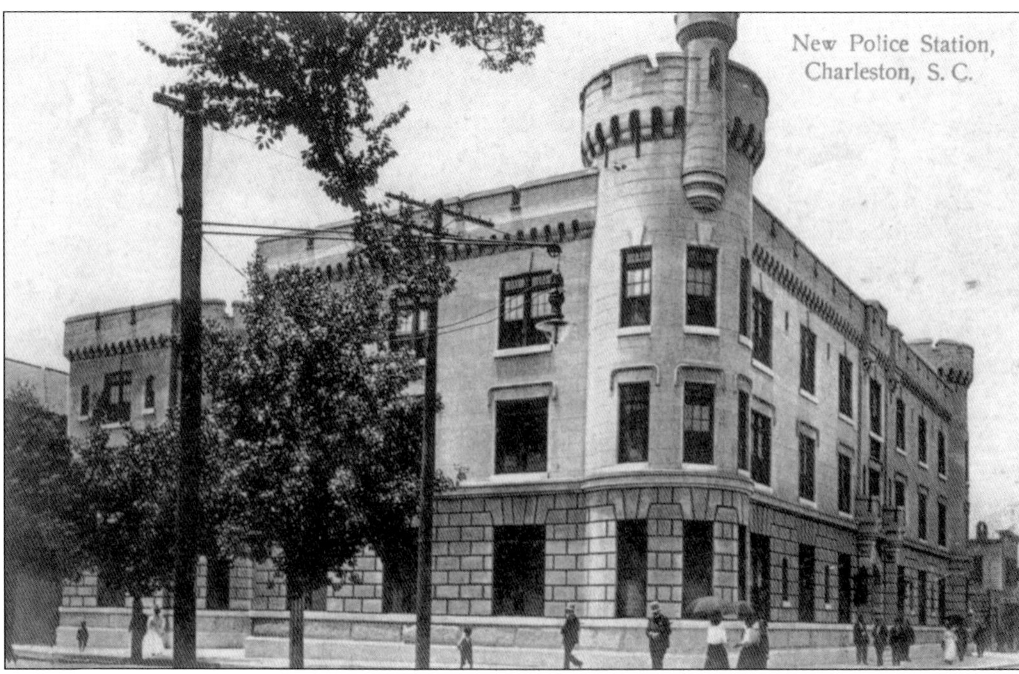

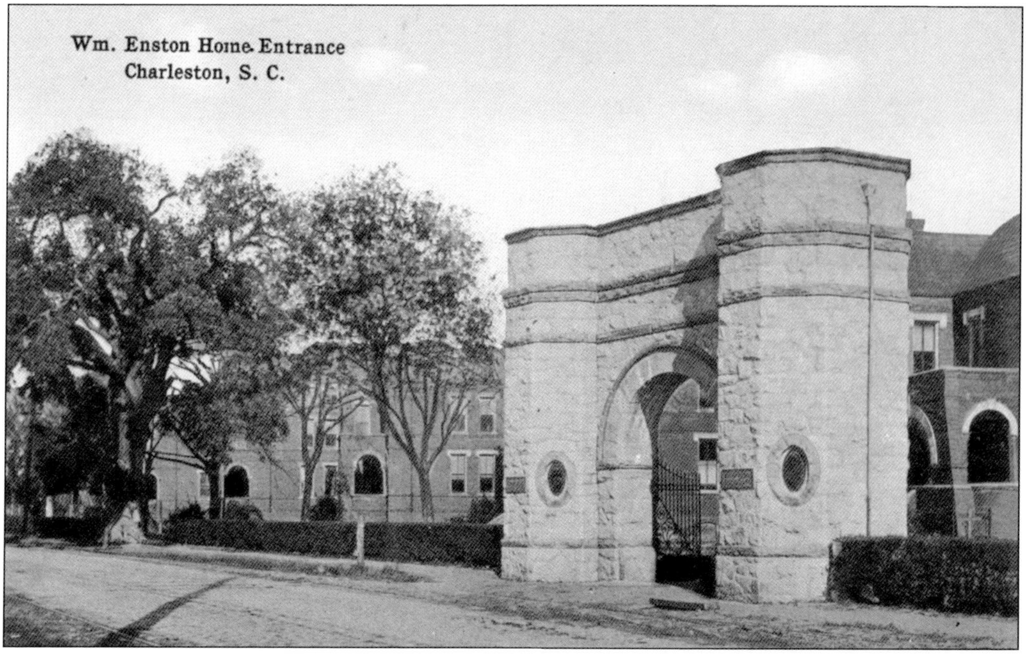

Located on King Street across from James Simons School, William Enston's Romanesque Revival, redbrick two-story cottages were built between 1884 and 1889 and lined either bricked village streets or King Street. Each had garden space for the cottage inhabitant's use. Of the 29 buildings, 24 were cottages for the village's residents. Additionally, there was an infirmary, a water tower to provide the residents with artesian water, an entrance gate, and a Memorial Hall, the building with the steeple. The Memorial Hall housed a bust of William Enston and a combination meeting room and small library. Enston was a cabinetmaker who relocated to Charleston from Philadelphia in 1833 and became very wealthy. He died in 1860, and his estate provided for the building of a home for some of Charleston's elderly (over 45 years of age), poor, or infirm.

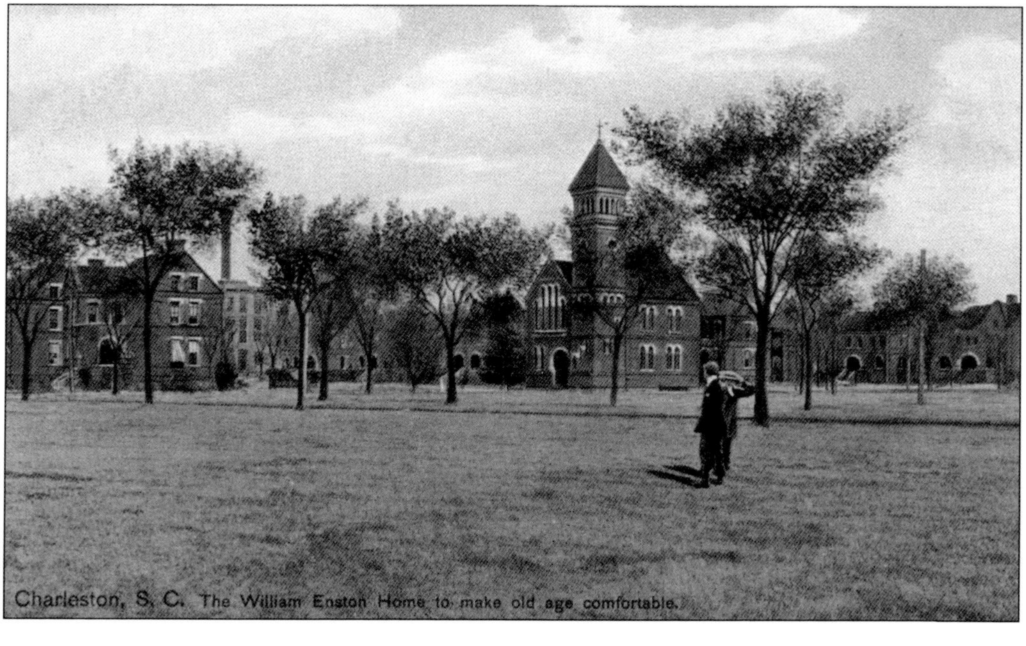

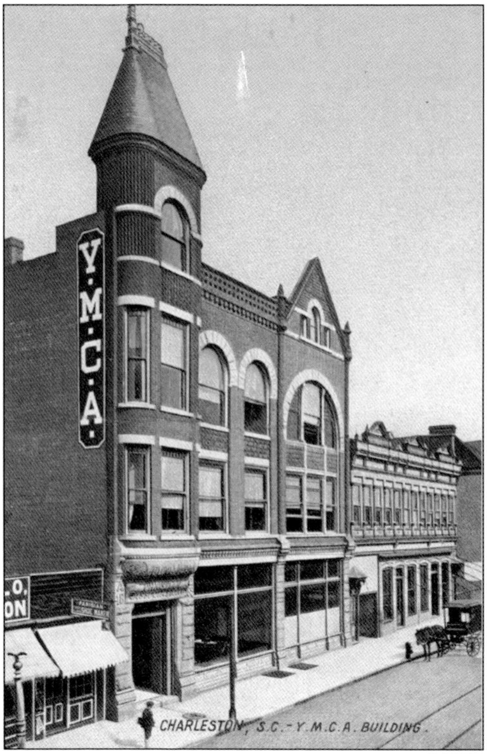

Located at 298 King Street, this YMCA served Charleston from 1889 until 1912. The three-story building had two stores on the ground floor for rent, as well as a gymnasium, pool, and bathing facilities. The second floor had the reception area with classrooms. The third floor had a kitchen for ladies to use for special events. The tower was an observation area for members.

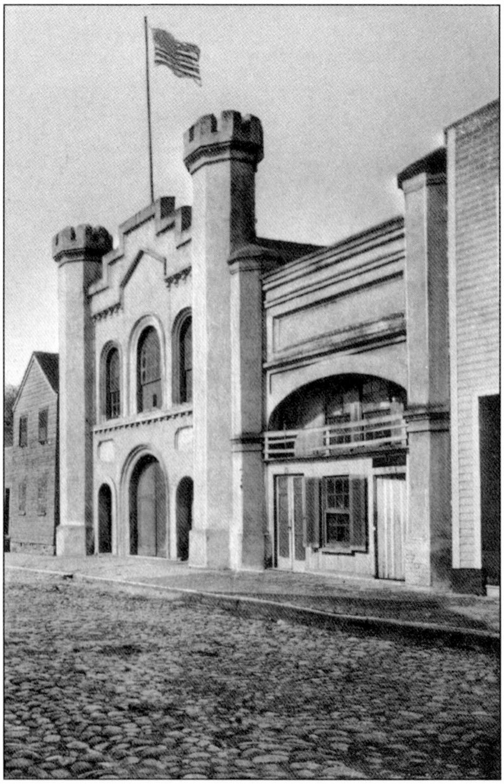

Old Slave Mart is located at 6 Chalmers Street, a cobblestone street. Prior to 1859, the site was part of Ryan's Mart, which extended to Queen Street. Ryan's Mart was named after a city councilman who sought to centralize all slave sales within the city. It ceased to be used for that purpose in 1863 and may be the last building still standing that was used for the sale of slaves. It now operates as the Old Slave Mart Museum.

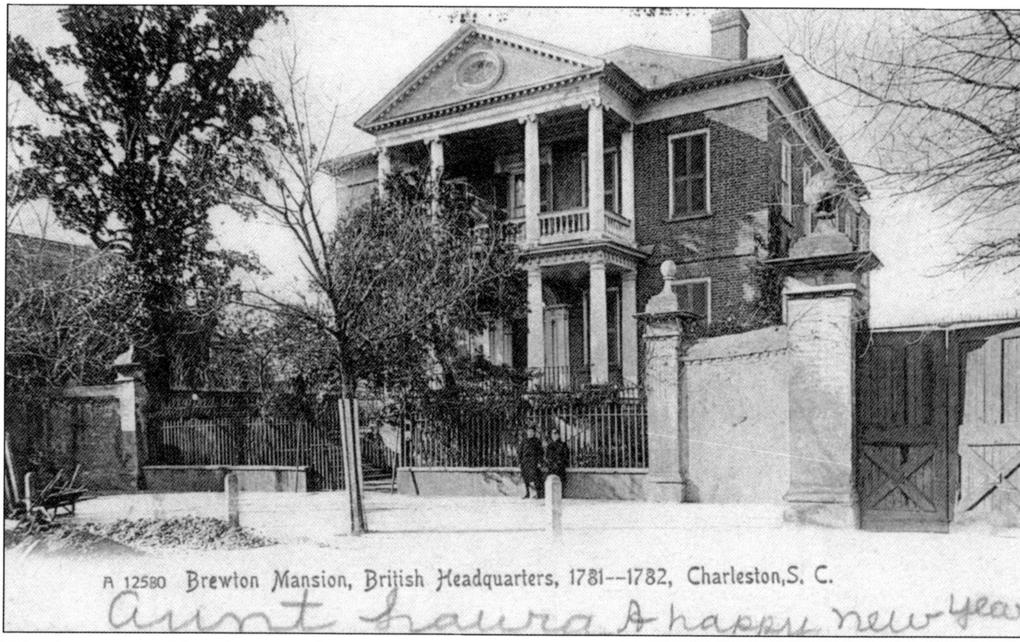

The Brewton Mansion, or the Pringle House, at 27 King Street, was built in the Georgian Palladian style by Miles Brewton in the 1760s. Brewton and his family were lost at sea in 1775. The house has stayed within Brewton's extended family, but it has been used by others. During the American Revolution, it was used as headquarters by both Sir Henry Clinton and Lord Cornwallis, and about 100 years later, as that of another occupying army, the Union's.

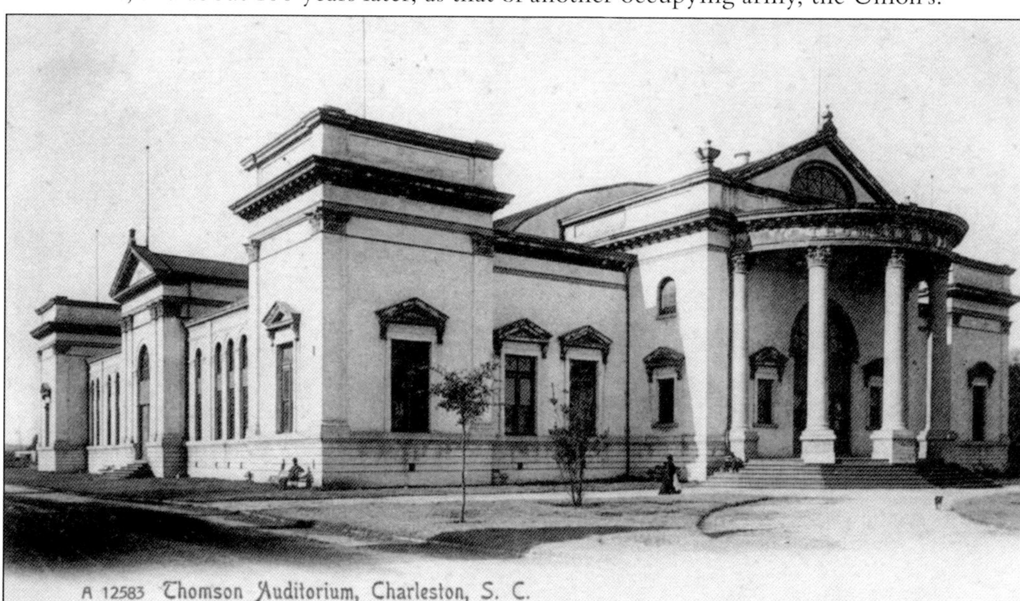

The Thomson Auditorium, fronting on Rutledge Avenue near Calhoun Street, was designed for and built to host the last United Confederate Veterans' convention of the 19th century, in the city where their war began, and was completed on April 27, 1899. Four palmetto trees from the Isle of Palms and two cannons lined and decorated its walkway. The May 10 convention opened with a full auditorium.

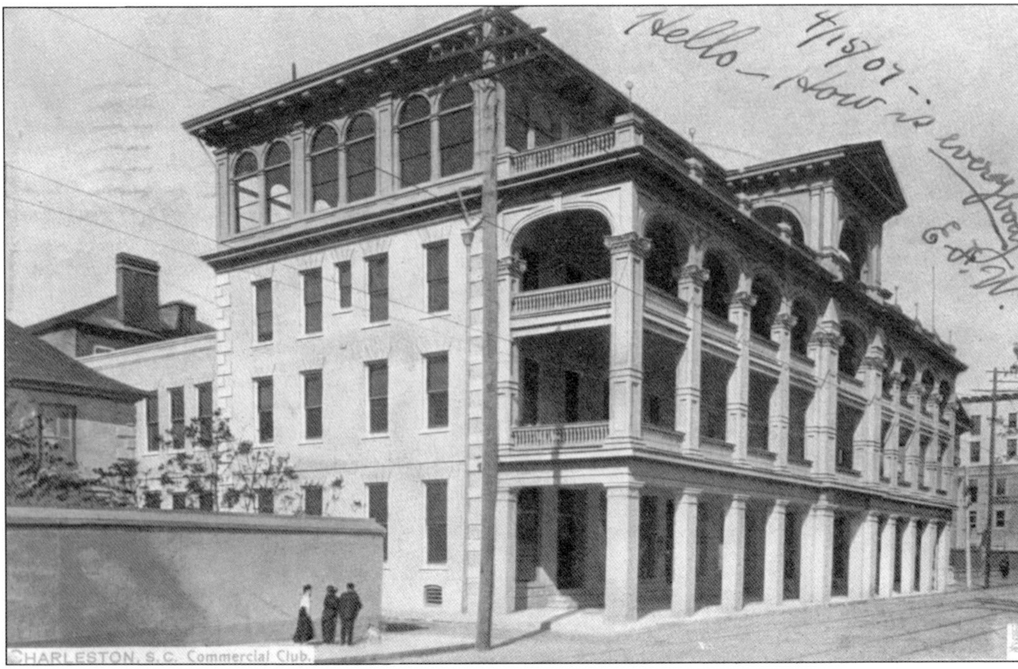

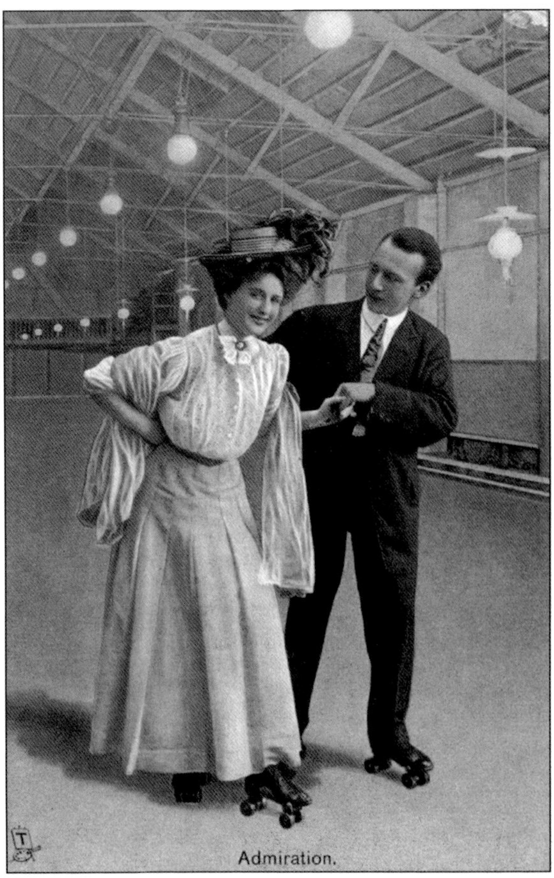

The Commercial Club, located on Meeting Street across from Washington Park, opened on September 15, 1903, with three floors with four bowling alleys, billiard tables, and a ballroom, as well as sleeping rooms for club members' usage and one, the first, open to the public, excepting the offices of the chamber of commerce. This opened the first floor's café, barbershop, and cigar store to all. Its purpose was to promote business in Charleston.

The top floor of the Commercial Building opened on September 29, 1905, for an evening of roller-skating. Its large auditorium/ballroom proved to be perfect for young couples and singles to come and skate. Lessons were offered beforehand, but once Metz's Orchestra started, it was time to skate, and for hours the ladies and their gentlemen enjoyed themselves.

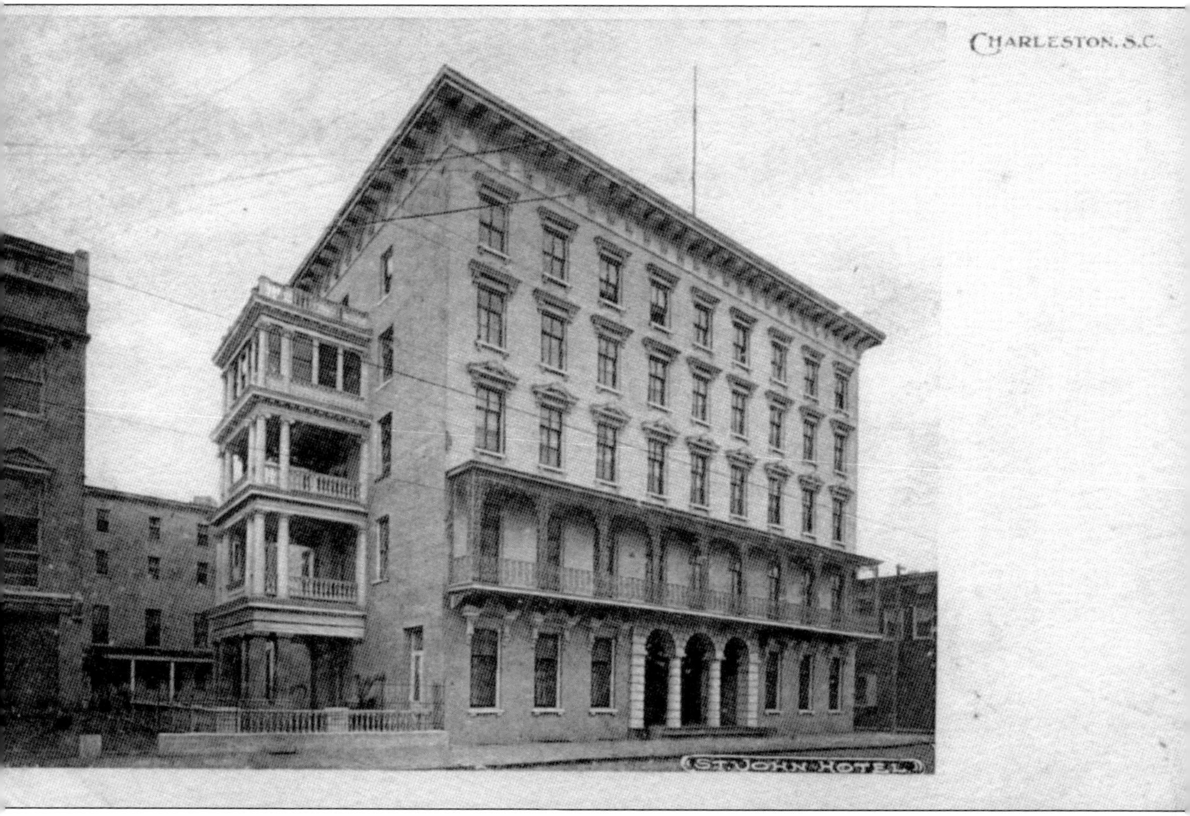

The St. John's Hotel was situated where the present Mills House is located, on the corner of Meeting and Queen Streets. The older Mills House that had been built in 1853 and was used for a time as Confederate general P.G.T. Beauregard's headquarters was renamed the St. John's Hotel after it had been remodeled. The hotel offered steam heat and over 50 bathrooms, with some attached to adjoining bedrooms, or en suite. Pres. Theodore Roosevelt came to Charleston for President's Day at the South Carolina Inter-State and West Indian Exposition. He, his wife, and their party stayed at the St. John's. In severe need of renovation by 1968, it was sold and demolished to build a new hotel. The new Mills House opened in 1970, using the balcony of the original St. John's in its design. That balcony had been part of the original Mills House, too. Robert E. Lee watched Charleston burn in the great fire of 1861 from the balcony of the older Mills House.

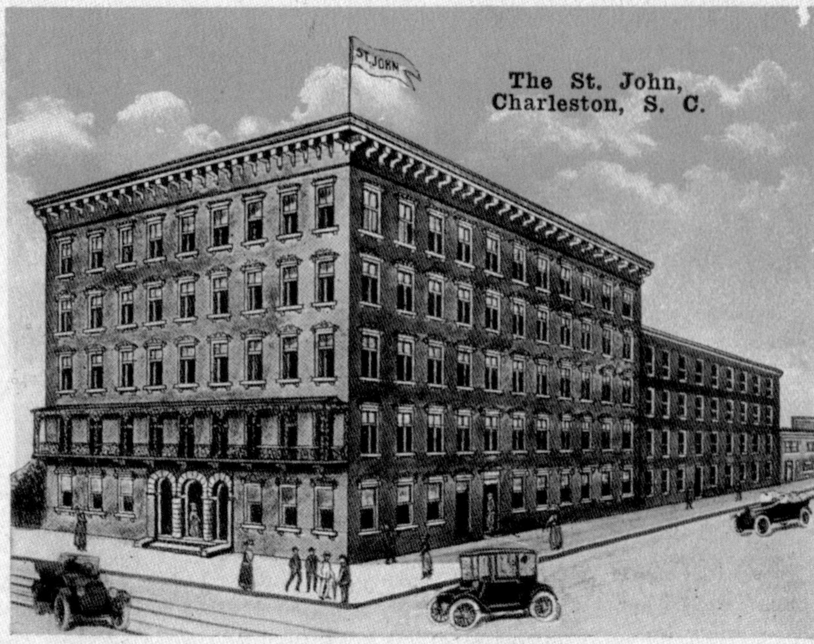

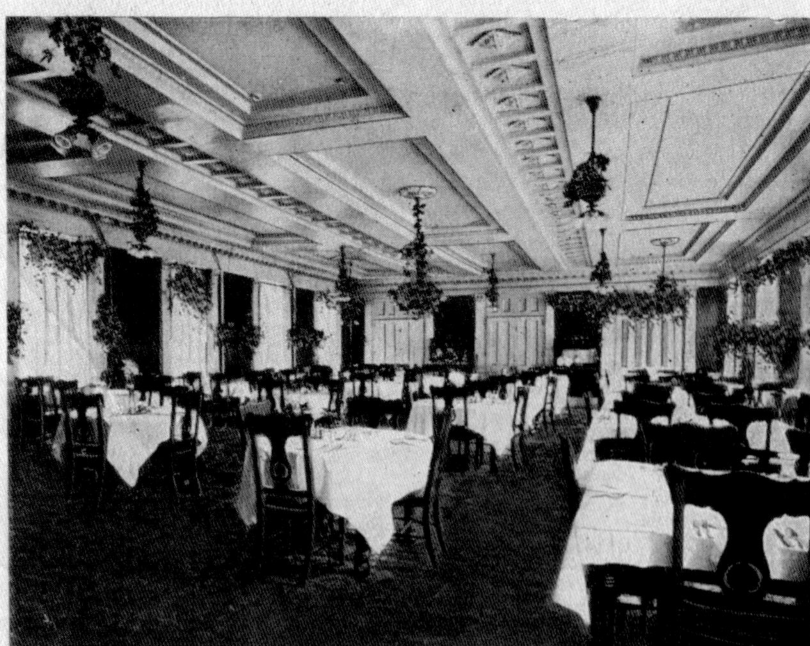

Dining Room

On November 9, 1905, the Hotel St. John hired seven girls from New York, who would be living at the hotel, to take over its waitressing duties. The St. John Hotel management thought that these professional waitresses might be both less clumsy and prettier than the waiters they had been using. They were also the first white waitresses ever hired to work regularly in a Charleston hotel.

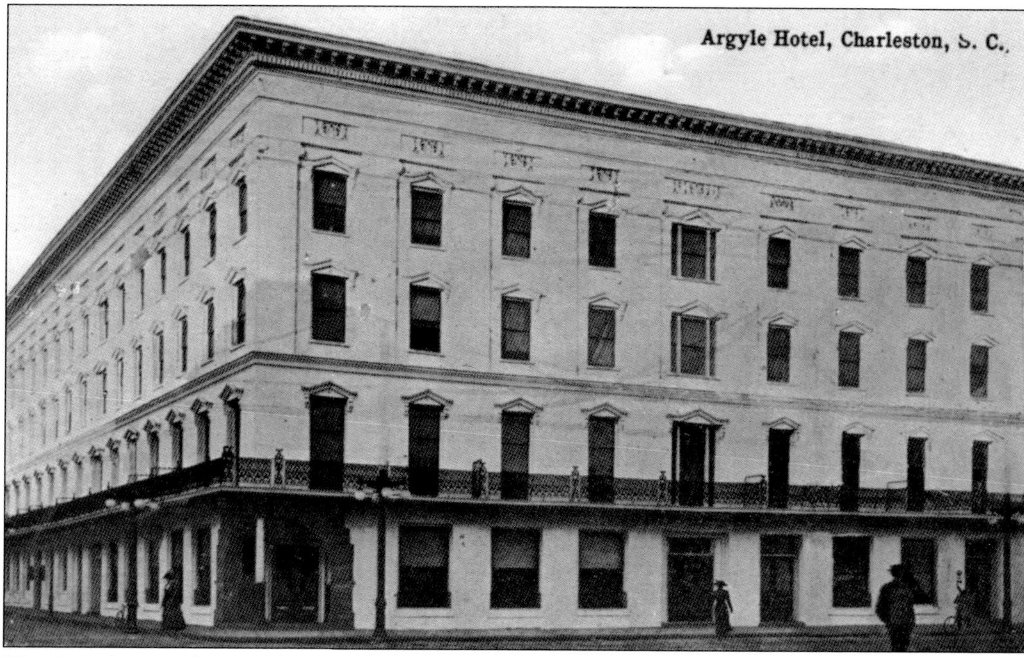

The Argyle Hotel opened on December 12, 1901, on the corner of Meeting and Hasell Streets. The same property operated as the St. Charles Hotel, but its owners changed its name after remodeling it for the visitors to Charleston for the South Carolina Inter-State and West Indian Exposition. It had 100 rooms that were steam-heated, with electric lights. Some had en suite bathrooms. It offered an elevator for its guest's convenience.

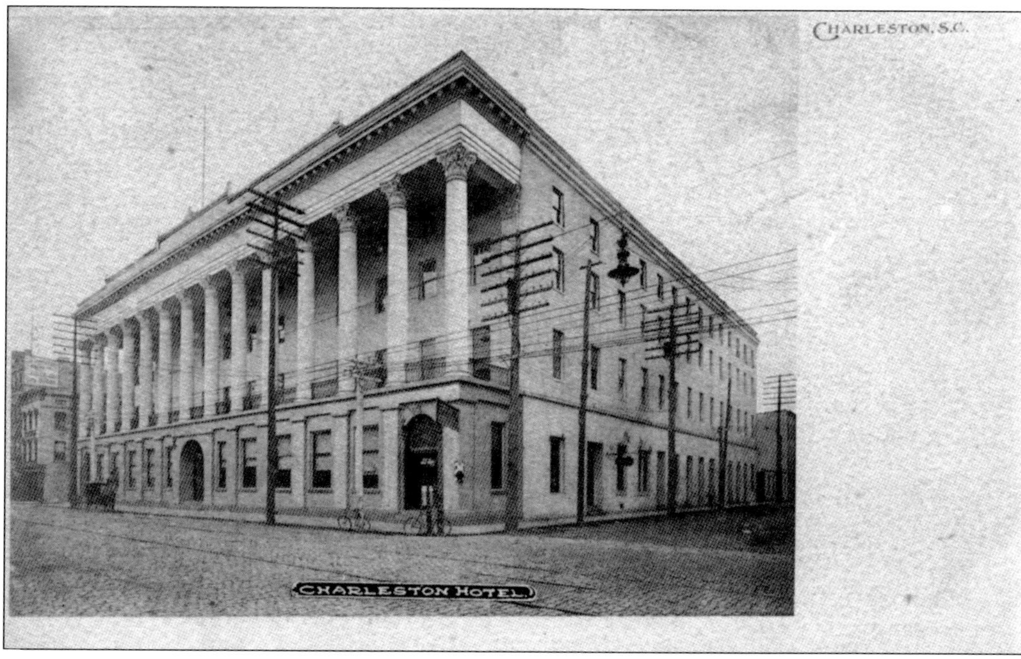

Secretary of War and future president William Howard Taft arrived at the Charleston Hotel in March 1907. The hotel fronted on Meeting Street and occupied the block between Pinckney and Hayne Streets.

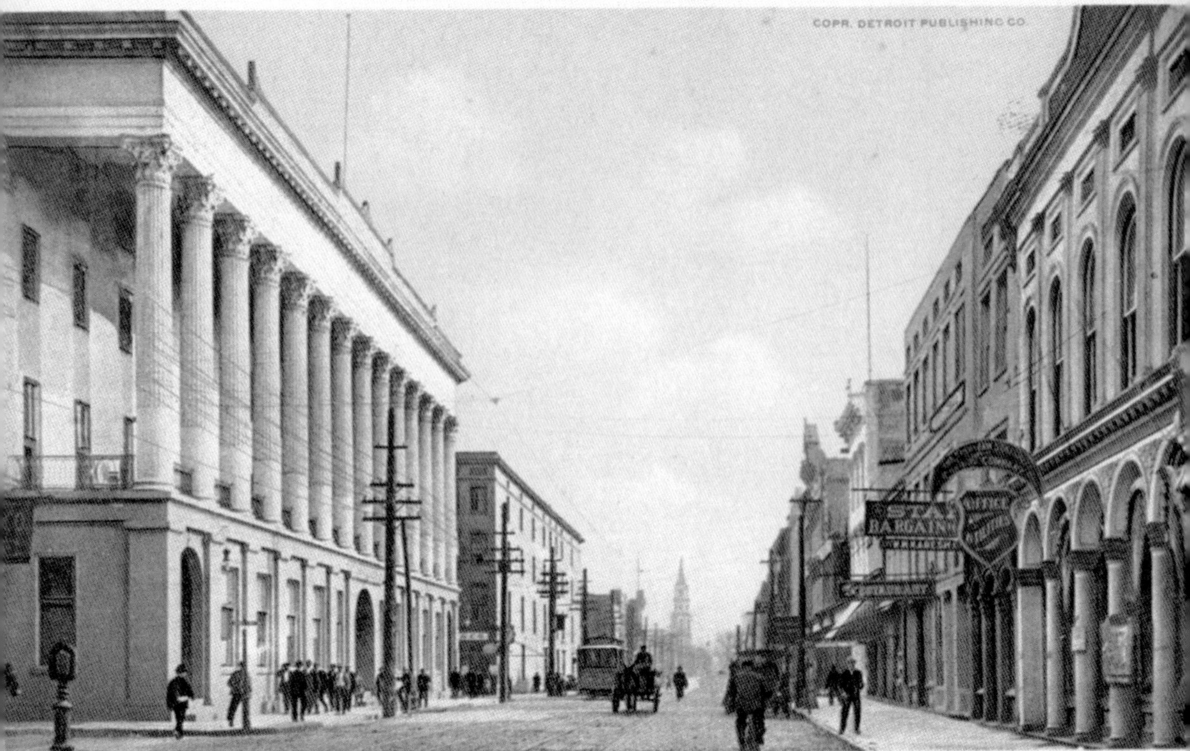

70254 CHARLESTON HOTEL AND MEETING STREET, CHARLESTON, S. C.

The *Charleston News and Courier* of May 19, 1913, reports on the possible bloody collision of two colleges. As one looks at the above image of the Charleston Hotel, which was located on Meeting Street at Hasell Street, imagine a column of Citadel cadets that year marching five abreast up Meeting Street on its shaded west side to the cadence of "one, two, three, four" at route step from church. People who watched remembered that similar phalanx not yielding to charging fire engines, while marching in a Washington's Day parade down King Street. As they marched opposite the Charleston Hotel, there turned from Hasell Street onto Meeting Street another group, moving two abreast, coming from another church, and like the cadets, seeking the shady side of the street. The two college groups were now on a collision course. When the two groups were mere feet apart, came the command "Column half right." As a man, the body halves right. Off the sidewalks go the leaders, their uniforms almost brushing against the (blue-and-white) dresses of the Confederate Home (College) girls. "Column half left'" came after the girls passed. The pending disaster gave way to chivalry.

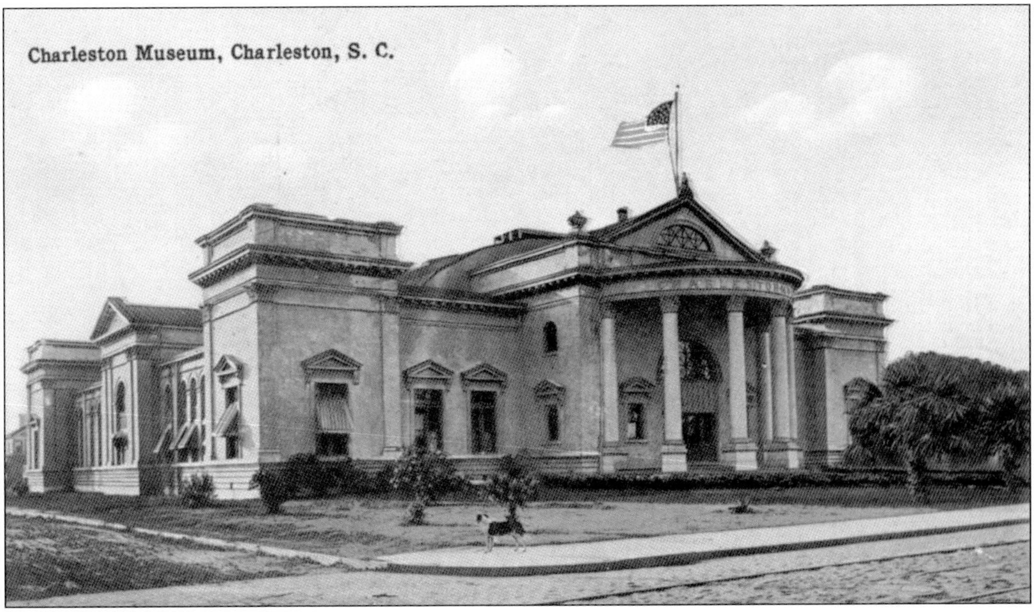

The Charleston Museum was located on Rutledge Avenue near Calhoun Street and opened on January 31, 1908. It began through the Library Society in 1773 and opened to the public in 1824. Its exhibits were moved to the College of Charleston in 1850, where they stayed until 1908. This building, already emptied, burned down in 1981. The columns are all that remain and are now the centerpiece of Cannon Park.

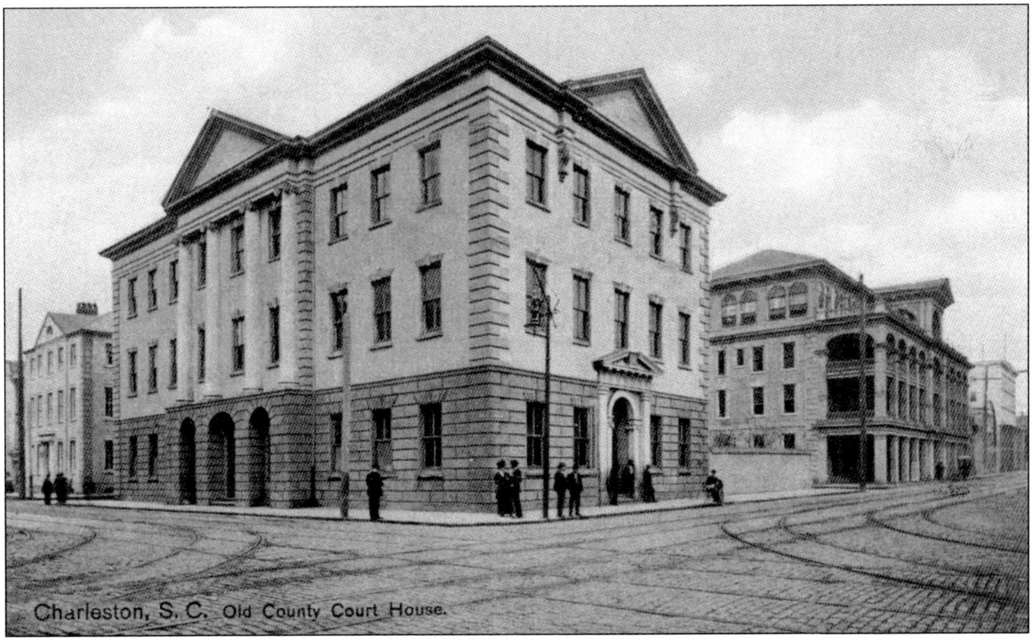

The first colonial courthouse was built on the corner of Meeting and Broad Streets in 1753 as part of the capitol. It came down in 1788 but was rebuilt by 1792. In addition to all of the courthouses, the new building housed the oldest museum in the United States and the Charleston Library Society before each moved into its own building. This courthouse has since been remodeled to look more like the 1792 courthouse.

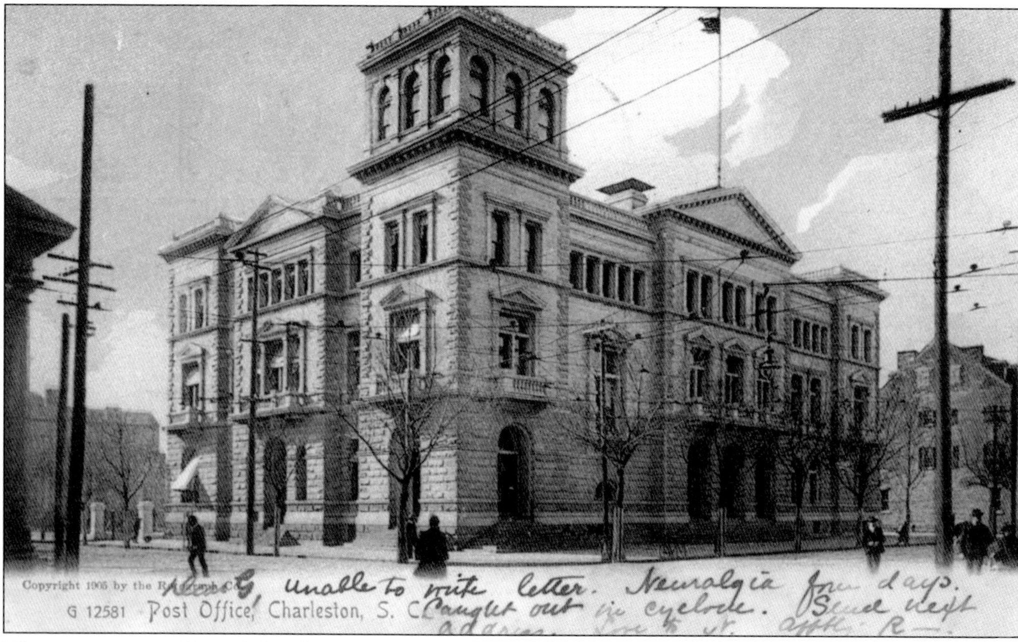

The new post office/federal court opened in 1896. The earthquake of 1886 contributed to it being built on one of the corners of the Four Corners of Law, representing federal law. Originally on this site was a guardhouse, built in 1769 and later remodeled. The old post office was the Exchange Building. The earthquake destroyed the guardhouse, damaged the old post office, and engendered sympathy for Charleston in Congress.

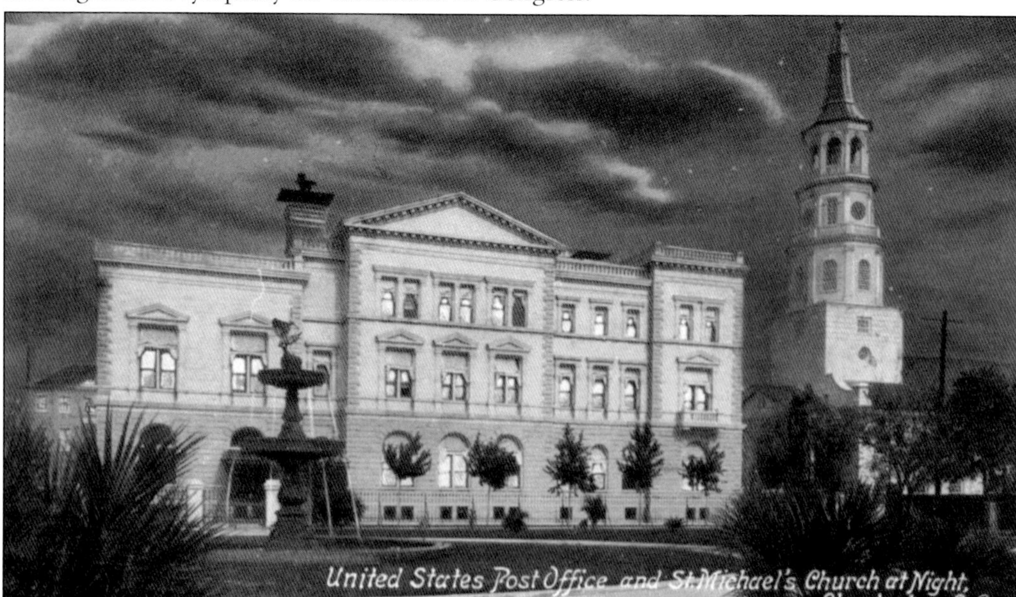

Post Office Park was located behind the new post office. With the Battery and Washington Park nearby, the postmaster did not see any reason to open it to the public when it could easily be viewed as one walked or rode by it. The park had fish in the fountain, a peacock, and a resident buck. Opening the park to visitors would have meant moving its animals. Today, the Hollings Judicial Center is located behind the post office.

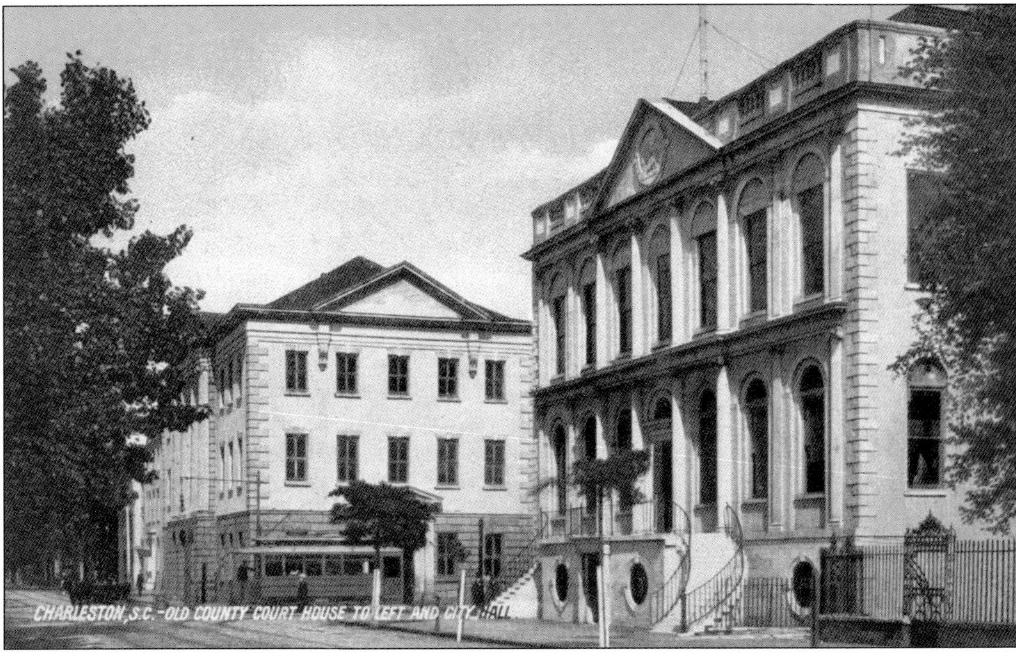

Charleston City Hall is located at 80 Broad Street and has been at that location since 1818. Beyond it and the trolley is the county courthouse. These two make up two of the Four Corners of Law, representing city and county law. Joining these two are the two buildings directly across Broad Street, the post office as federal law, and St. Michael's Church, the law of God.

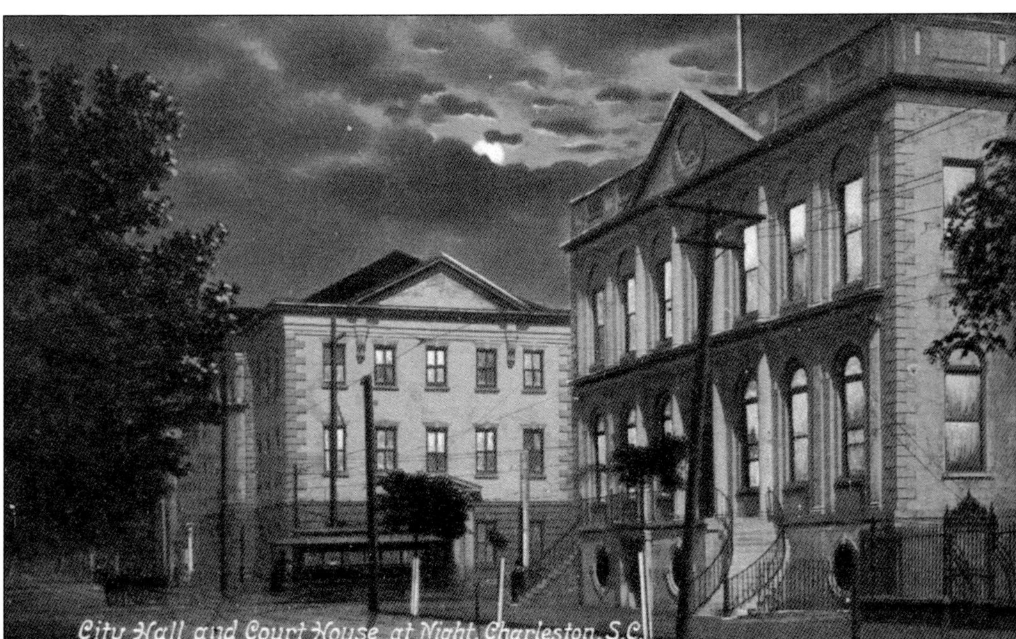

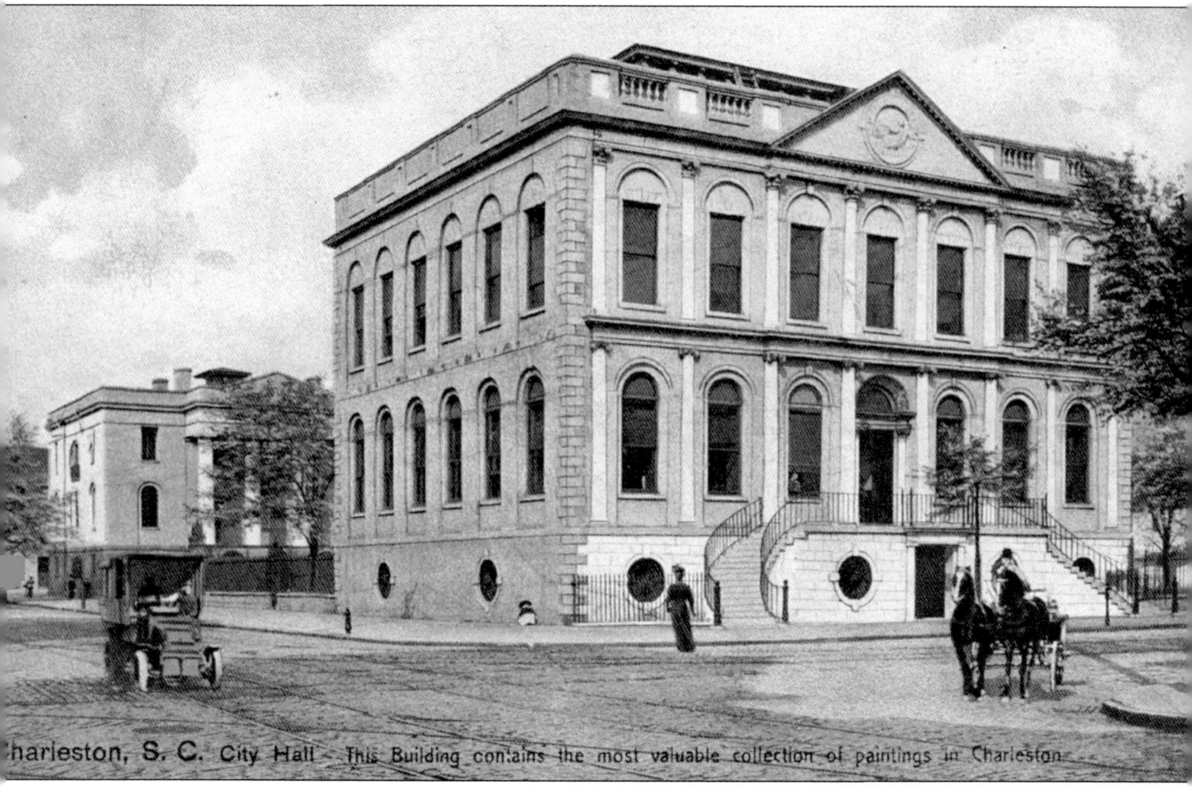

Charleston's city hall is located on a corner of Meeting and Broad Streets and is one of the Four Corners of Laws, as Robert Ripley of *Ripley's Believe It or Not!* labeled the four corners where Broad and Meeting Streets cross. In the Grand Modell of old Charles Town, which laid out the city from the Battery area to Beaufain Street, the lot where it sits was for a public market. In 1800, it became one of the eight national branches of the Bank of the United States. In 1818, the property and building were returned to the city; it became Charleston's city hall. On its second floor is city council's meeting room and an art gallery. Among the gallery's paintings are a full-length portrait of George Washington painted by John Trumbull in 1792 and a painting of Pres. James Monroe by Samuel F.B. Morse.

Five

Beaches, Gardens, Parks, and Cemeteries

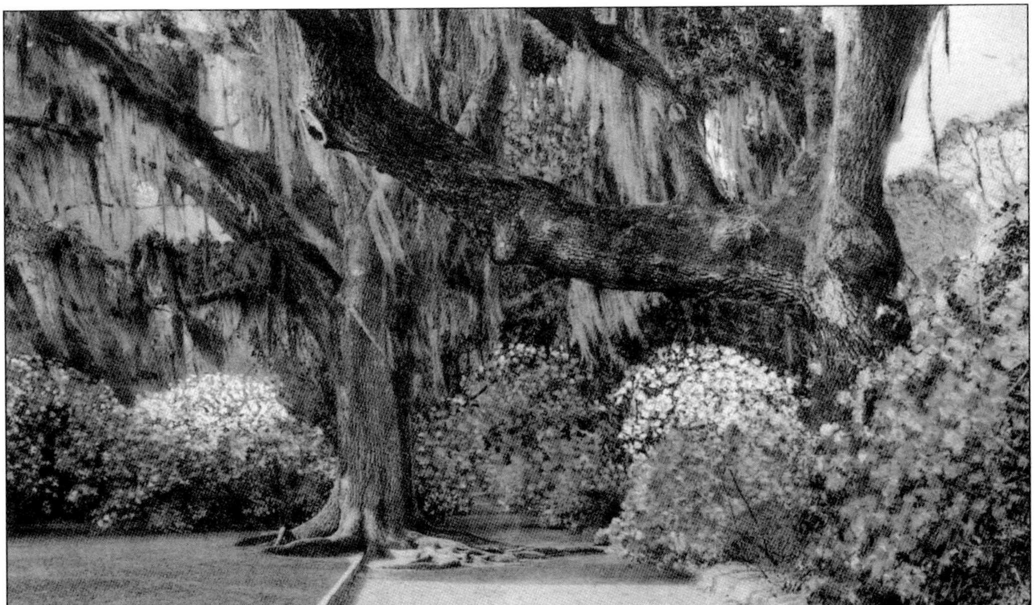

Magnolia Plantation and Gardens was begun by the Drayton family in 1676 but did not open to the public for almost 200 years. In 1870, boats started landing at Magnolia-on-the-Ashley with visitors. While it has swamplands with wildlife and some tall, moss-laden trees, the site is most famous for its azaleas and camellias.

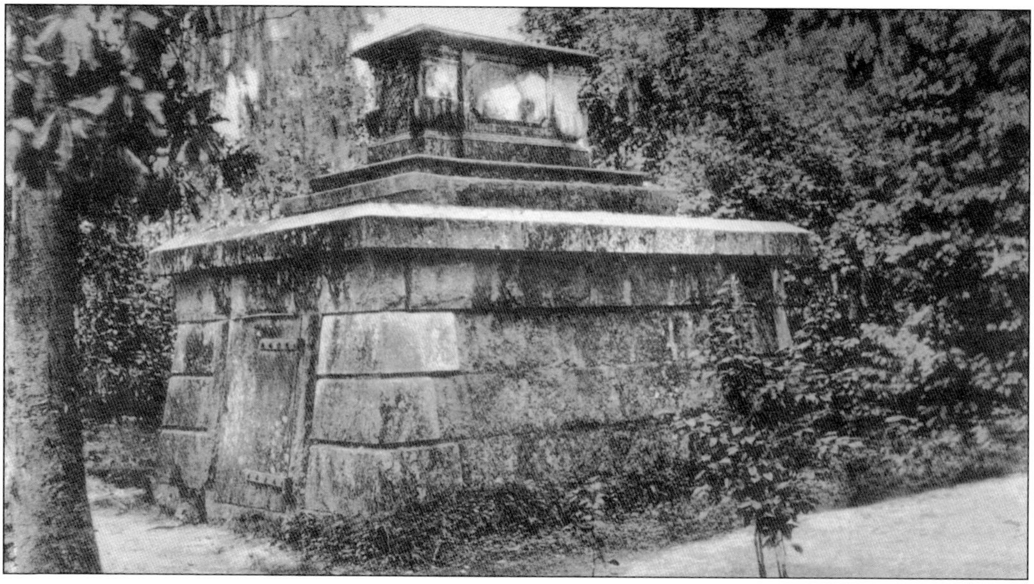

The tomb of Arthur Middleton (1742–1787) is located at Middleton Place. While his father, Henry, opposed independence from Great Britain, Arthur, who succeeded him when he resigned from the Continental Congress over independence, signed the Declaration of Independence. When Charleston came under attack, Arthur joined the fight. He and two other signers of the Declaration, Edward Rutledge and Thomas Heyward Jr., were subsequently captured by the British. Arthur was imprisoned in Florida. He returned home in 1781.

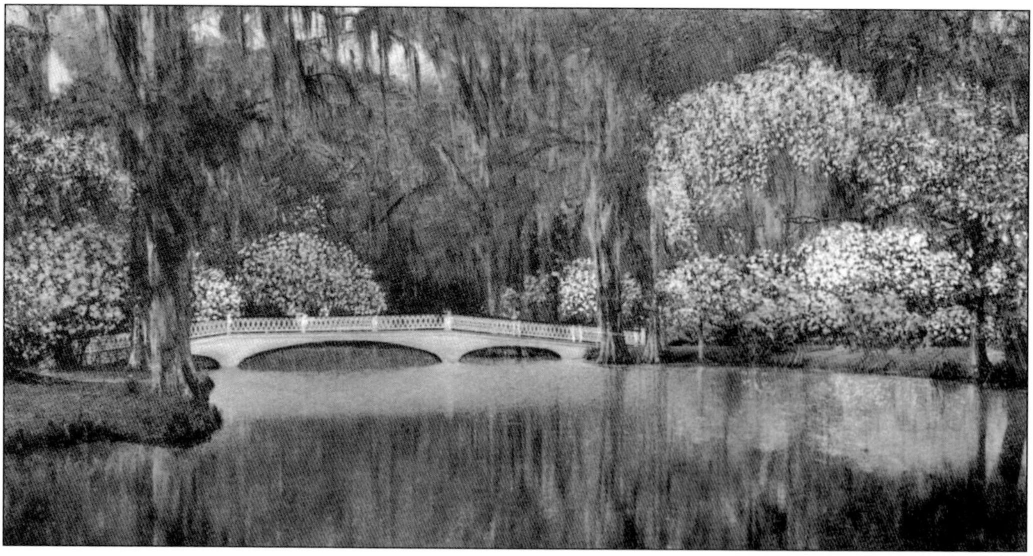

Magnolia Plantation and Gardens is located on Ashley River Road. The plantation was begun 100 years before the Declaration of Independence, in 1676, when Thomas Drayton and his wife, Ann, built their first house and small garden on the property. It became, through the efforts of its slaves, a working rice plantation. John Grimke-Drayton, nephew of Charleston's noted abolitionist sisters Sarah and Angelina Grimke, and an Episcopal minister, began the serious gardening, planting camellias about the property, and he may have been the first to introduce azaleas to America. After the Civil War, economic times were difficult. So, in 1870, Magnolia-on-the-Ashley opened to visitors.

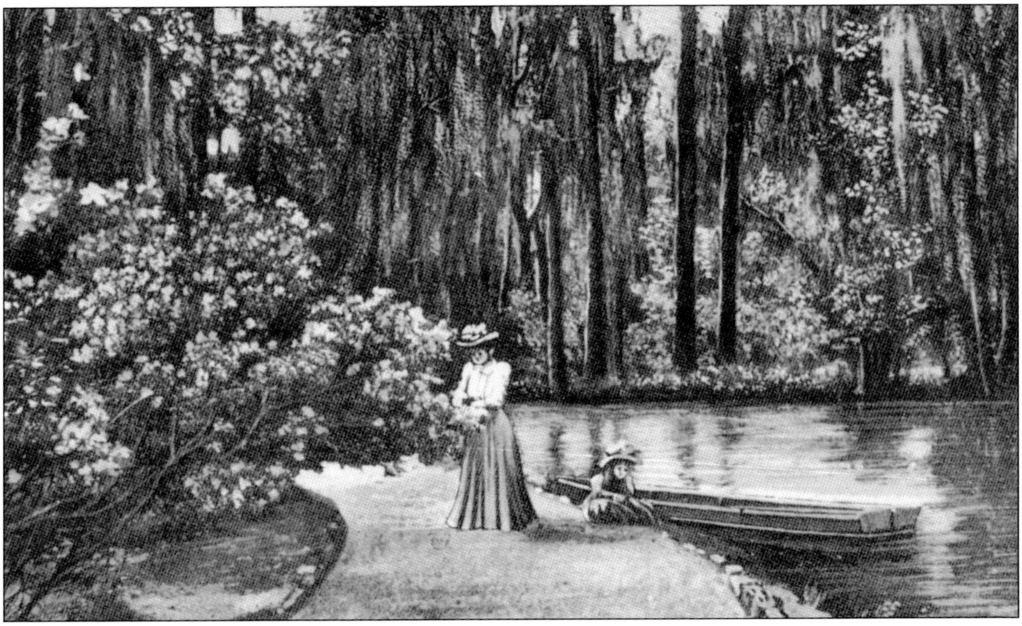

These ladies, mother and daughter, may have enjoyed an automobile ride to Magnolia Gardens this afternoon, December 3, 1909. According to the *Evening Post* of the day before, members of the Christian Automobile Club were to line up from the Commercial Club to the Battery, after Saturday's business hours, and be ready to leave at exactly 12:30 p.m. with a packed lunch. The drive had rules in that no car could pass the lead car, which would travel at 10 to 12 miles per hour, the legal speed limit. They arrived at 1:45 p.m., just in time for a late lunch and stroll before the return trip.

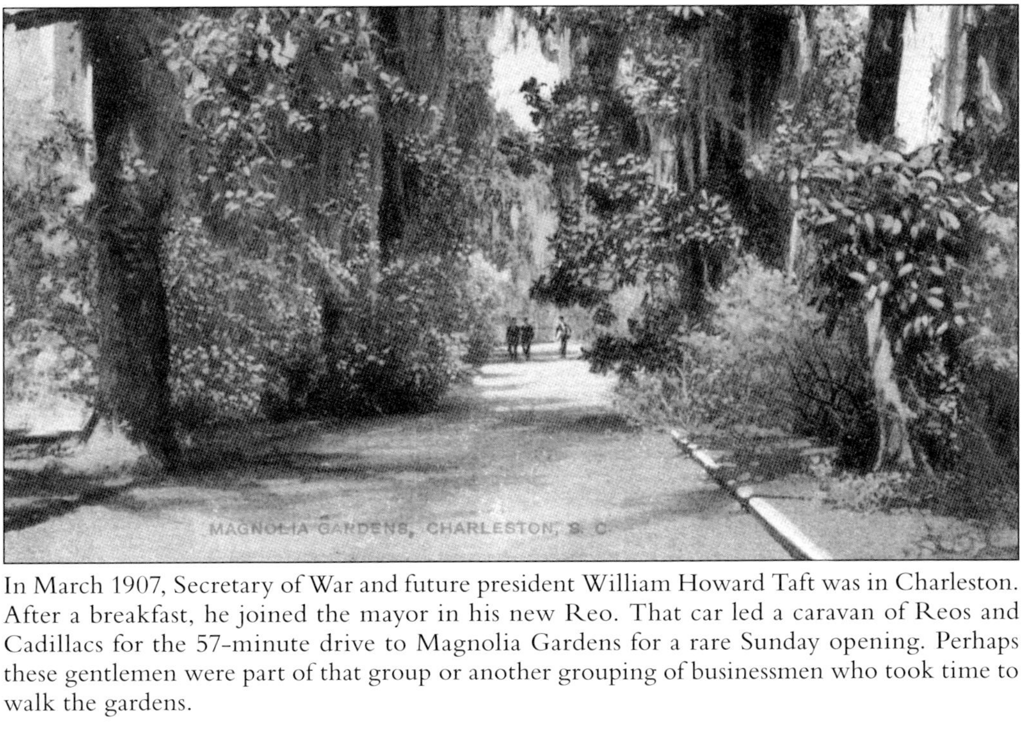

In March 1907, Secretary of War and future president William Howard Taft was in Charleston. After a breakfast, he joined the mayor in his new Reo. That car led a caravan of Reos and Cadillacs for the 57-minute drive to Magnolia Gardens for a rare Sunday opening. Perhaps these gentlemen were part of that group or another grouping of businessmen who took time to walk the gardens.

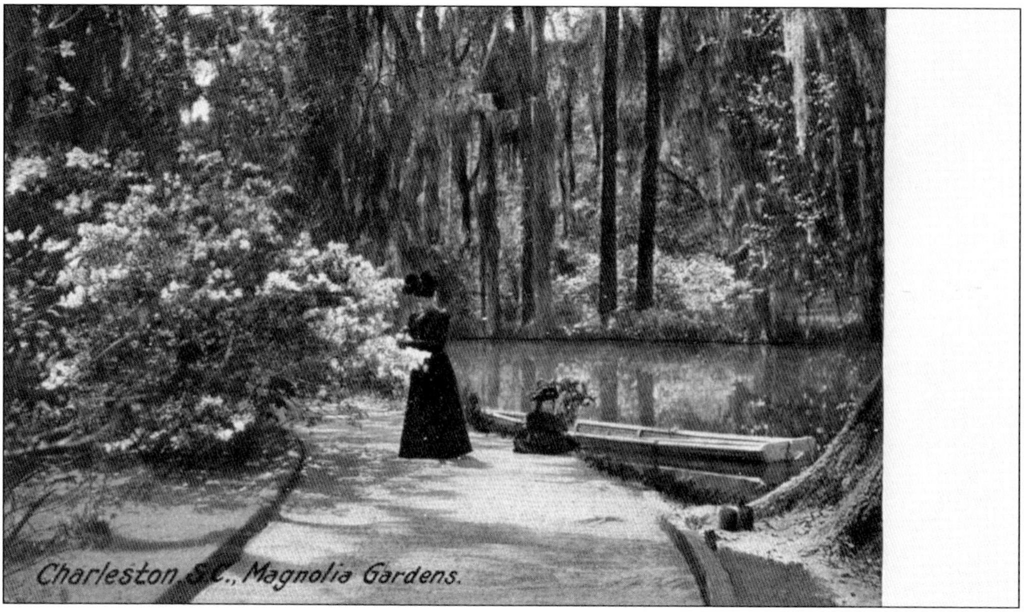

Magnolia Gardens usually did not open on Sundays, but the *News and Courier* of March 21, 1913, notes that the gardeners wanted to give those who could not visit during the week the opportunity to see them while they were at their peak. The steamer *E.H. Jackson* was scheduled to run usual weekday hours on those Sundays. Magnolia Gardens' owners' share of the profits were committed to helping the sick and poor blacks who lived near the gardens.

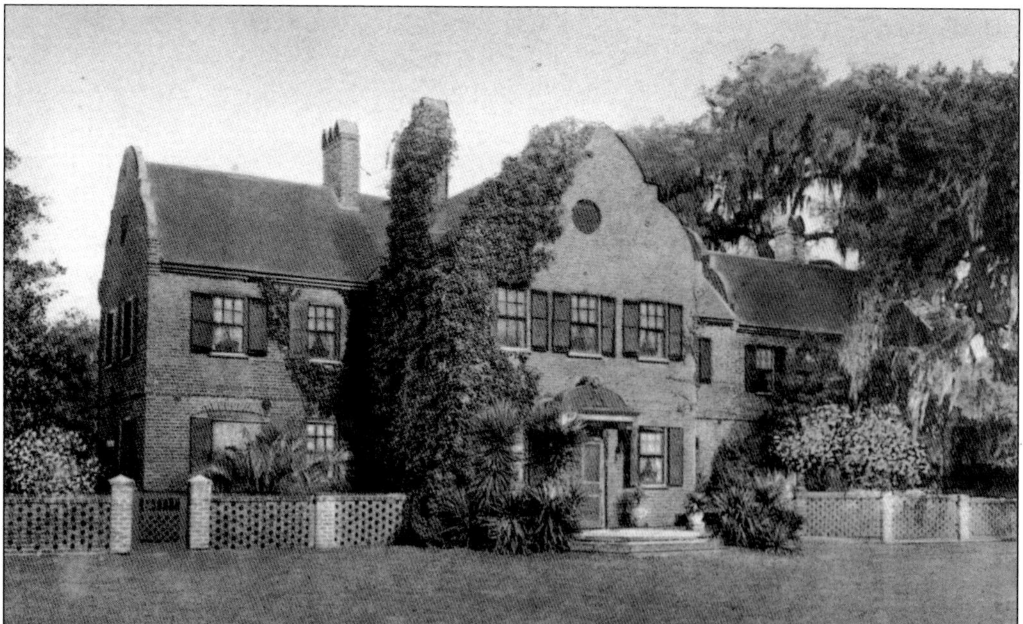

Henry Middleton was responsible for laying out Middleton Place Gardens before 1765, including the houses. During both the Revolutionary and the Civil Wars, Middleton Place was raided. The raiding Union forces were with Sherman and burned the houses. They may have been looking for William Middleton, who had signed the Ordinance of Secession for South Carolina.

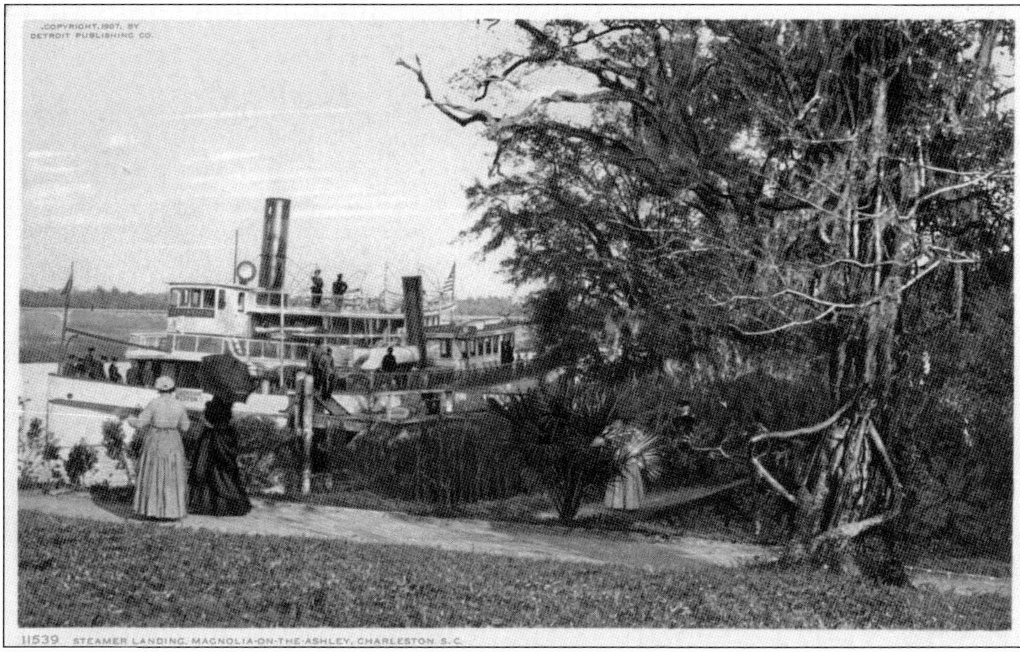

Motion pictures of Magnolia Gardens were taken on April 25, 1915, the last of three separate filming sessions. They were to be taken by Magnolia Film Company of Augusta, Georgia, for Pathé Bi-Weekly News. Pathé News films appeared nationwide and beyond. The movies were expected to be quickly released and would have promoted both Magnolia Gardens and Charleston.

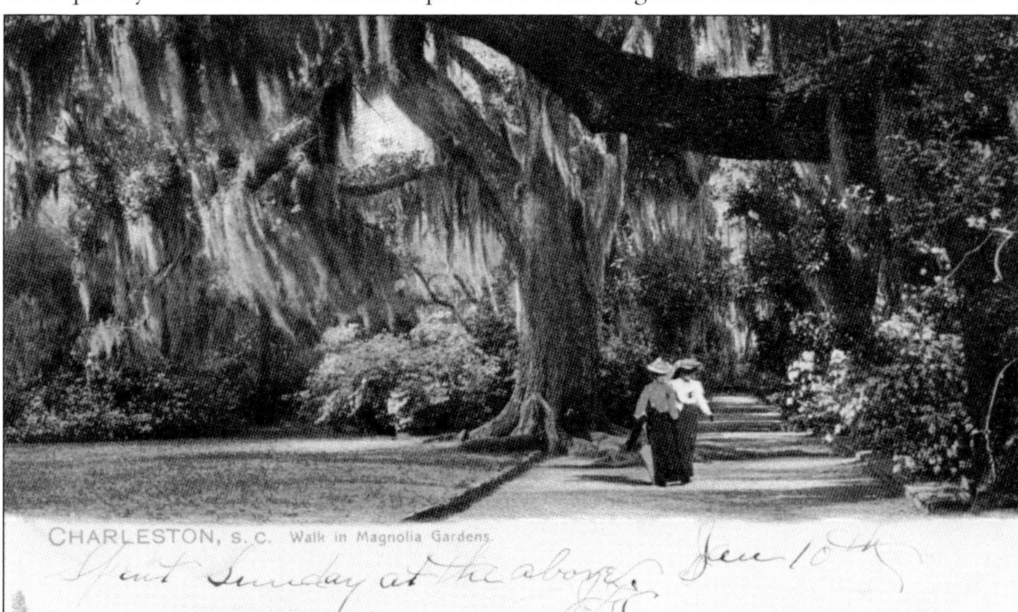

The *News and Courier* of March 21, 1911, notes that those who wanted to enjoy an afternoon at Magnolia-on-the-Ashley could now make the trip upriver on the steamer *E.H. Jackson* multiple times a day. Those who set out for the short cruise would enjoy seeing the original Charles Town site, as well as the old dueling site and Bull Plantation before getting to the japonicas and azaleas.

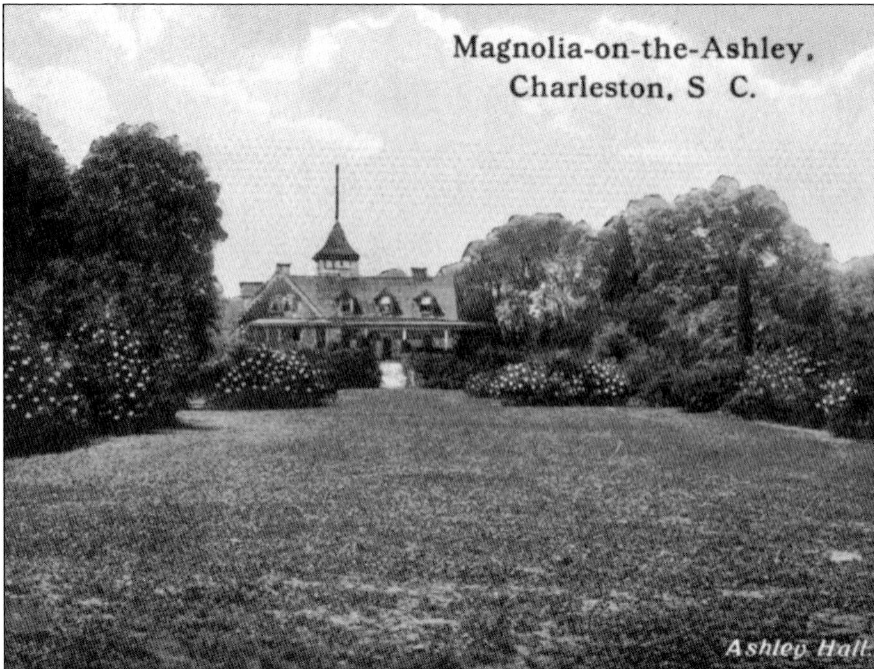

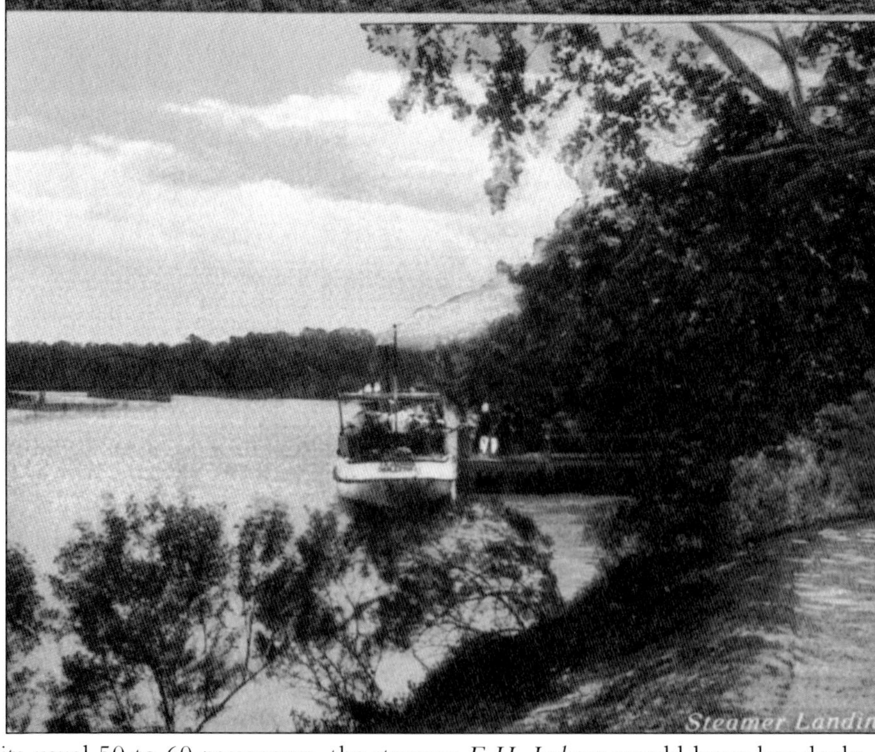

With its usual 50 to 60 passengers, the steamer *E.H. Jackson* would leave her docks, headed toward Magnolia-on-the-Ashley's gardens. After leaving the docks, she passed the Battery with its White Point Garden and imposing mansions, turned up the Ashley River, and passed through the draw of the new bridge that crossed it. The boat passed the fertilizer factories and tree-lined banks as it steamed towards the gardens.

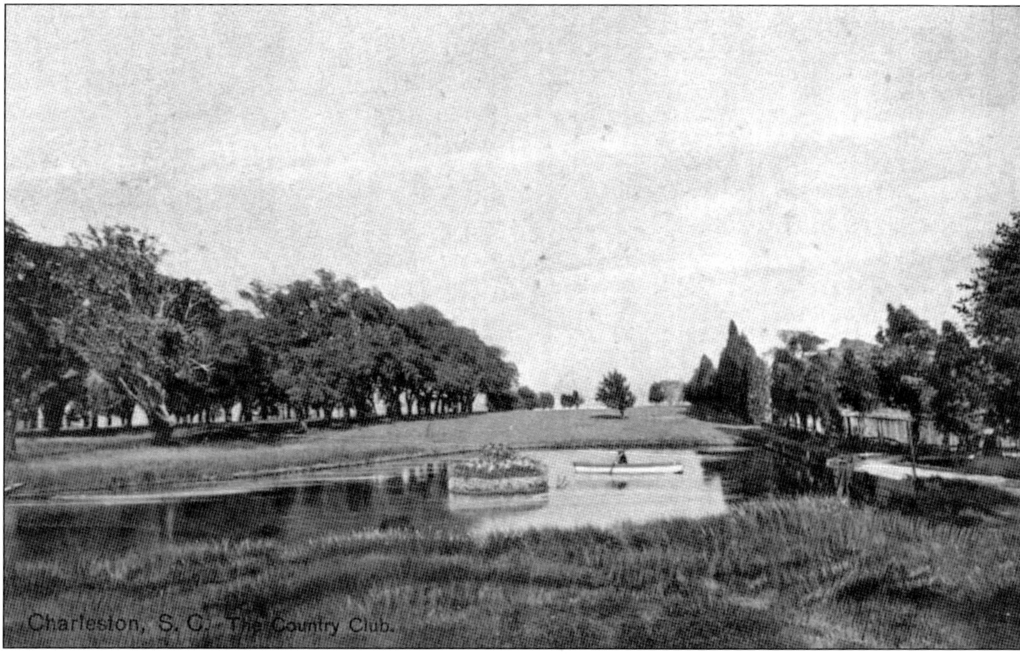

Charleston's country club began with a meeting of a majority of the members of the Chicora Golf at the Carolina Yacht Club in June 1901. The members decided to look into dissolving their club in favor of a country club. The country club's charter was recorded on July 22, 1901. Membership was $25 for men and $10 for ladies. The country club officially opened on Thanksgiving Day 1901, but both gentlemen and lady golfers used the course for weeks before the scheduled formal opening. The club was opened on what had been the grounds of the Belvidere farm. The farm's old Colonial house had been renovated and a piazza added on its east side facing the river. It had both a golf course and a tennis court and could receive members or guests by carriage or boat.

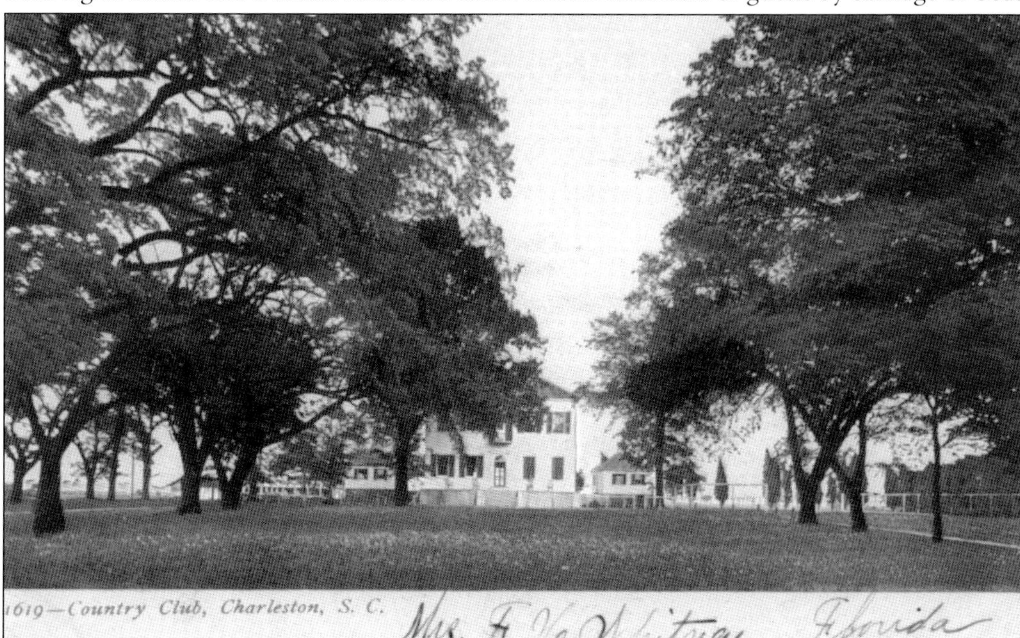

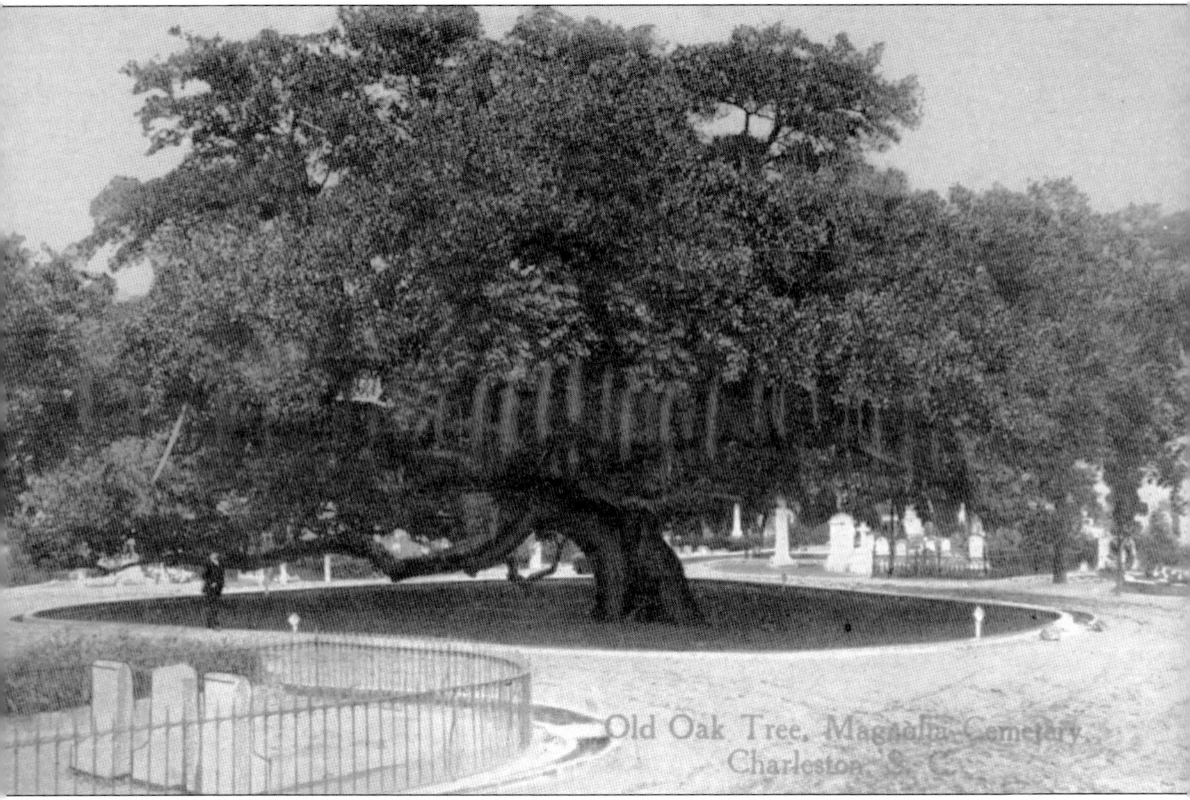

Concerned readers could consult the March 12, 1910, edition of the *News and Courier* for a report that the storm damage done to Magnolia Cemetery's great oak several years before had, finally, been addressed by tree doctors, and its gash had been repaired with cement. The old oak tree still greets Magnolia Cemetery visitors. It has grown older with Charleston and may have witnessed all 300 years of its history.

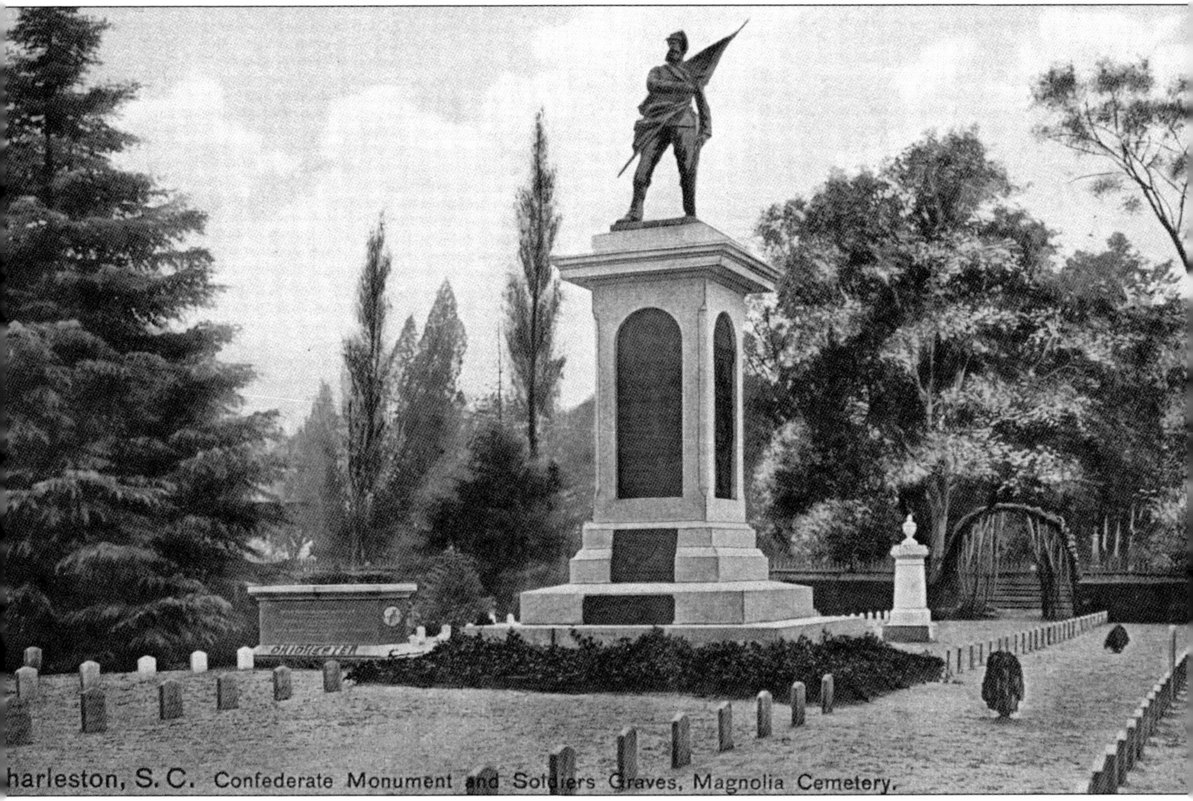

A monument with a bronze Confederate soldier, clutching both his flag and his rifle, watches over about 3,000 Confederate dead at Magnolia Cemetery, including some brought home from Gettysburg and reburied here and the dead of the Confederate submarine *H.L. Hunley*, who recently joined their comrades, under the same watchful eyes. Gen. Wade Hampton spoke at its 1897 unveiling. May 10, the day that "Stonewall" Jackson died, is set aside in South Carolina as Confederate Memorial Day. Every year, that day is observed at Magnolia Cemetery. The *News and Courier* of May 11, 1901, covers the Confederate Memorial Day that took place almost exactly 50 years from the day the shots that began the war whose dead they were remembering were fired from the Battery, just a few short miles away. It is noted that flowers, wreaths, and crosses were placed on the graves of the Confederate dead by the Daughters of the Confederacy, among others.

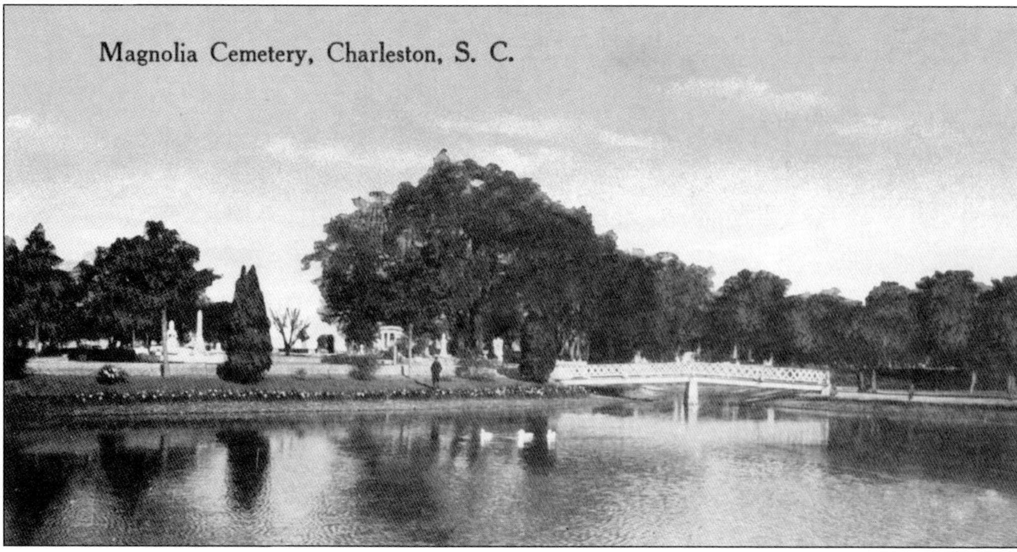

Magnolia Cemetery was dedicated in 1850 with a dedication speech delivered by local and nationally known artist Charles Fraser. Fraser is buried at St. Michael's Church. In addition to the 3,000 Confederate dead, Magnolia Cemetery is the final resting place of multiple governors, representatives, senators, and judges of South Carolina, as well as authors William Gilmore Simms, Frank Bunker Gilbreth Jr., and Josephine Pinckney

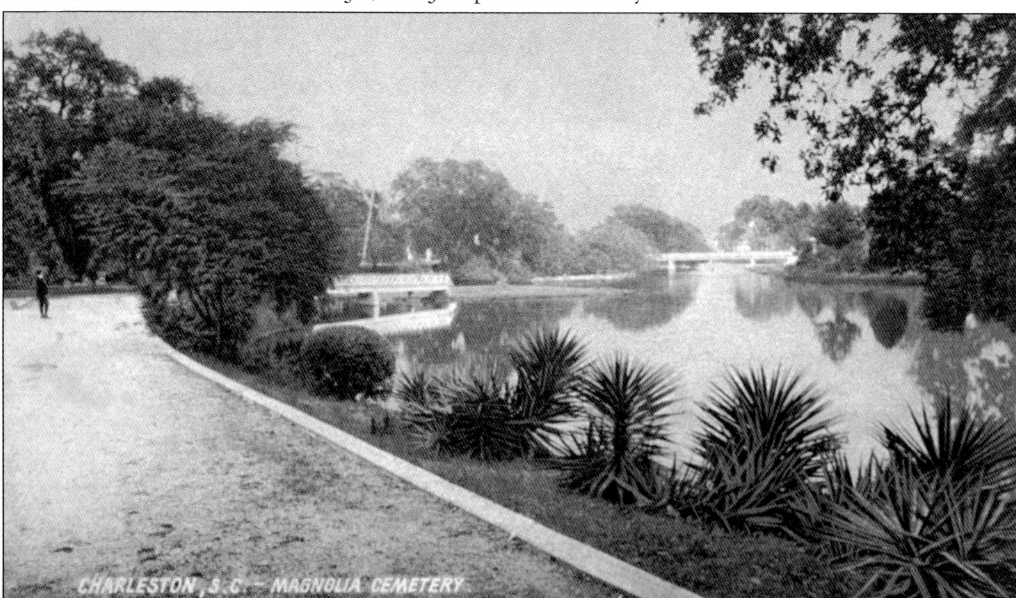

The *Charleston Courier* of November 19, 1850, includes an announcement of the dedication of Magnolia Cemetery: "The dedication of the grounds at Magnolia Cemetery to the sacred purposes of Sepulture, will take place in solemn form and with appropriate ceremonies, This Day, the 19t instant, at half past 11 o'clock A.M. Professor Robinson and Mr. Speissegger, having kindly volunteered their aid, two original Odes written for the occasion, by gentlemen of this city will be sung by a full choir with the accompaniment of piano. After a Dedicatory Prayer by the Rev. WM. C. Dana, an Address will be delivered by Charles Fraser, Esq. and a Poem, entitled 'The City of the Silent', by W. Gilmore Simms, Esq."

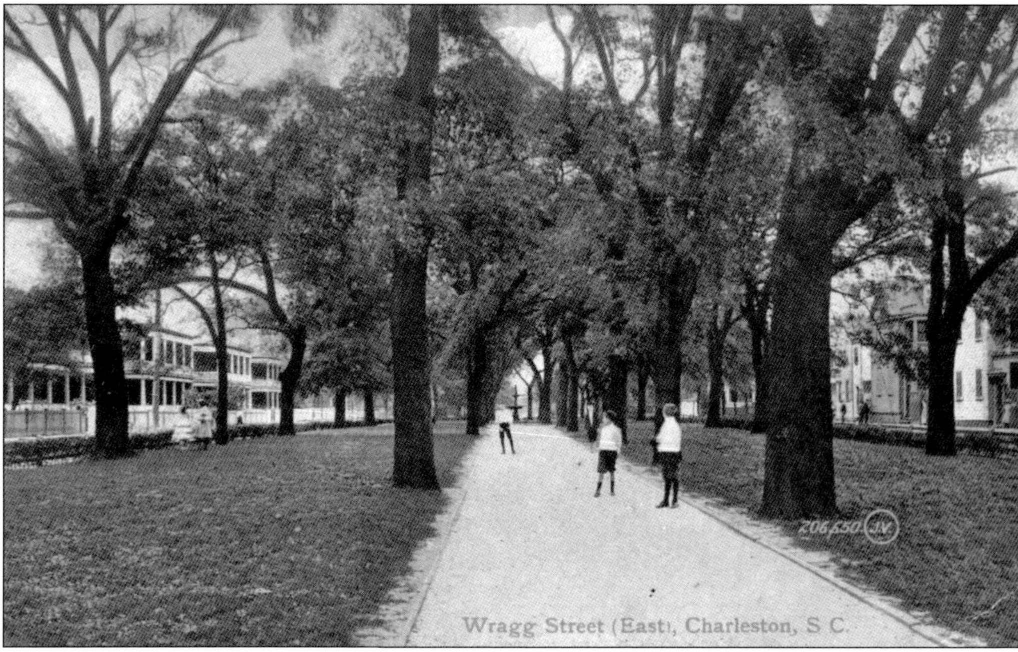

These boys are playing on Wragg Mall, located on Meeting Street. It is now sandwiched between the Charleston Museum and Courtenay School. To the left are what were seven identical rental houses built by William Aiken. Only two of the seven are still standing. Five were demolished due to the expansions of Courtenay School, the last two in 1957.

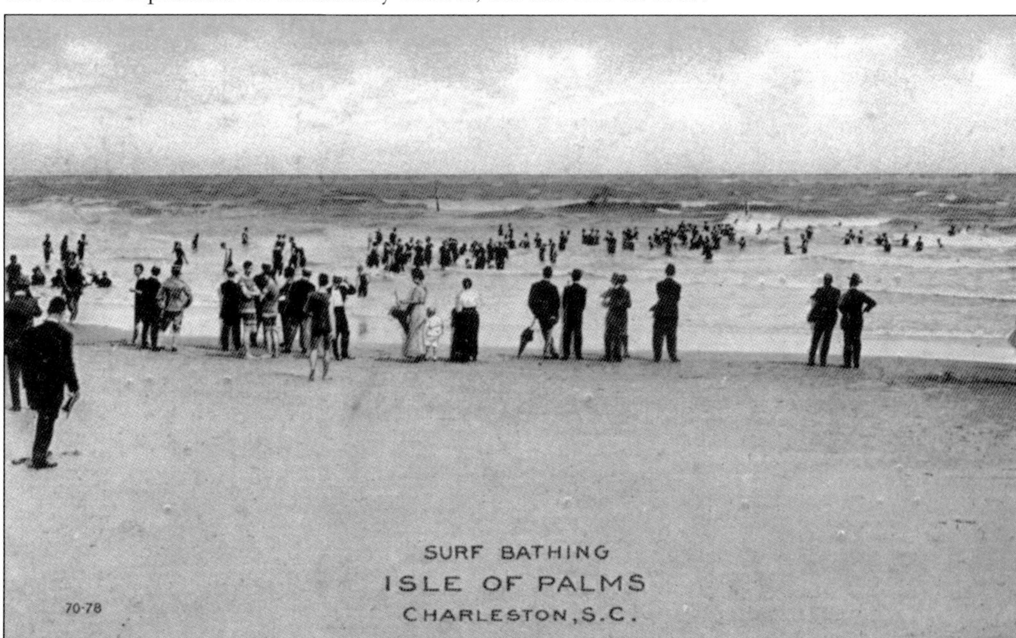

There are few beachgoers wearing swimwear outside of the water. Most of the people enjoying the beach sands and the sounds of the surf are wearing regular street clothing, including long dresses, long-sleeved blouses, suits, and hats, with a few even carrying parasols or umbrellas. Perhaps these beachgoers are in town for business or a convention and just wanted to see the ocean.

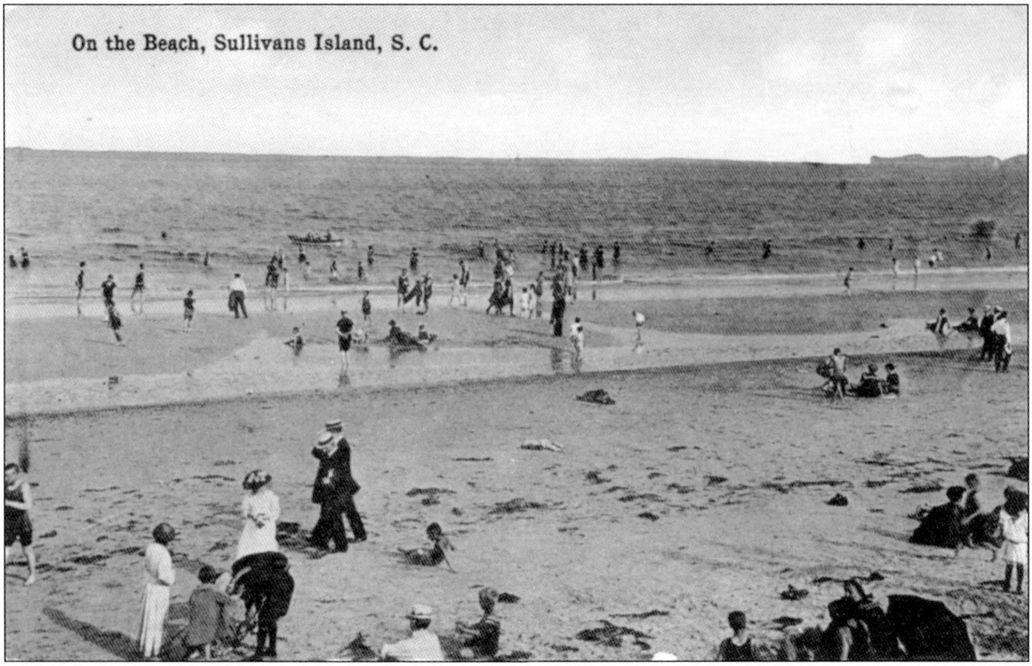

While Isle of Palms offered a pavilion and rides from Coney Island, Sullivan's Island offered beachgoers the same sun, sand, surf, and ocean breezes. More people here are sitting on the beach and watching, as do beachgoers of today. Edgar Allan Poe was once stationed on the island at Fort Moultrie.

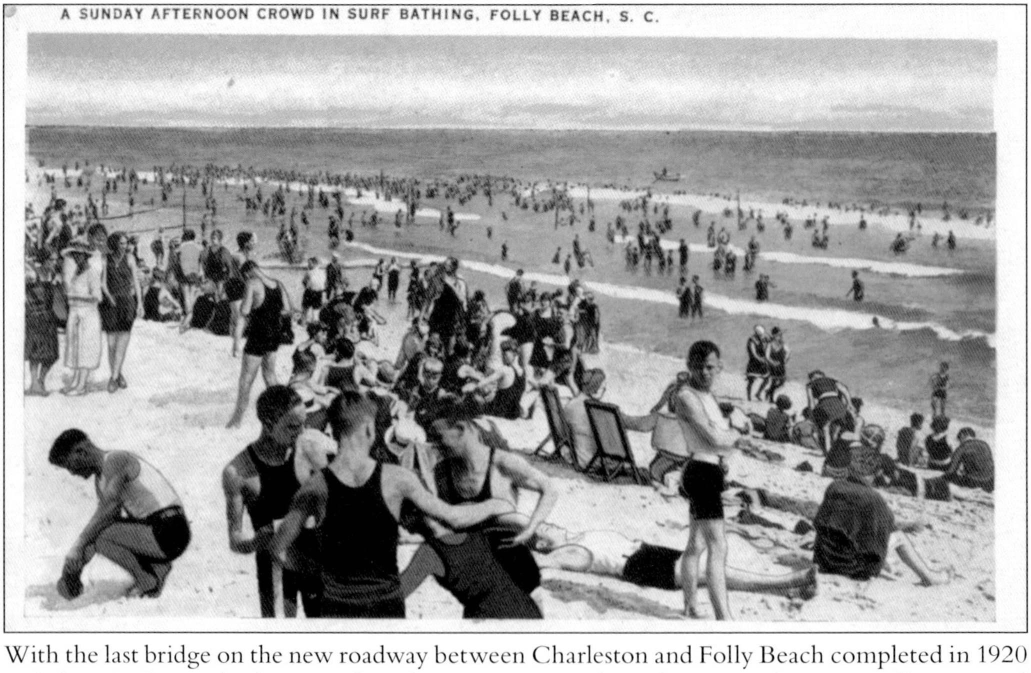

With the last bridge on the new roadway between Charleston and Folly Beach completed in 1920 and the trip from Charleston only a short 45-minute drive from Broad Street, Folly attracted beachgoers in large numbers, like those pictured here. George Gershwin lived on Folly Island while writing *Porgy and Bess*, which is based on Charlestonian DuBose Heyward's novel *Porgy*.

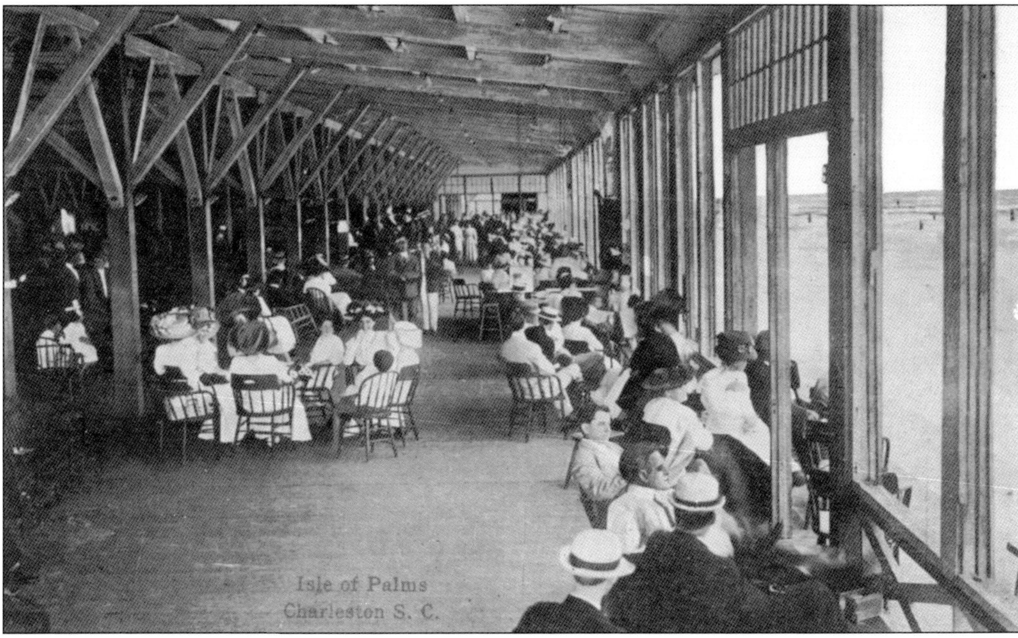

In addition to allowing people to get out of the sun, enjoy an ocean breezes, have lunch, and view beachgoers in and out of the water, the Isle of Palms Pavilion hosted evening concerts and hops, or dances. Bands like Metz's Military Band played as the couples danced the night away before taking the late trains back to Charleston.

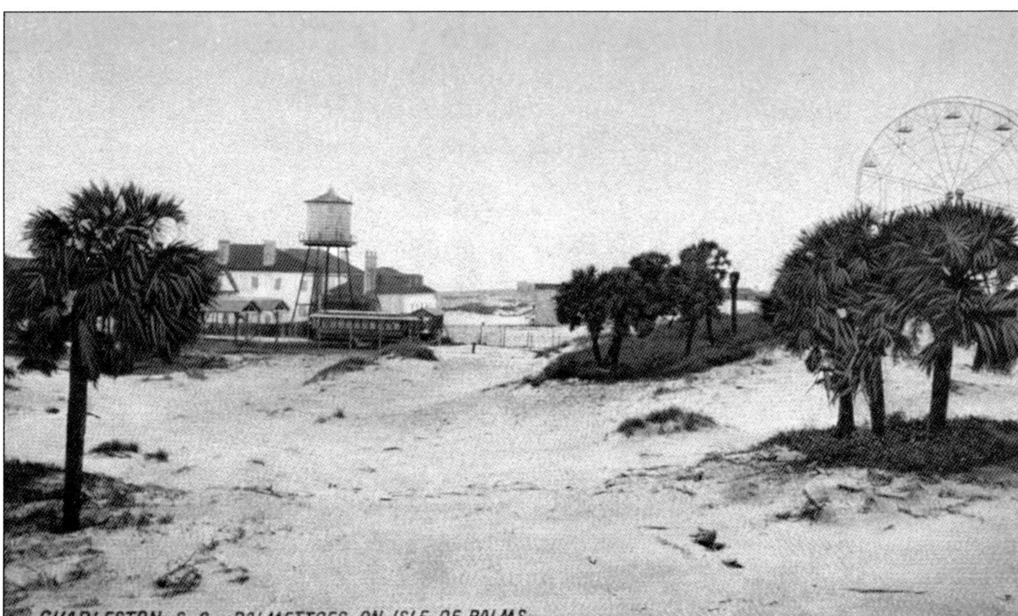

Beyond the sand dunes, one can see the Isle of Palms' towering Ferris wheel above the palmetto tree to the right, the island's water tower, and the train that brought the daily visitors from the Mount Pleasant–side ferry landing to the beach.

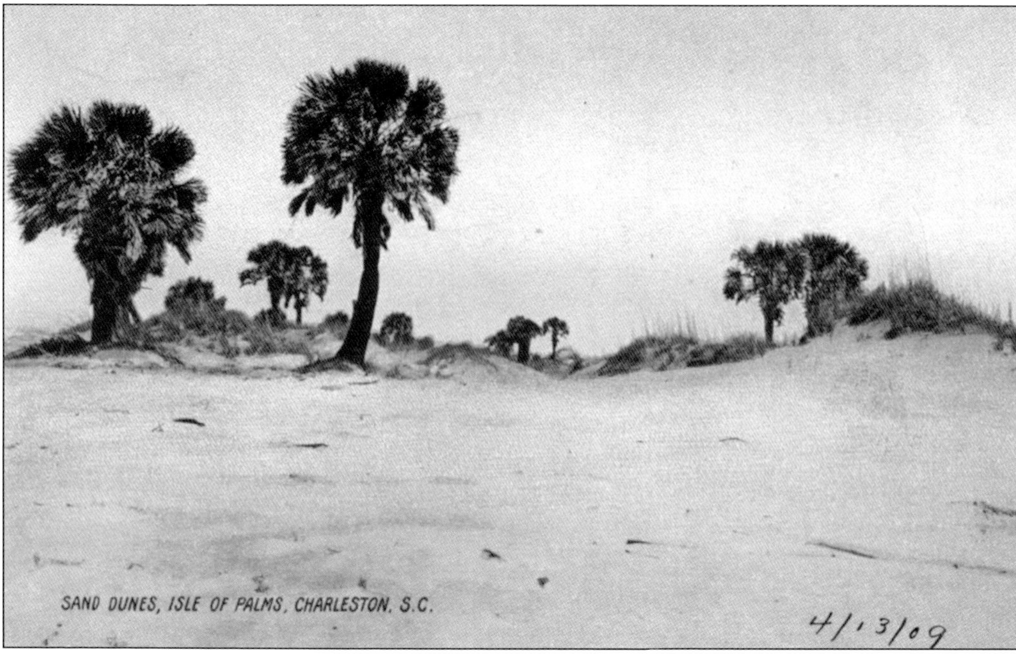

The palmettos of the Isle of Palms are the type of trees used to make Fort Moultrie, which saved Charles Town from the British and from which South Carolina received its nickname, the Palmetto State, and part of the design of the state flag. Perhaps these dunes were where the Solax-Blanche Company filmed its Spanish-American War battle scenes for *Her Own Way*, filmed on the island in 1915.

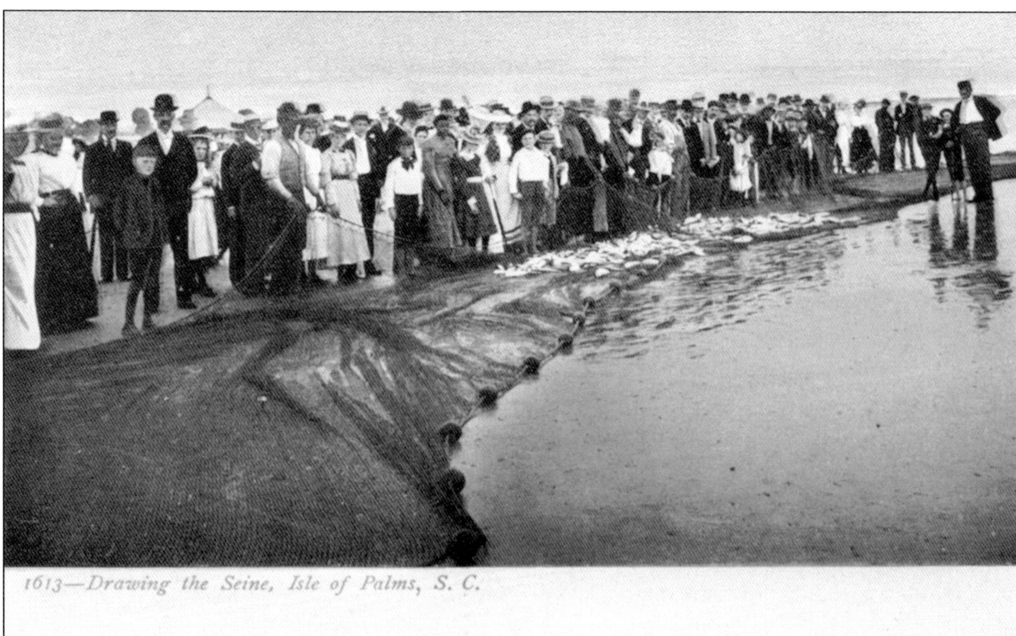

A seine is a net that can be dragged through the water to catch fish. It used to be a beach pastime to get the maybe hundreds of beachgoers at the Isle of Palms to help drag the seine through the waters for fish about 5 o'clock in the afternoon, hoping to catch enough to feed the group.

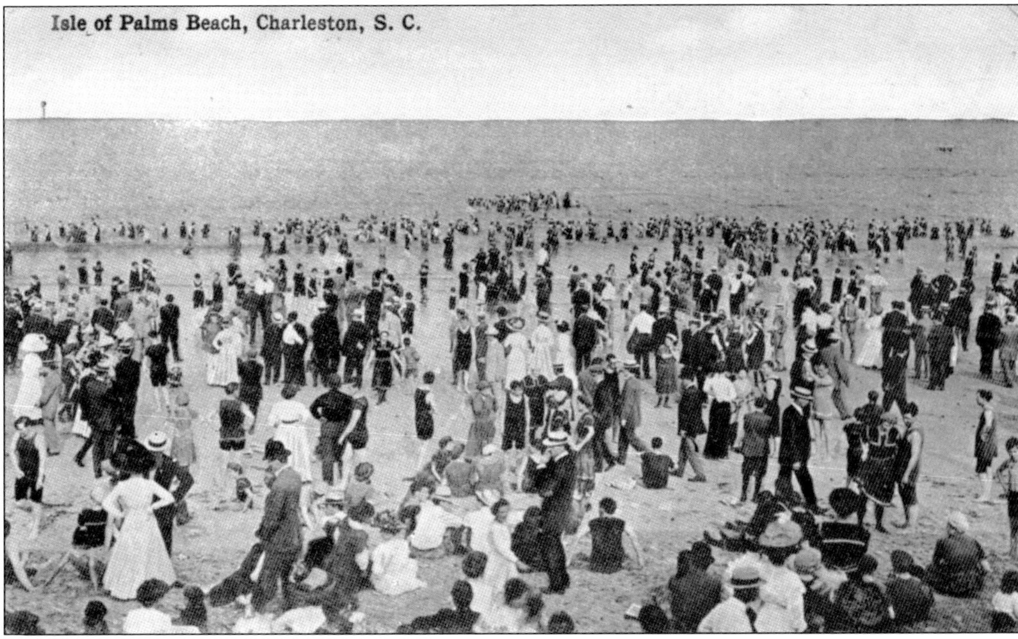

Most of the beach crowd seems overdressed. Perhaps they are still dressed from some earlier event in Charleston, or they came to the Isle of Palms dressed for something different than swimming. The Isle of Palms was popular with young couples who would come to walk the beaches, ride the rides, or dance the night away on the pavilion.

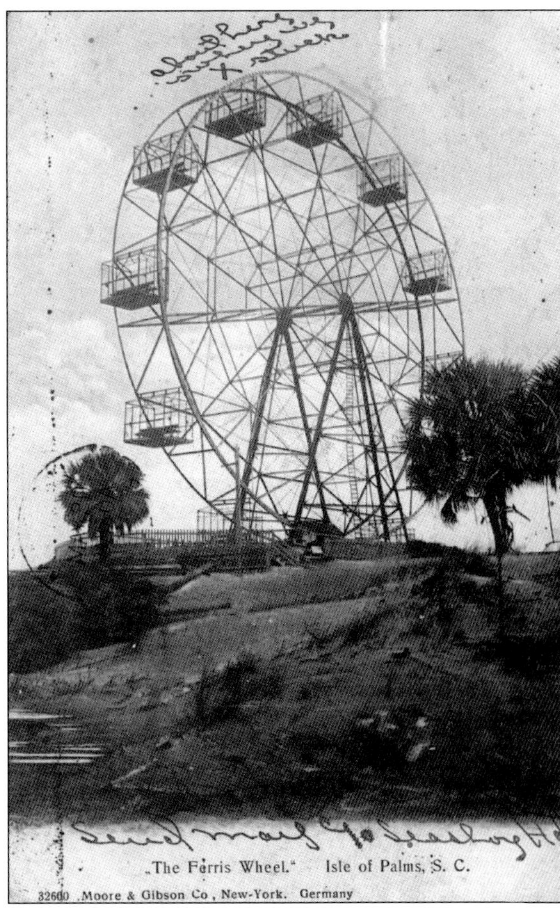

A Colonel Shaw purchased the electrically operated 120-foot-tall Ferris wheel from Coney Island in 1898, along with a steeplechase and merry-go-round for use on the Isle of Palms. For 10¢, one of the wheel's 12 cars gave a rider a bird's-eye view from 150 feet of the beach, the beachgoers, the island itself, and beyond.

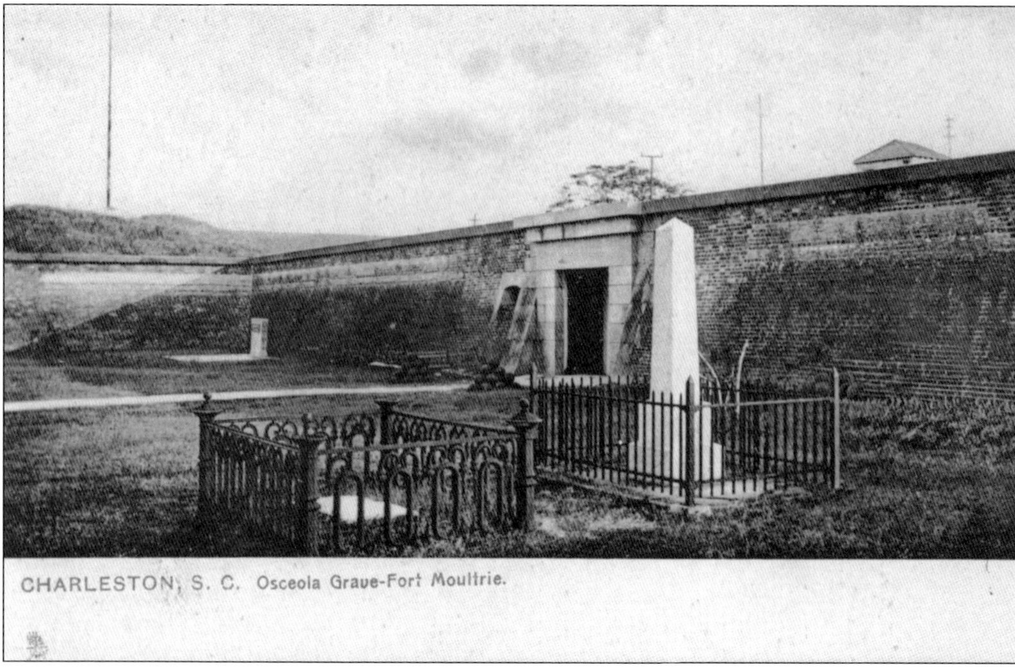

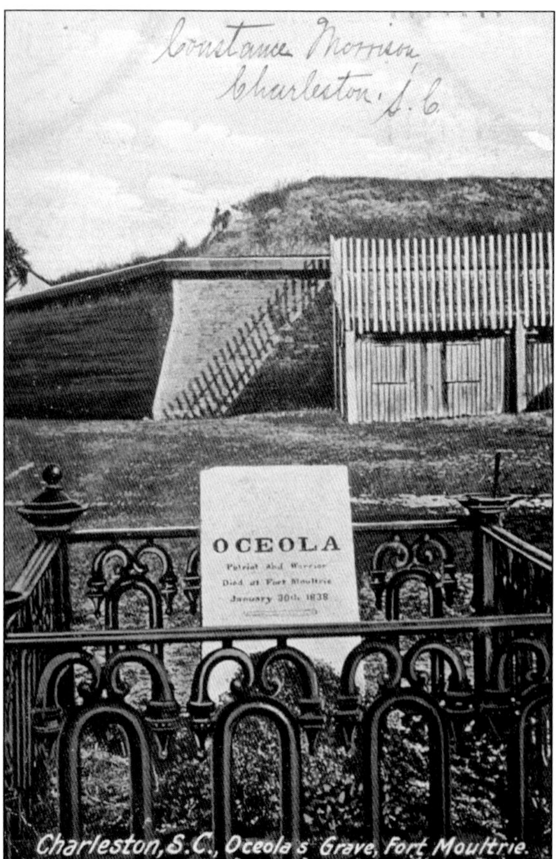

Little Owl was born to a Creek Indian mother and a white father named William Powell in 1803. During the Red Stick Wars in Alabama, Andrew Jackson killed hundreds in Battle of Horseshoe Bend and burned their villages. Survivors such as Little Owl and his mother made their way to Florida and joined other displaced Creeks, who called themselves Seminoles. Osceola, as Little Owl came to be called, now a Seminole chief, waged a guerilla campaign against the ever-encroaching Americans who wanted all Creeks and Seminoles removed to Oklahoma.

Seminole chief Oceola (Osceola), captured in Florida on October 21, 1837, under a flag of truce, died imprisoned at Fort Moultrie on January 30, 1838. Osceola had a throat problem that had continued for days. He was offered medicines and medical treatment by local doctors but refused them, preferring a tribal doctor who had previously treated him for a similar problem.

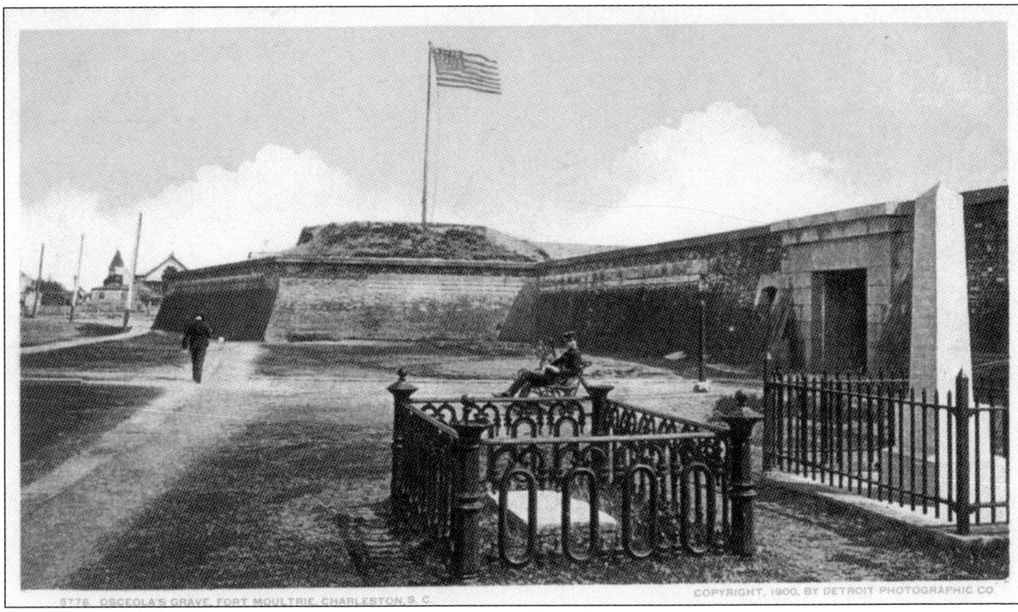

Sullivan's Island's Fort Moultrie was named after Gen. William Moultrie. It was originally constructed of spongy palmetto logs. British warships trying to take Charles Town had to sail past it, exposing themselves to its cannon fire to get to Charles Town. So, on June 28, 1776, they attacked it. British fire had little effect on the small fort. The fort's fire kept Charles Town free and safe, for the moment.

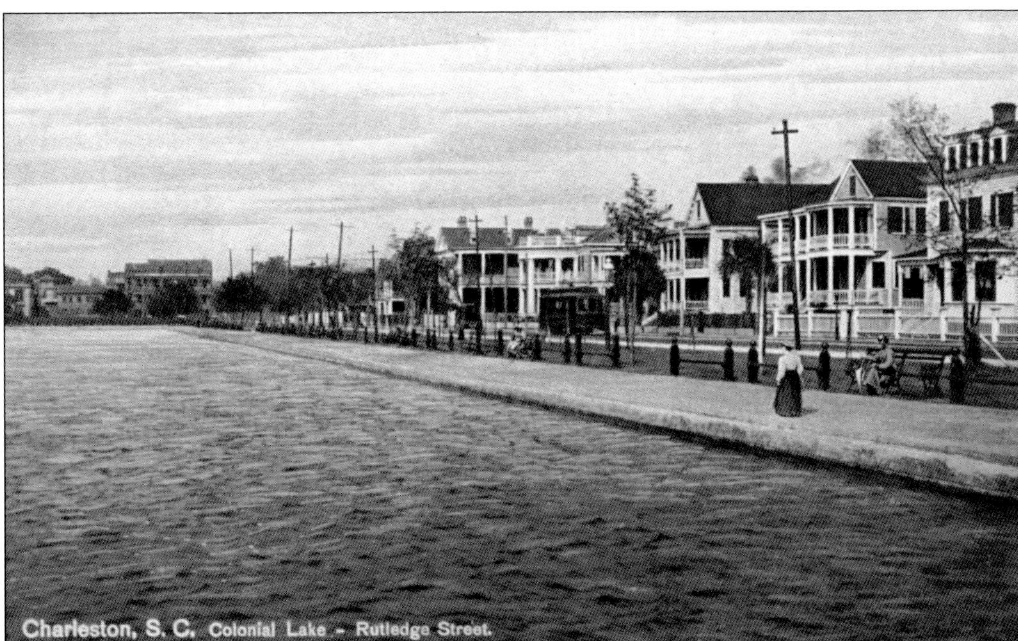

The lake between Rutledge and Ashley Avenues and Broad and Beaufain Streets, sometimes referred to by locals as the "Pond," was named Colonial Lake in 1881. Its area had been set aside as a colonial common for public use in 1768. The concrete embankments that define the lake were completed in 1885. Locals sometimes used boats to fish, and there were boat races in it.

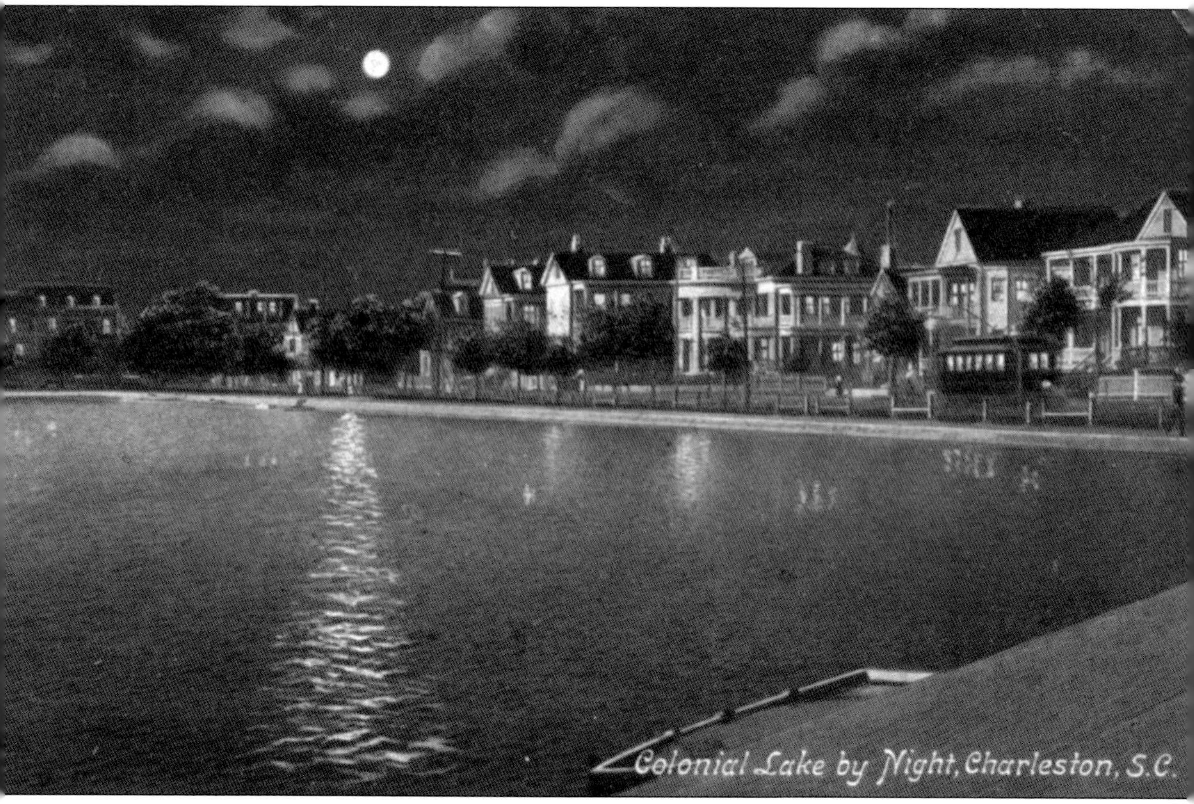

Two men, one a white carpenter and the other a black truck driver, reported to the *News and Courier* that each had been at Colonial Lake cooling himself the evening of Thursday, August 21, 1902, when each heard strange noises coming from the lake. Shortly, something crawled out of the lake and onto its shore. The truck driver said that at the sight of the creature, he ran down Broad Street, without stopping, until he ran into the Old Post Office. The carpenter described the creature as having the head of a huge frog with large fangs and eyes, arms and shoulders like a man, but a serpent-like body covered in large scales. He left quickly, too. This frog-man was seen again the evening of April 16, 1903, on the lake's bank near Broad Street and Rutledge Avenue.

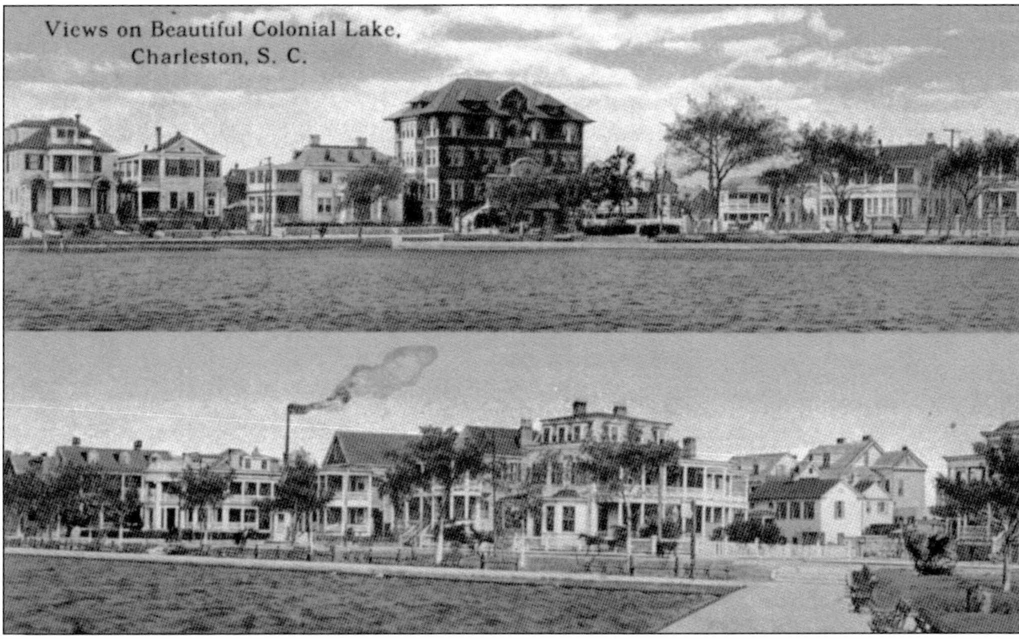

In the top half of this postcard is what was the Baker-Craig Sanatorium, which was located on the corner of Ashley Avenue and Beaufain Street, facing Colonial Lake. It opened on Thanksgiving Day 1912. The building, furnishings, and equipment needed to open the sanatorium cost about $100,000. The sanatorium closed and the building was converted into condominium units.

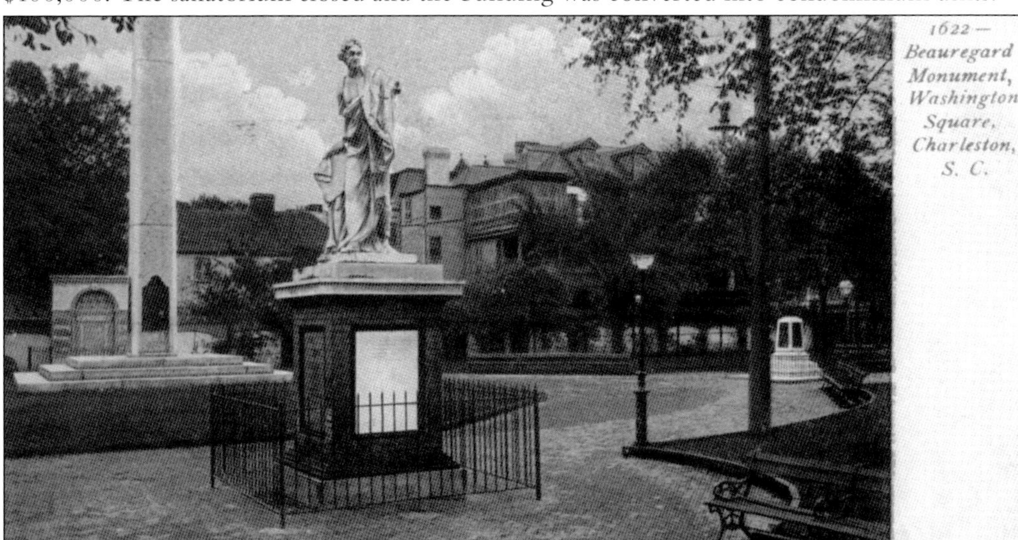

In the center foreground next to the lady in pink is a statue of William Pitt, a member of the British Parliament. Charlestonians, in appreciation of his opposition to the Stamp Act erected this statue to him in 1770. Originally, it stood not too far from here, where Meeting and Broad Streets come together. By chance, several years later, during the American Revolution, a British cannon firing from James Island took off the statue's arm. In 1794, it was removed to the Charleston Orphan Asylum, where it stayed until placed in Washington Square in 1881. The wounded statue is now housed in the Charleston County Judicial Center, just across the street from this location.

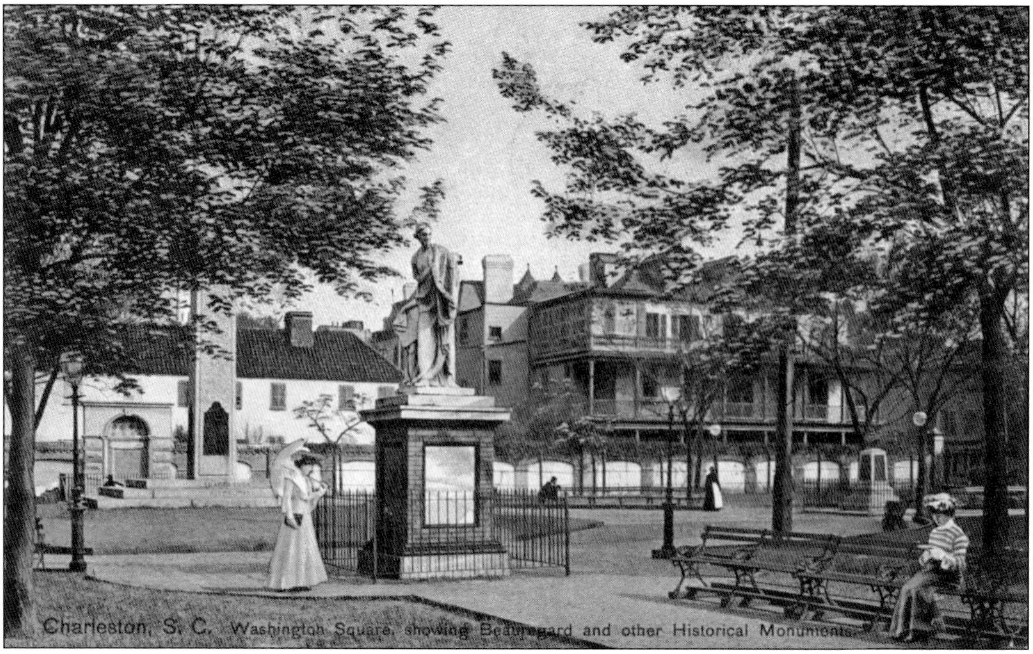

On the afternoon of March 10, 1901, the Washington Light Infantry marched to the Confederate Home on Broad Street, picked up the ladies of the Confederate College and escorted them the short walk to Washington Square Park, where they placed flowers and wreaths on the Washington Light Infantry Monument, which rises just beyond the Pitt statue. The ceremony concluded with a bugler playing "Taps."

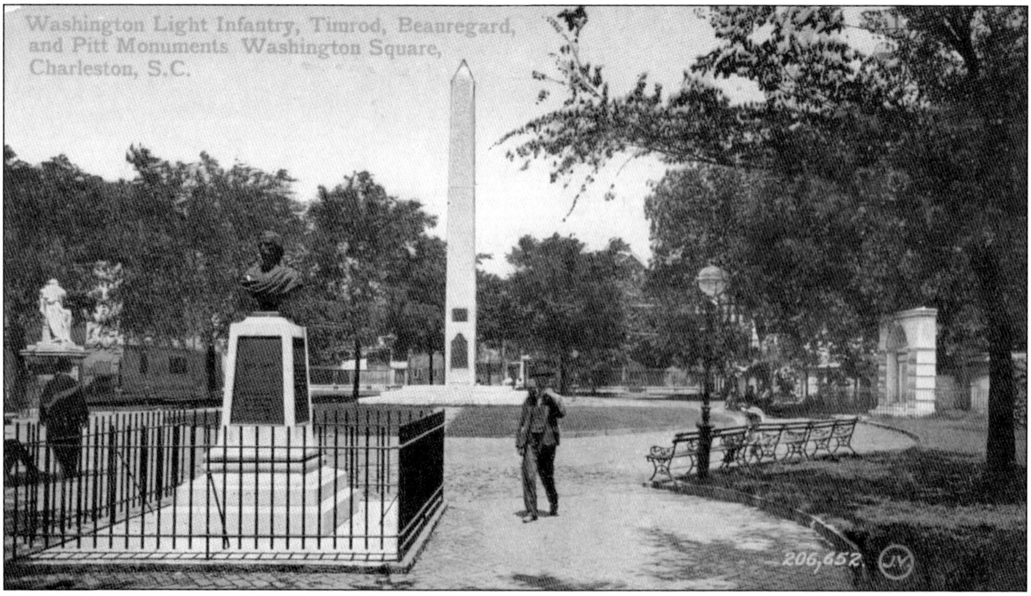

The statue that watches over the Broad Street entrance to Washington Square Park is of poet Henry Timrod, who is often referred to as the Poet Laureate of the Confederacy. His poem "Carolina" was resolved by the state's general assembly in 1911 to be the lyrics to the state's anthem. Behind Timrod is the obelisk dedicated in 1891 to the Washington Light Infantry for its service in the Civil War.

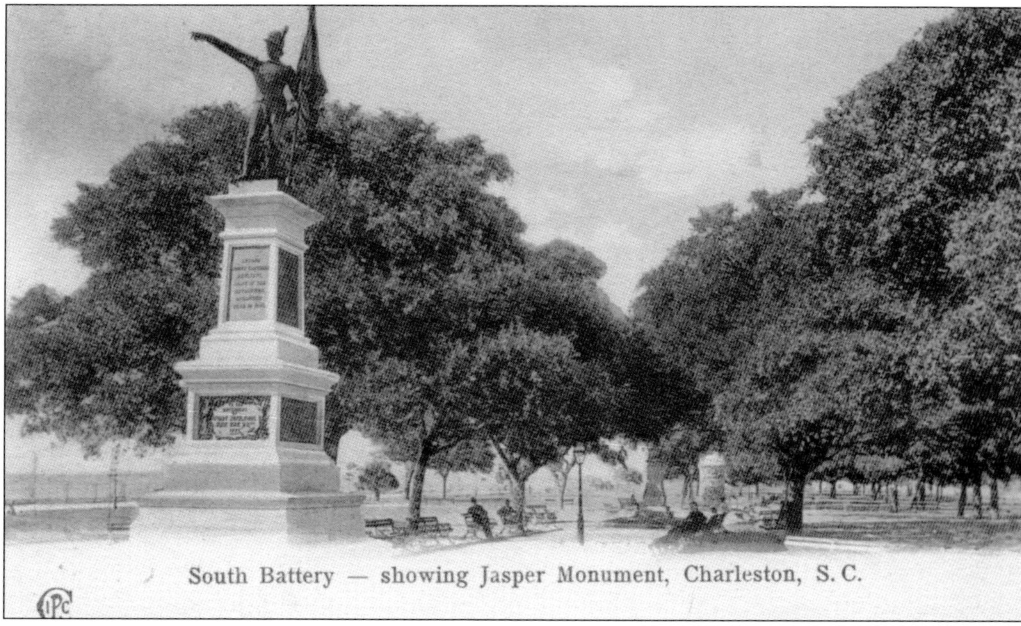

The Battery's Sergeant Jasper Monument is really a monument to the defenders of Fort Moultrie. It was unveiled on Carolina Day, June 28, 1877, the 101st anniversary of the battle that temporarily saved Charleston. Sergeant Jasper's heroic bravery, recovering and replacing the fort's fallen flag, made him appropriate to appear on the statue. Present at the unveiling was Jasper's surviving granddaughter, a resident of the Confederate Home.

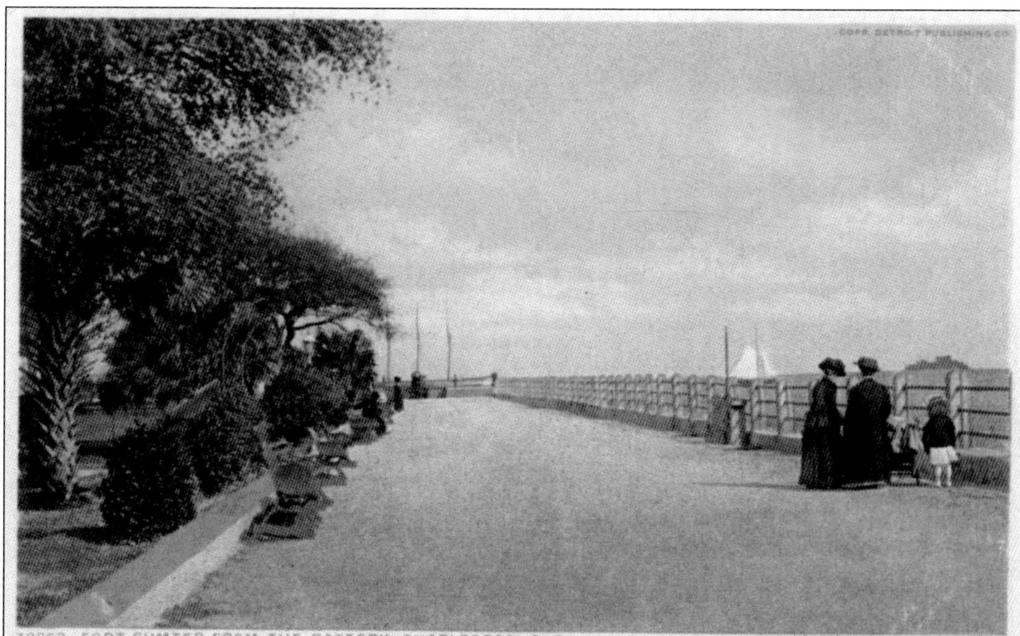

These ladies and their charges stop to talk where East Bay, Meeting, and King Streets all end, and where many Charlestonian say the Ashley and Cooper Rivers come together to form the Atlantic Ocean. It was originally known as Oyster Point because of the shells that washed up there. Today, the park is known as White Point Garden, still paying homage to the oyster shells.

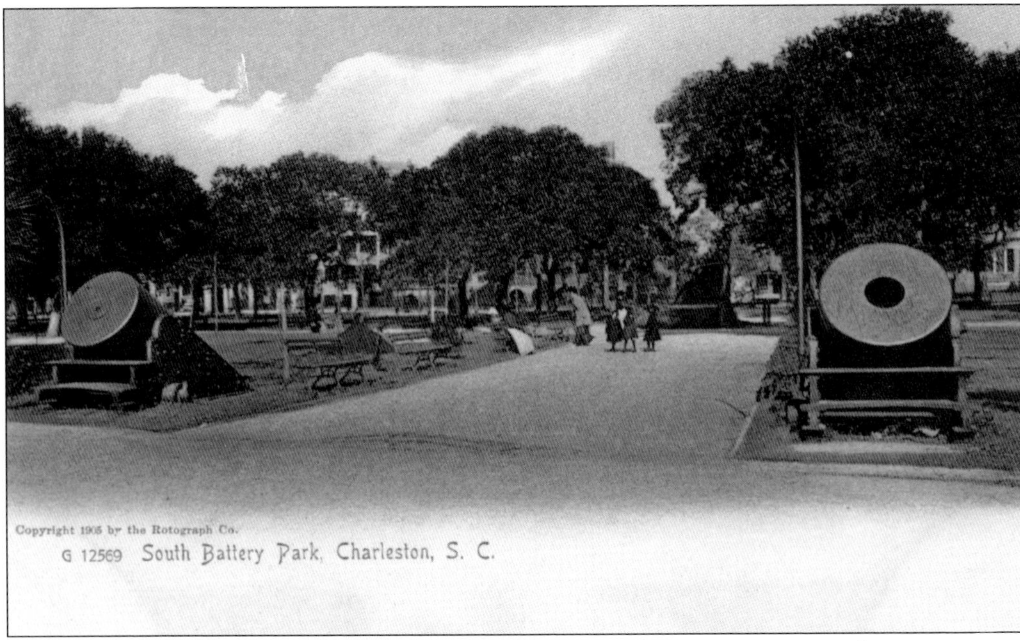

The three young girls, all wearing dresses, hose, and hats, are with their mothers or nannies. They, unlike little girls today, were probably not allowed to climb on the Civil War mortars that guard the entrance to their little kingdom and were once used in a war to defend it.

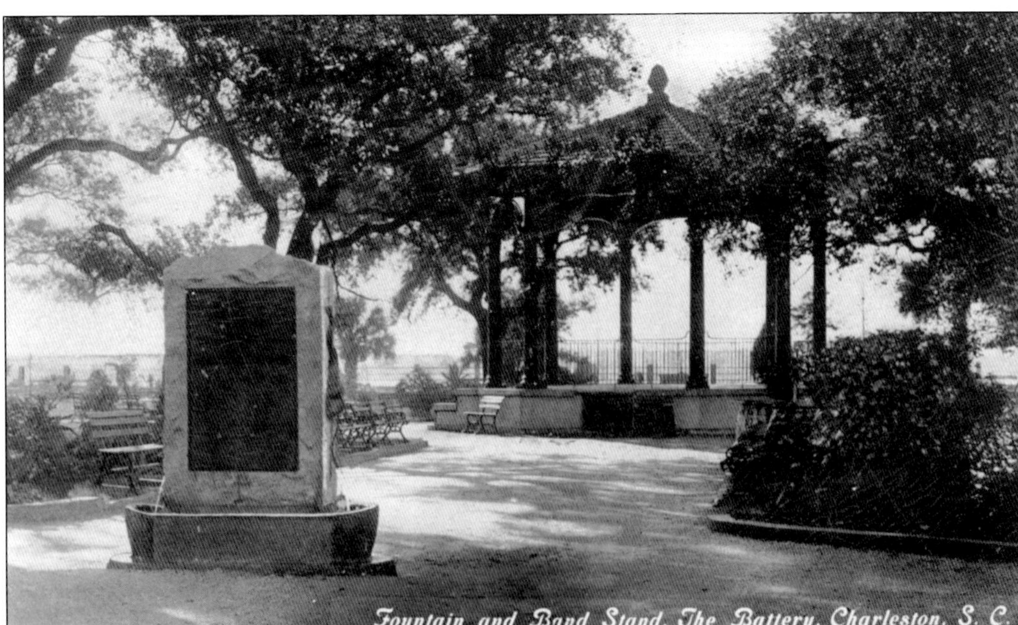

On June 28, 1907, Metz's Military Band gave the first concert in celebration of Carolina Day from the bandstand built in the center of White Point Garden by Martha W. Carrington, as a memorial to her mother, Martha F. Williams. The fountain in the foreground was erected by the Daughters of the Confederacy and Memorial Association in 1899.

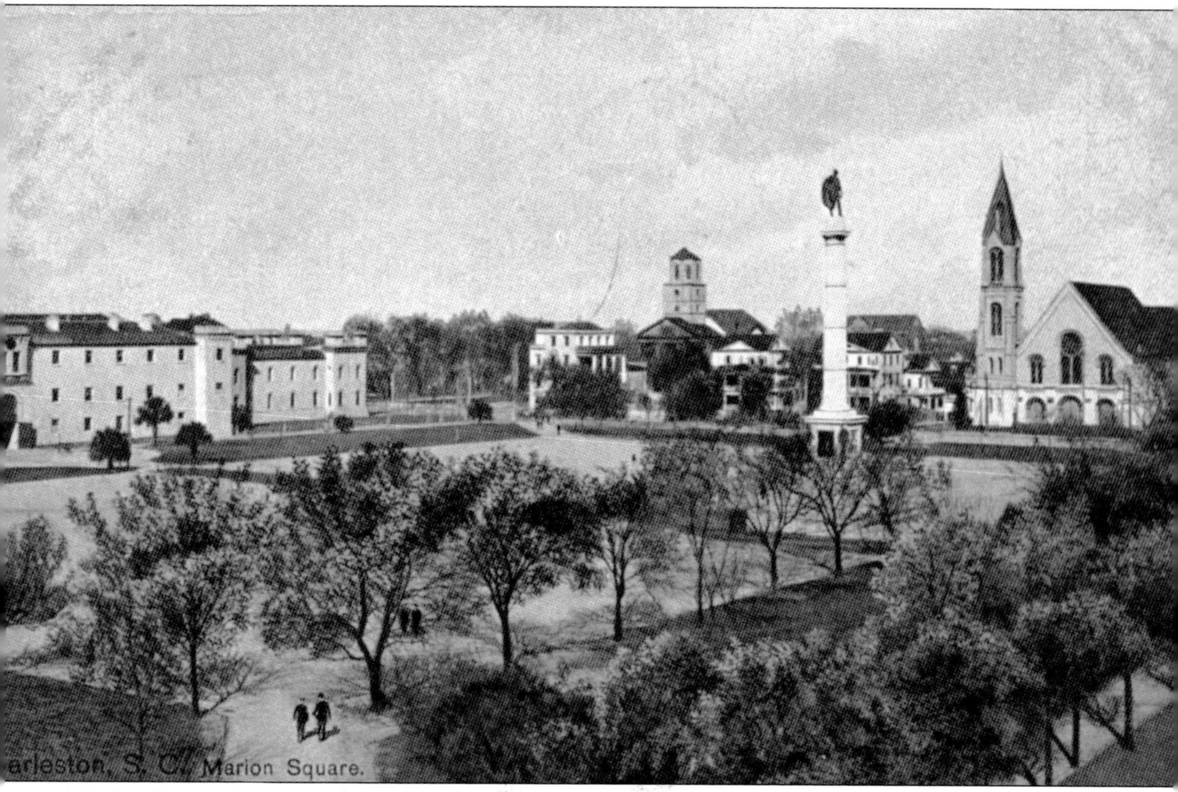

Marion Square is a green lying between Meeting and King Streets and facing Calhoun Street. This perspective may be from the top of the Charleston Orphan House. To the left is the South Carolina Military Academy, or the Citadel. To the right of it are the steeples of Second Presbyterian Church and Citadel Square Baptist Church, with John C. Calhoun rising between them, keeping watch over his street and city.

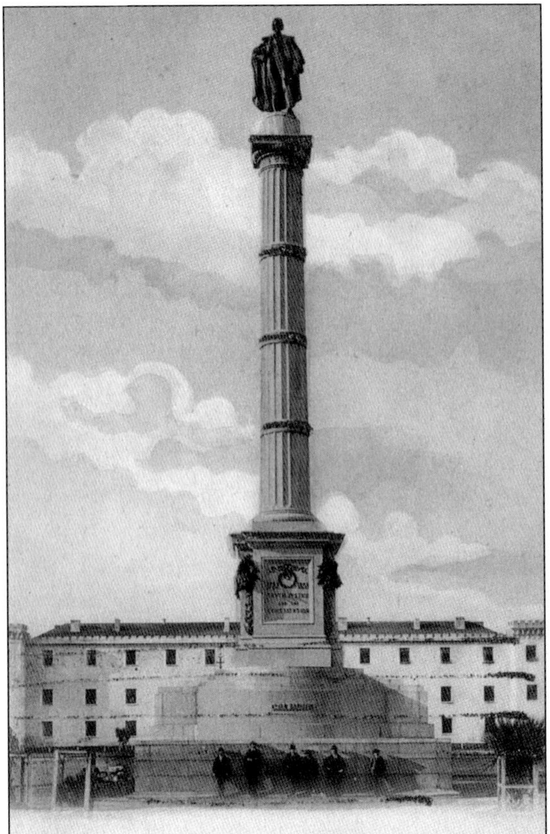

Calhoun Monument, Charleston, S. C.

The 1896 monument to John C. Calhoun on Marion Square is the second such statue on that same pedestal to South Carolina's native son, who in 1957 would be voted among the top five all-time US senators. He had been a war hawk in Congress before the War of 1812 and vice president to both Pres. John Quincy Adams and Pres. Andrew Jackson. He resigned as Jackson's vice president to represent South Carolina in the Senate. The first statue was not big enough for such a man; this 13-foot Calhoun by New York sculptor J. Massey Rhind on an 84-foot-high column and pedestal was. Ironically, the money for the monument, raised before the Civil War, had been invested in US bonds. These had been hidden from Union occupying soldiers sewn into the skirts of Mary Amarinthia Snowden.

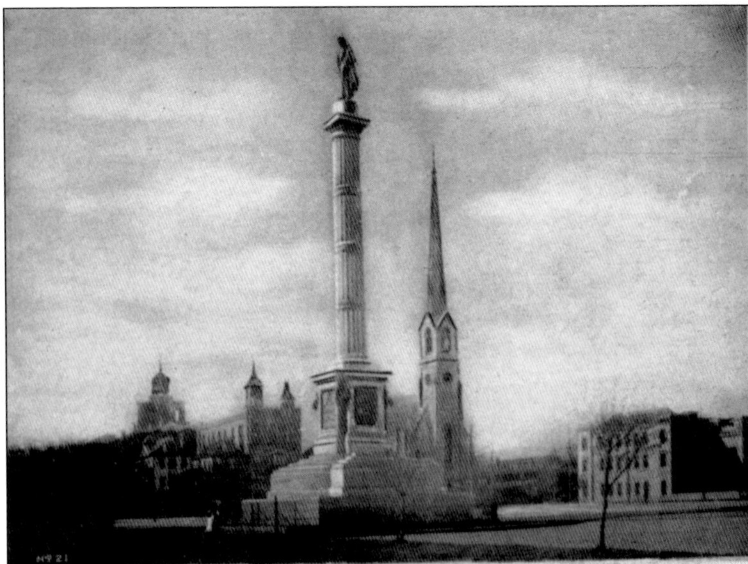

CHARLESTON, S.C.

ORPHANS HOUSE. CALHOUN MONUMENT MARION SQUARE

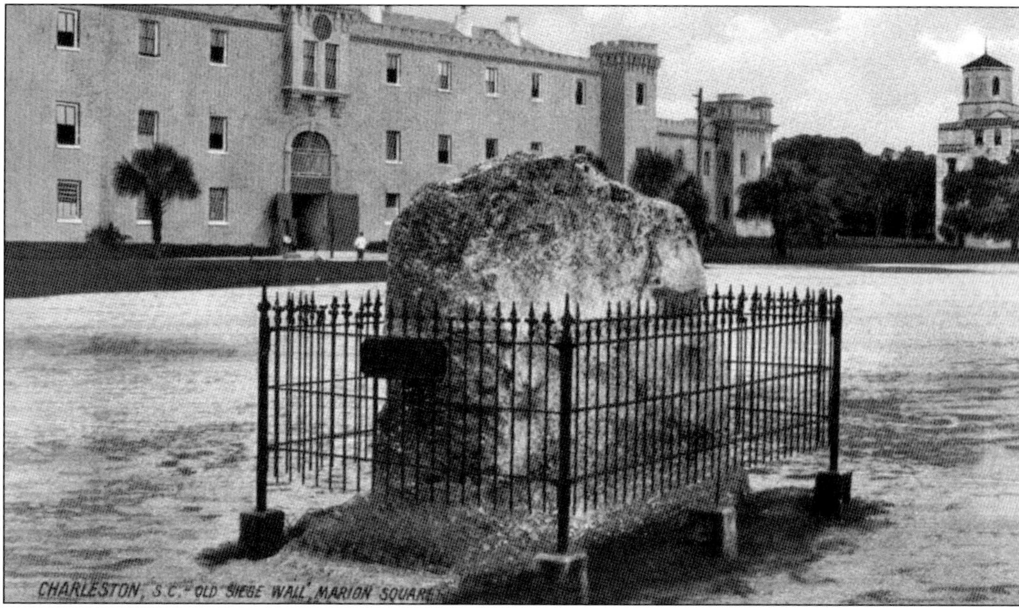

This remnant of Charleston's Old Siege Wall is made of tabby, a type of concrete made from oyster shells, lime, water, and sand. The wall was built in 1759 and taken down after the Revolutionary War. Its plaque reads, "Remnant of Horn work. May 1780, Siege of Charleston." Near here is where American general Benjamin Lincoln surrendered his 6,000 men and Charleston to the British in 1780.

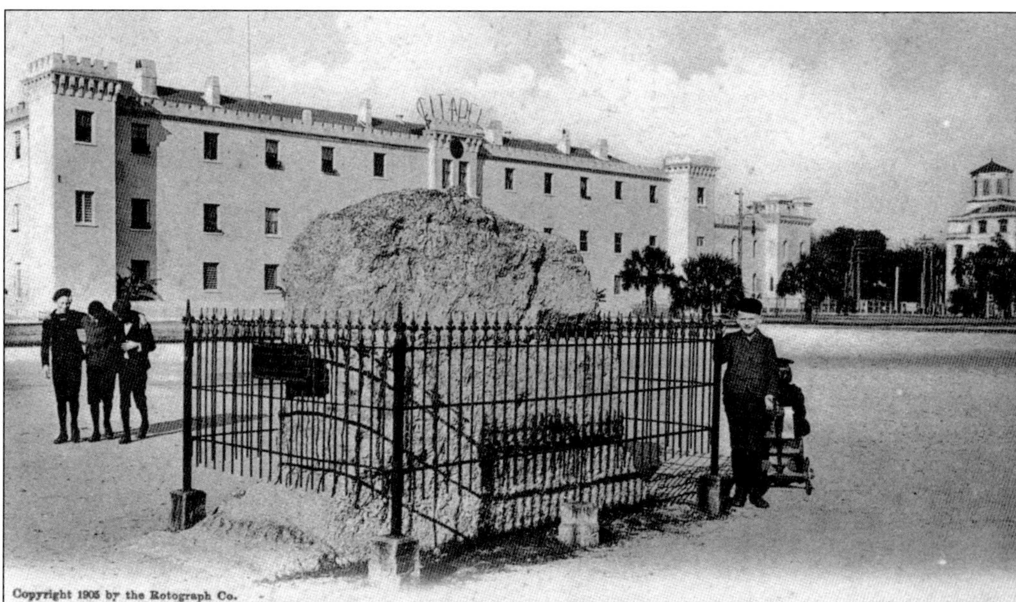

These young guys may be on Marion Square to play about the tabby wall remnant, but on November 11, 1910, they may have been among some 3,000 white schoolchildren present to hear Pres. William Howard Taft's five-minute speech. He did not speak from the bandstand; it was not built until 1944. President Taft made a similar speech at the newly built Colored Industrial School on President Street shortly afterwards.

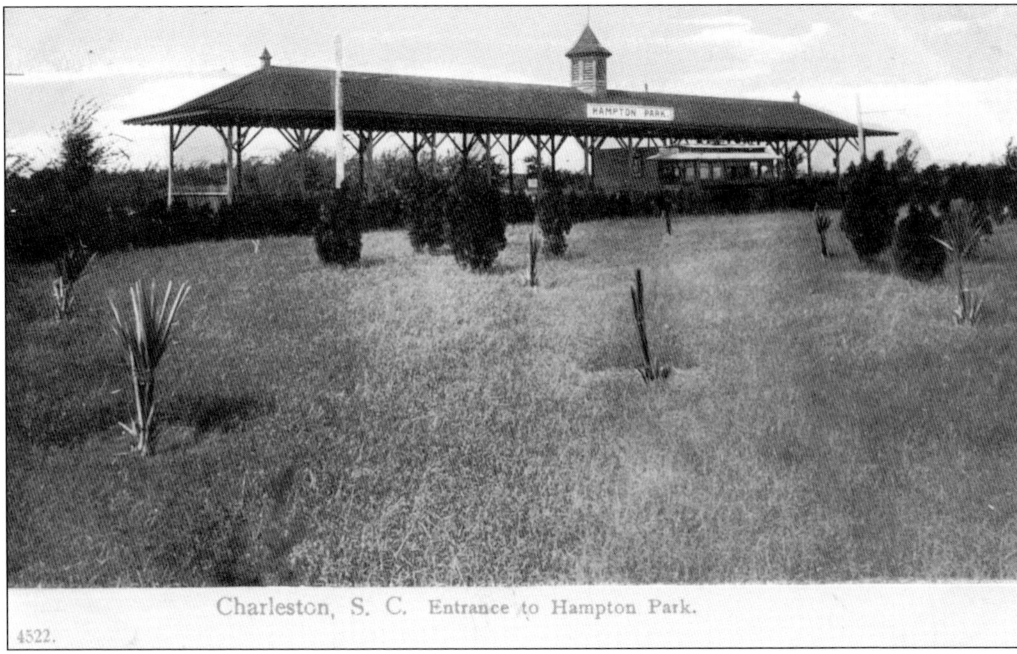

In July 1903, the Charleston City Council voted to buy land for a new city park to be named Hampton Park in honor of Gen. Wade Hampton, a native Charlestonian, and place a statue of the general in the park. The land, formerly part of the Rhett Farms, was purchased for $35,000.

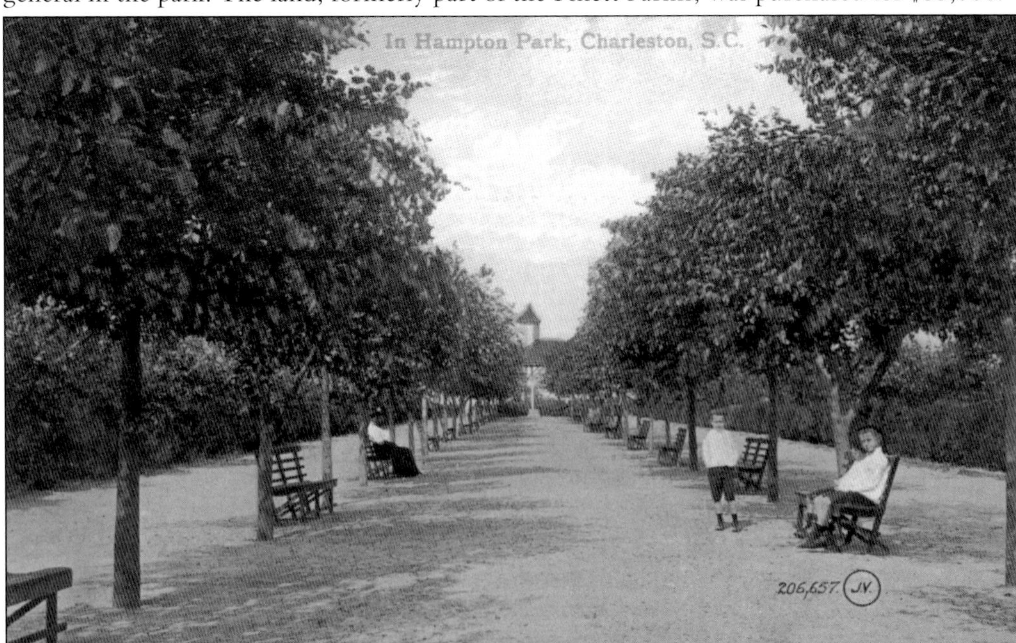

Perhaps the boys seated here in Hampton Park, as their nanny watches, are anticipating the football game to come on the park's field. It had been announced that on November 24, 1904, there was to be a big game between the Charleston Athletic Club and Furman University. The game turned out to be not as exciting as the anticipation. Some 1,500 fans watched as Charleston won 39-0 on a muddy field.

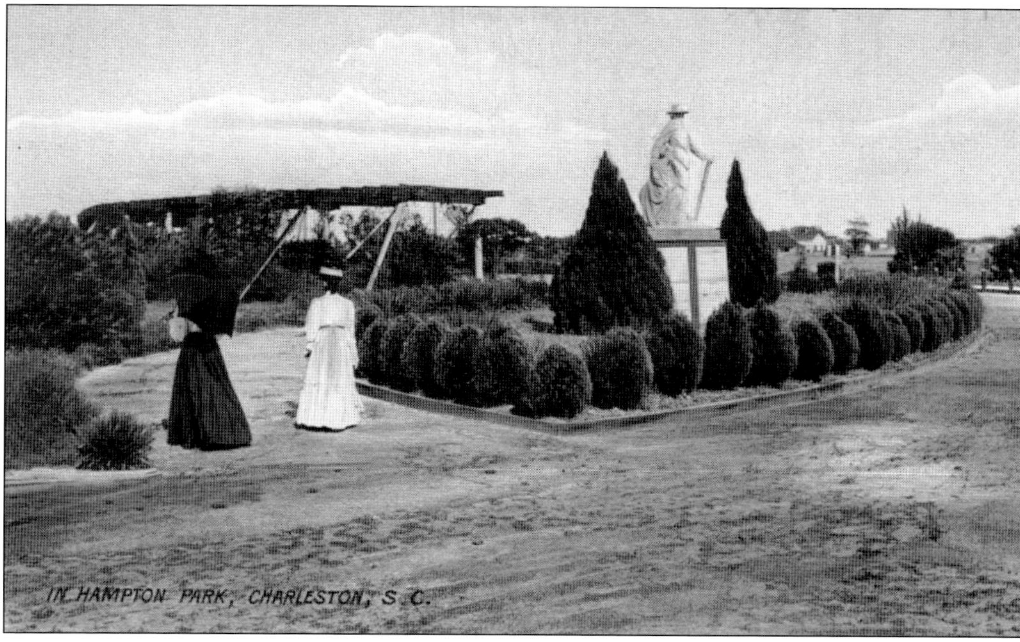

The ladies appear to be dressed for a sunny Sunday stroll through Hampton Park. Perhaps they will stop to enjoy the chrysanthemums on their way to the sunken gardens. There, they can stop and watch the ducks and swans before enjoying an afternoon concert by Carl Metz's Military Band before taking the trolley home.

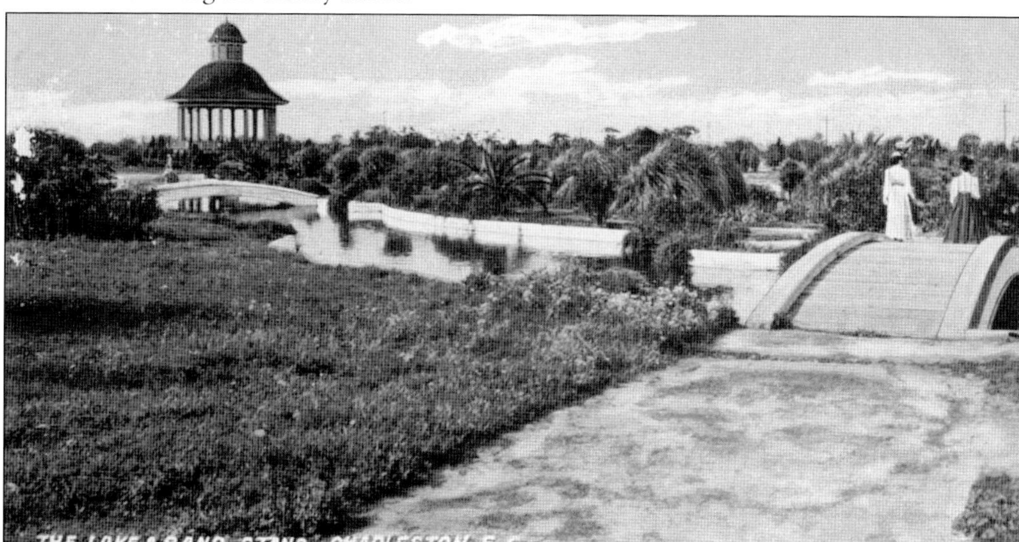

The two ladies crossing the bridge might be headed to watch the basketball game reported in the January 11, 1915, edition of the *Evening Post*, when Memminger School's sextet of girls met Savannah Girls School's team. "The attendance at the game at Hampton Park was such as to fill the grandstand and a number of automobiles. The cheering and songs of the Memminger supporters was a feature. The players were arrayed in natty uniforms, the most distinguishing feature being the illustrious yellow ribbons in the headgear of the home team." Despite losing to the Memminger girls 18-5, the Savannah girls had fun with the other girls, both before and after the game, and a rematch was scheduled for Savannah.

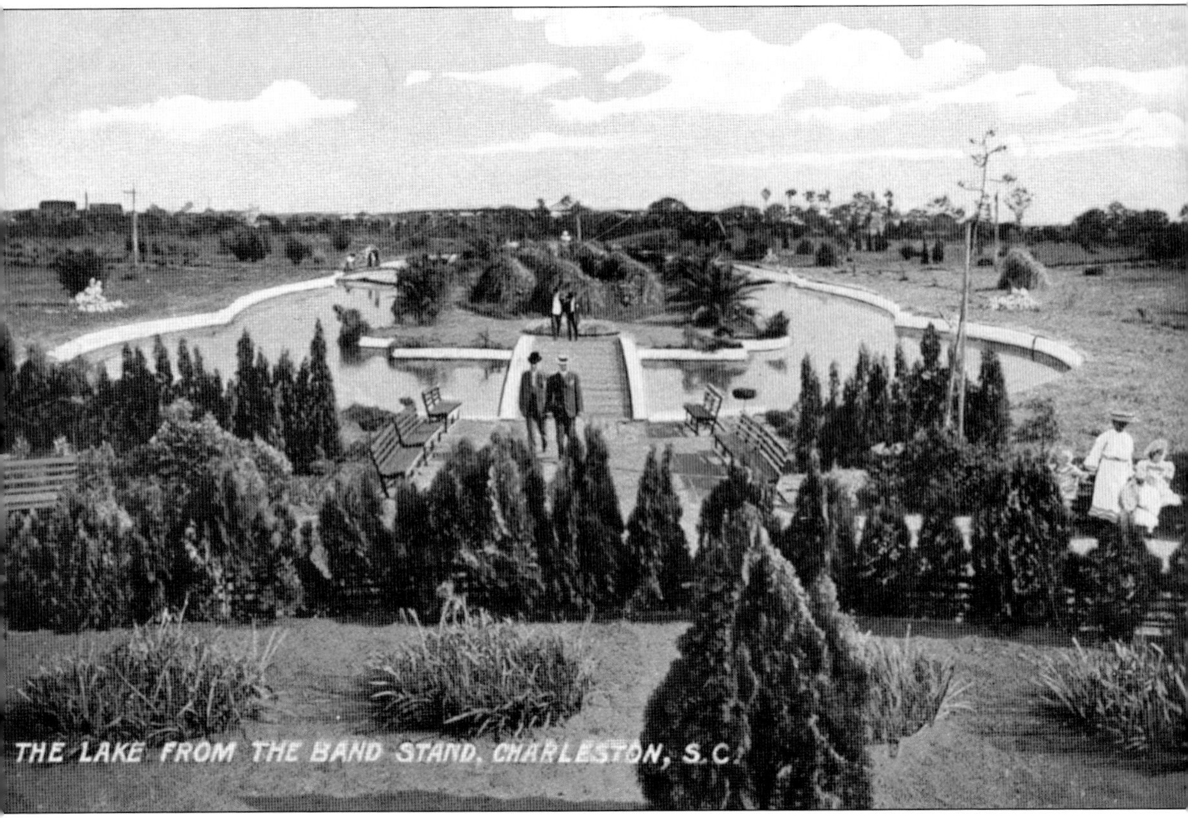

Enjoying the sunken gardens could have been a prelude to listening to a concert from the bandstand or something even more exciting. According to May 1904 editions of the *Evening Post* and the *News and Courier*, at the ball field part of Hampton Park there was an outdoor production called *The Last Days of Pompeii*, complete with chariot races, gladiator fights, and a fireworks interpretation Mount Vesuvius's volcanic eruption in AD 79. Among the hosted guests of the production company, on different nights, were the children of the Charleston Orphan House and those of the City Orphan Asylum, as well as the ladies of the Confederate Home College, with their teachers.

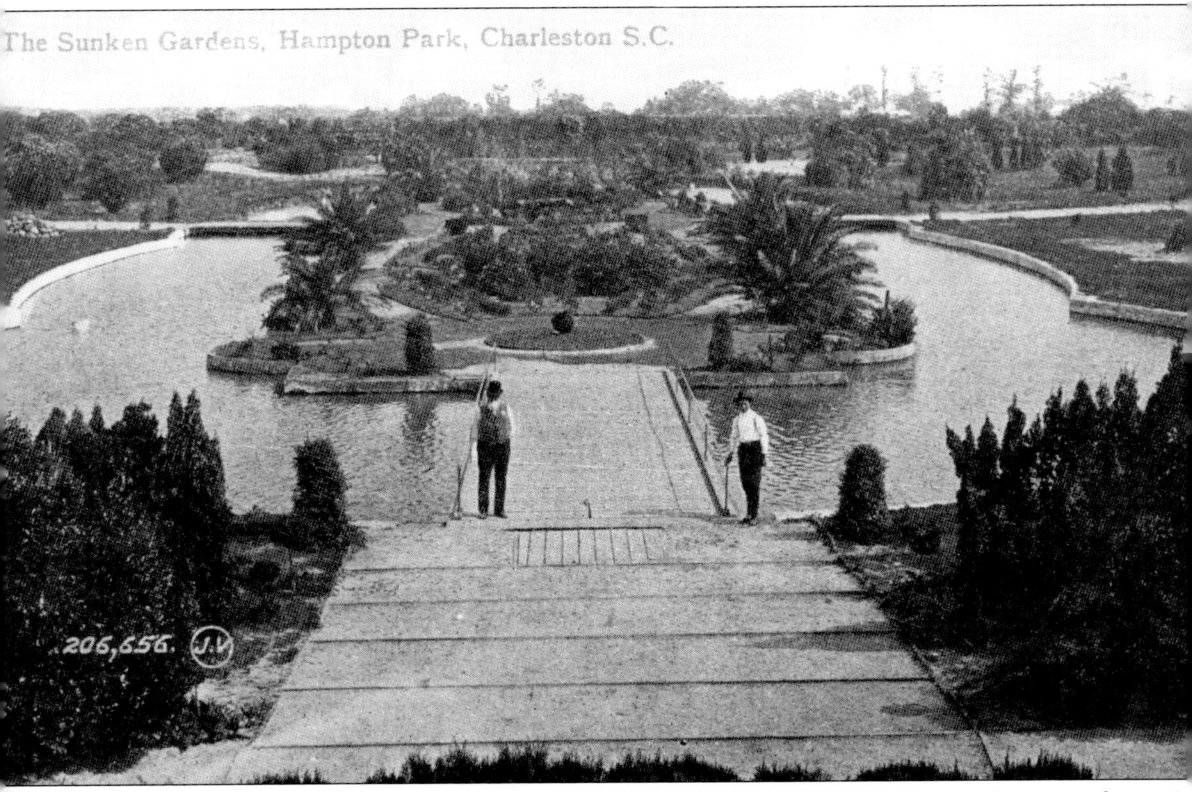

It looks like the two gentlemen may be enjoying their walk through the sunken garden area of Hampton Park that was left from the 1901–1902 South Carolina Inter-State and West Indian Exposition. They may be a couple of out-of-town businessmen or just two local residents taking a relaxing walk.

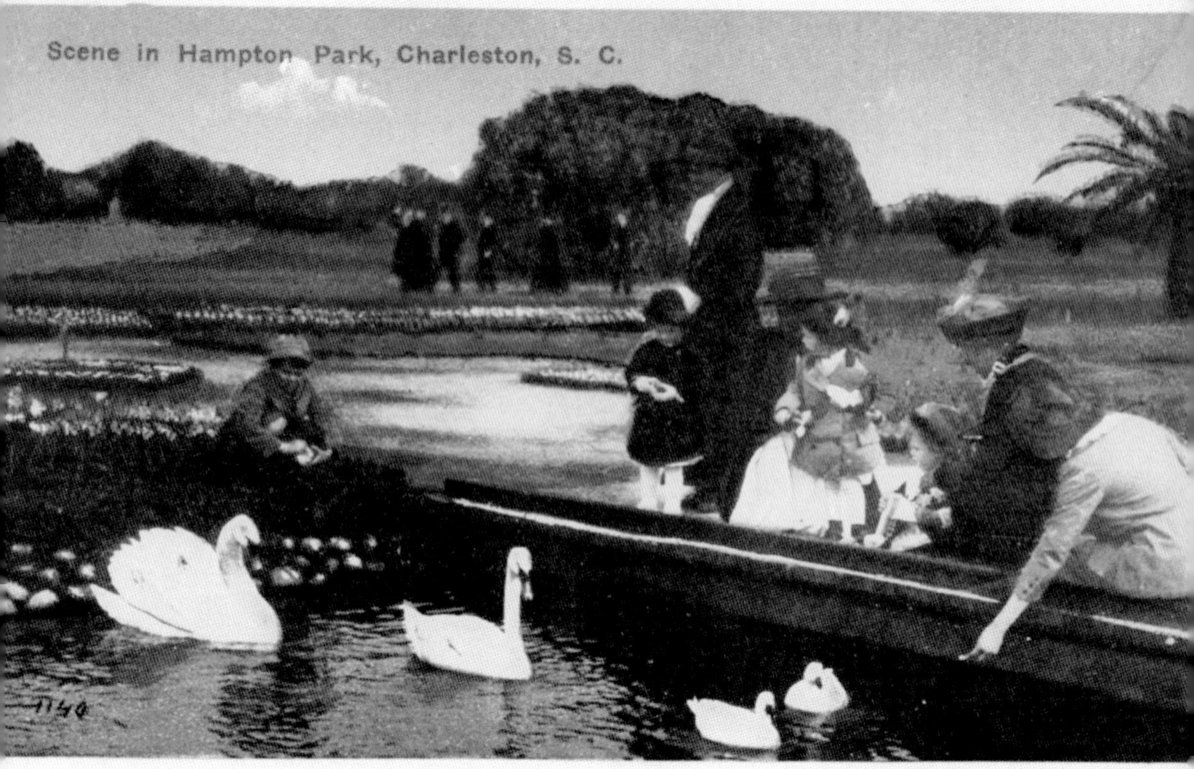

The *Evening Post* of June 13, 1908, reports that Hampton Park had bought five swans—two cocks and three hens—for $100 and built them a house in hopes of raising a larger colony. The swans swimming about in the Sunken Garden Lake proved to be a big attraction to the ladies, young and old.

Six

Dockside, Ships, and Shipyards

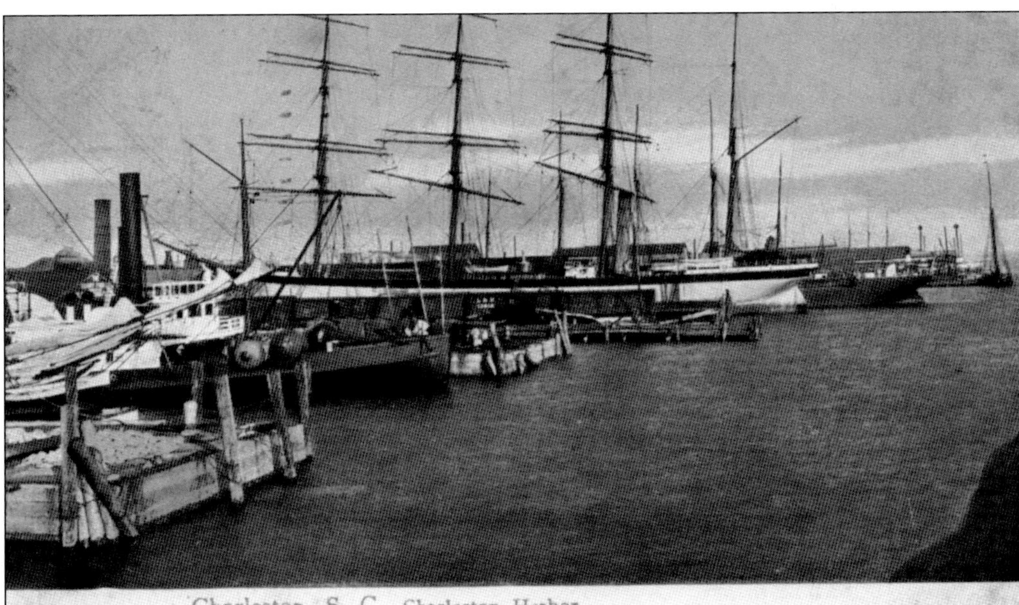

The Charleston docks and waterfront were home to all types of boats and ships, from the fleet of small boats called the "Mosquito Fleet," used for fishing or island taxis used to bring rural-grown crops to market, to private yachts, coast- or ocean-running sloops, cruise ships, and naval vessels like the USS *Charleston*. Additionally, along the waterfront, docked ships picked up delivered goods, from bananas to cotton.

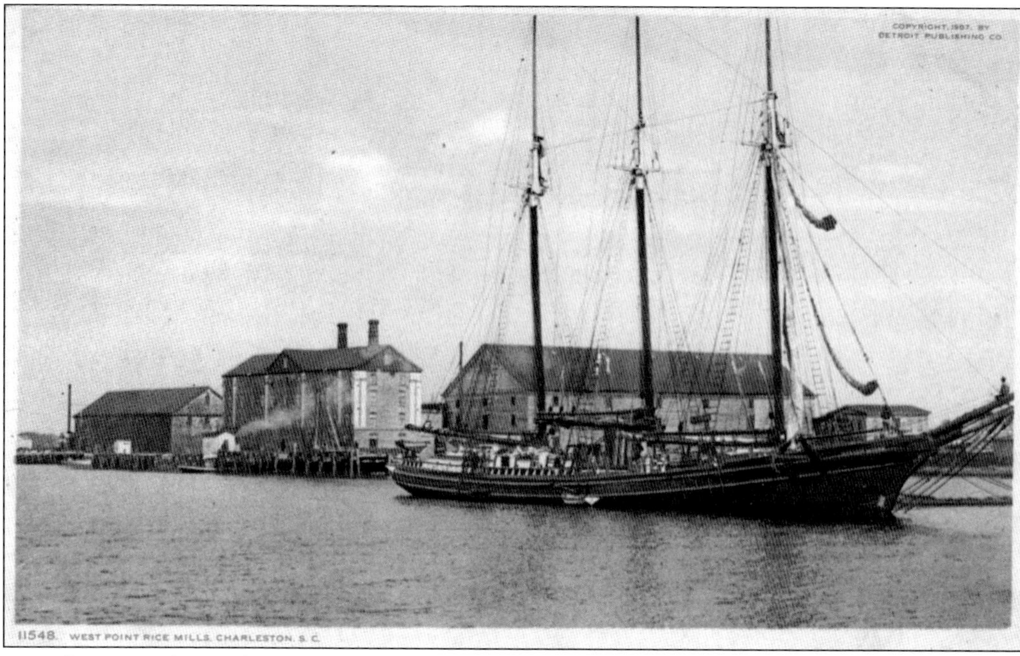

Rice from South Carolina usually arrived on barges, but Georgia rice arriving at the West Point rice plant in Charleston, on the Ashley River at the end of Calhoun Street, might arrive by sloop. The only mill of its type east of Louisiana, it could process about 2,000 bushels of rice in its usual 12-hour workday.

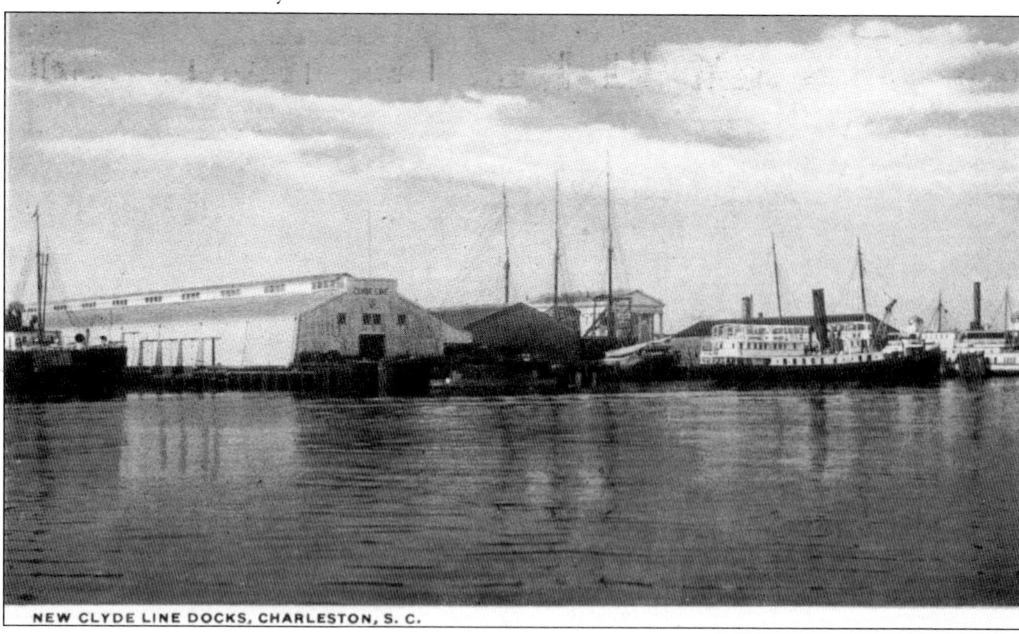

Clyde Steamship Company operated regular cruise routes from Charleston to Jacksonville, Florida, and New York. Four ships left out of and returned to Charleston for these two-day cruises: the *Arapahoe*, the *Apache*, the *Lenape*, and the *Mohawk*. They offered passage to first-class, intermediate, and steerage passengers on most cruises and carried cargo. These new docks were opened in 1914 to replace those previously destroyed by fire.

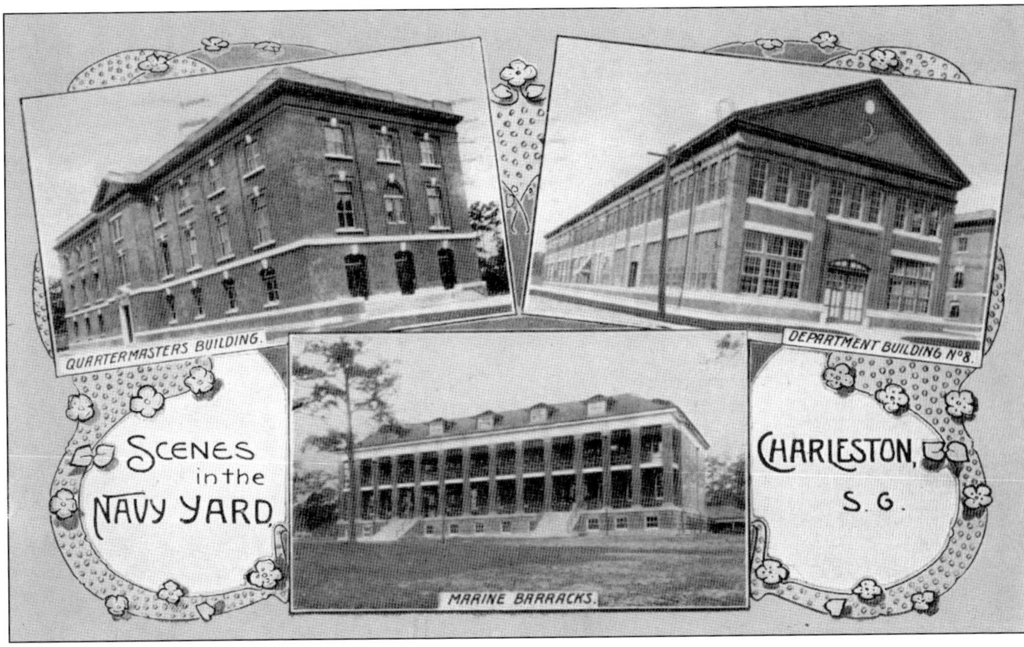

It was announced on January 11, 1901, that the naval and dry dock facilities at Port Royal were to be abandoned in favor of a new facility to be located at Charleston. Capt. Edwin Longnecker, USN, who had entered the Navy in 1861, took formal command as commandant of the new navy yard August 1, 1902. He oversaw the facility's building program until being redeployed two years later. During World War II, its employment peaked at over 25,000 employees. Its need ceased with the end of the Cold War and it closed in the mid-1990s.

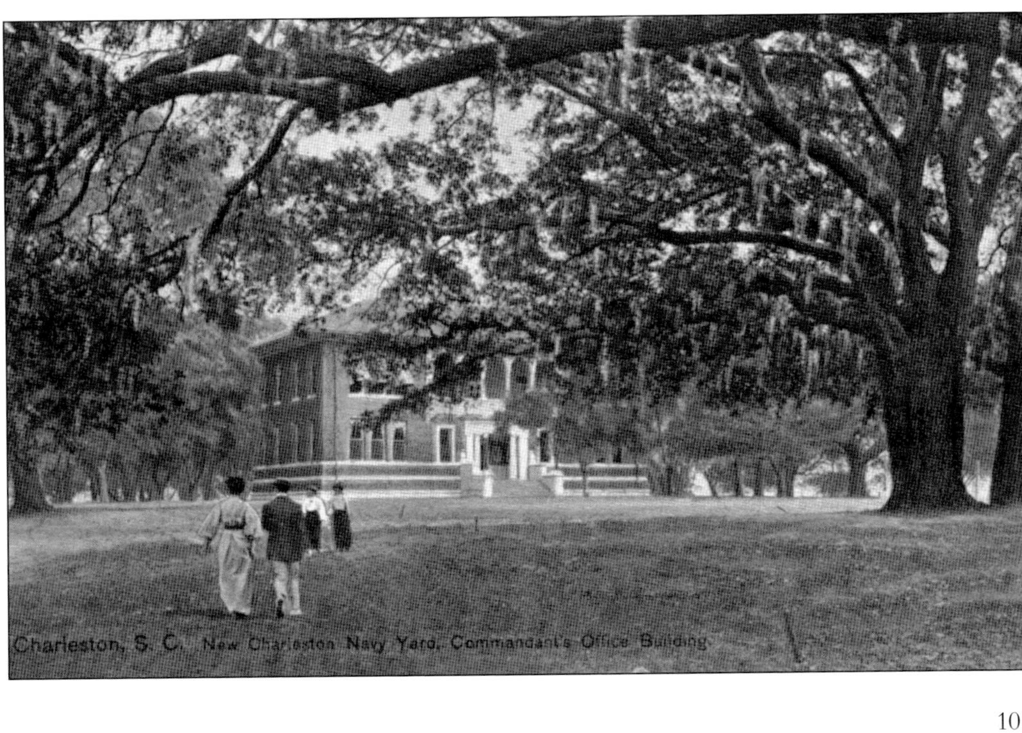

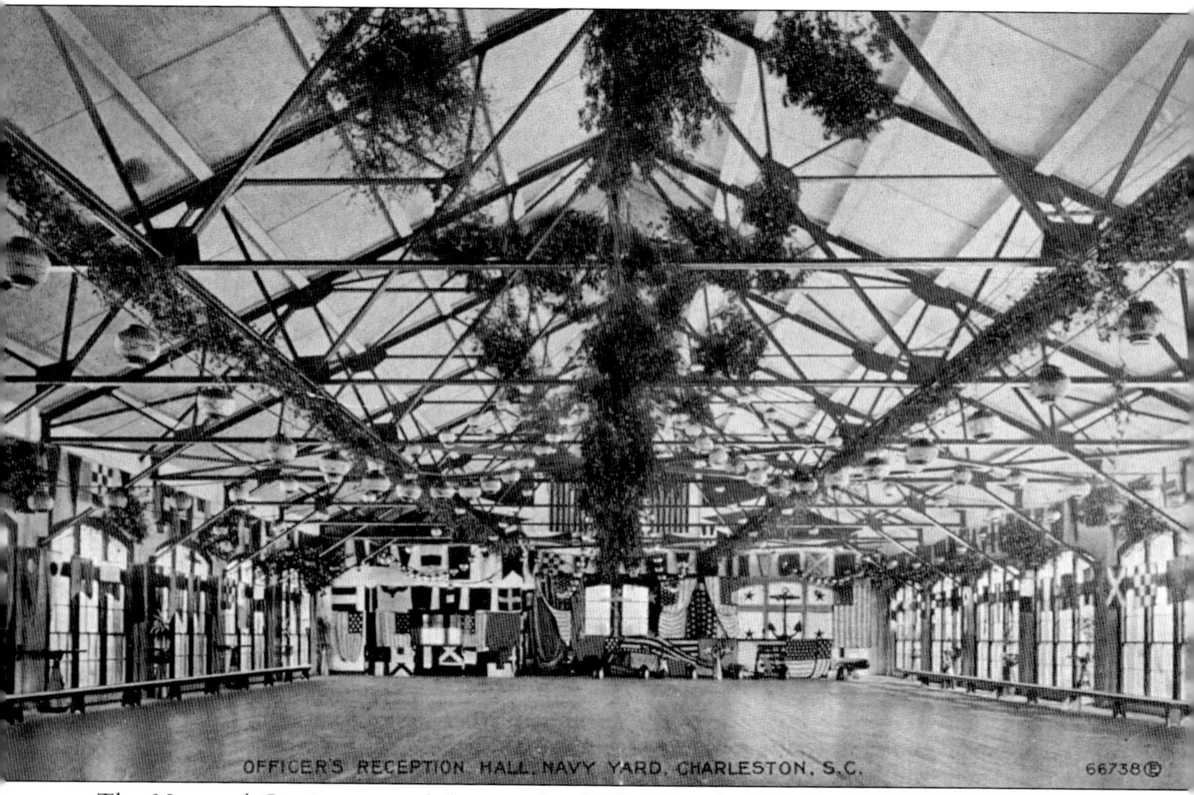

The *News and Courier* reported than on April 13, 1910, the Carolina Yacht Club hosted some 600, with the officers of the battleship USS *South Carolina* as the guests of honor. The dance was held at the Officers' Reception Hall at the base. The hall had been decorated with palmetto leaves, moss, and flags

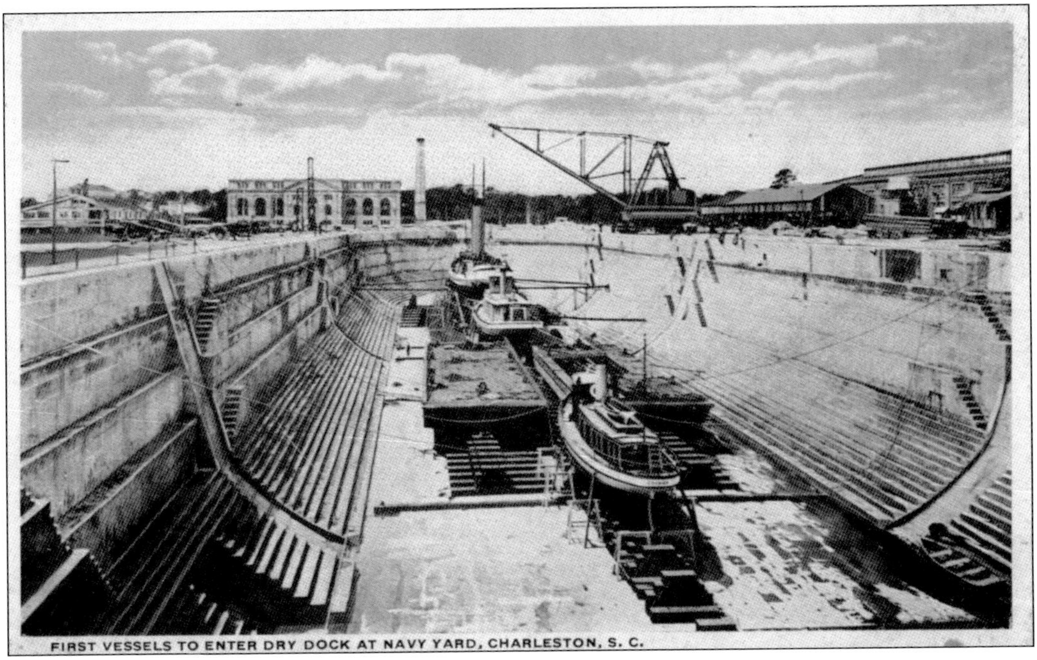

Charleston Navy Yard was opened on the Cooper River, about a five-minute trolley ride from downtown Charleston in 1901. It opened with dry-dock facilities, as well as officers' quarters and other such buildings necessary for its immediate operations. Its facilities were capable of handling repair work on ships both big and small, as well as building ships such as the USS *Tillman*, a destroyer, constructed here between 1918 and 1919. The ship, the first built at these facilities, was named for South Carolina's former governor and senator Benjamin Tillman. The base continued operations until 1996.

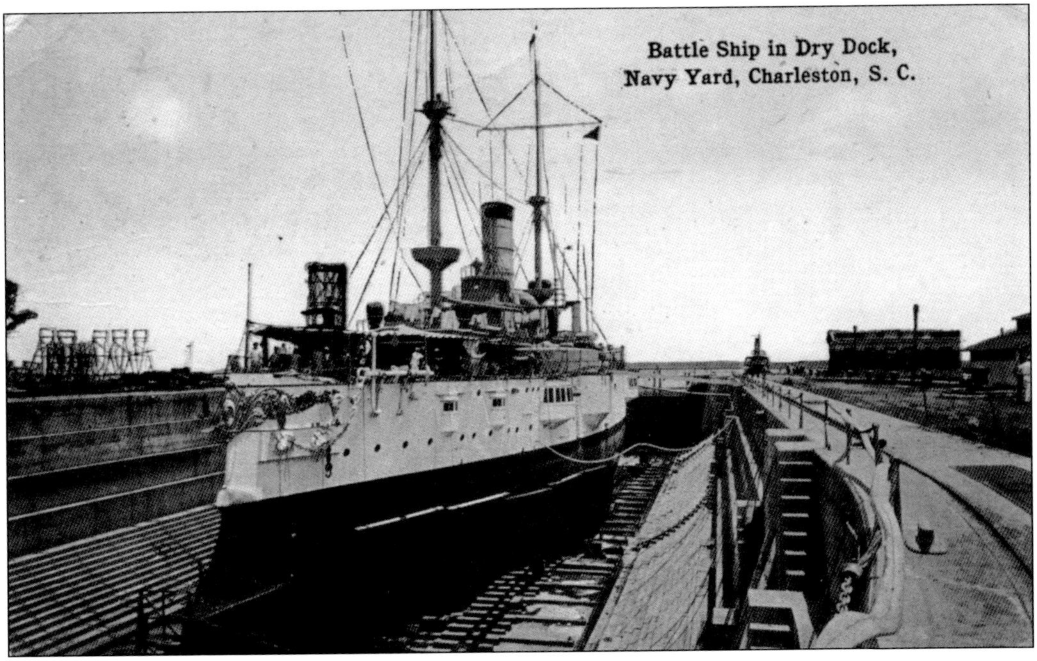

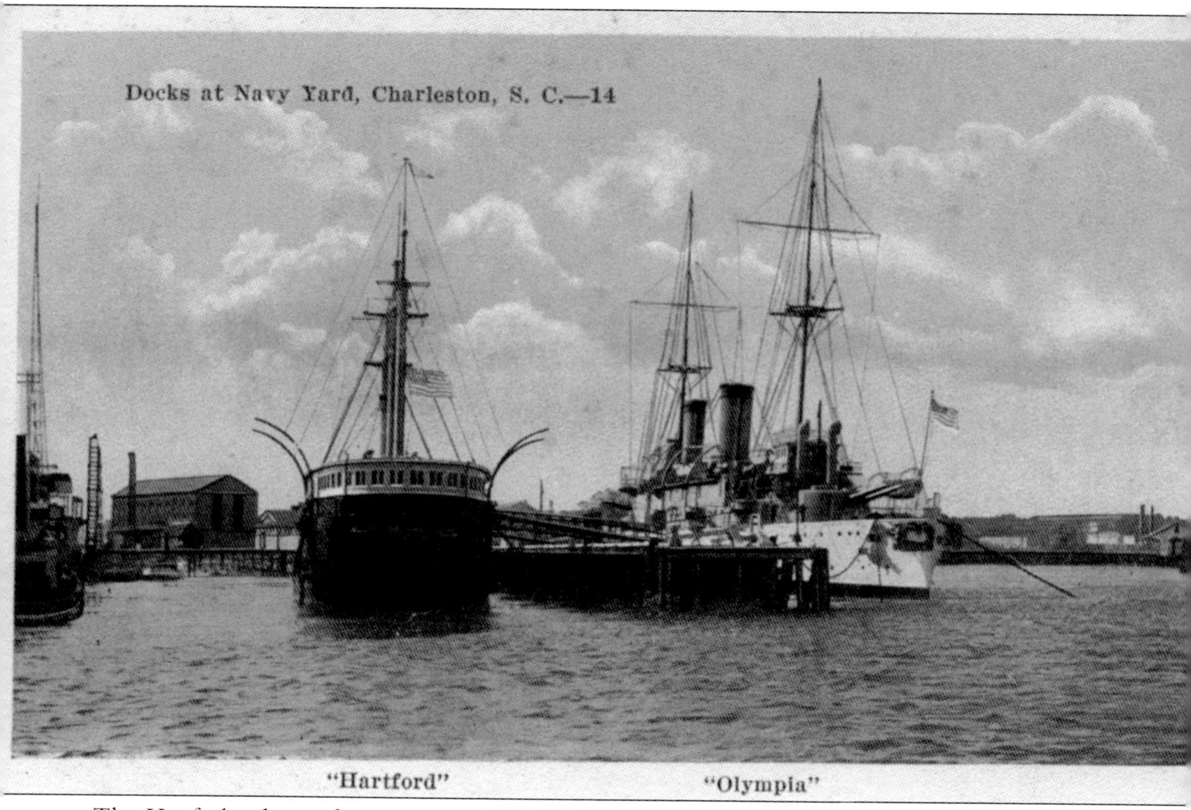

The *Hartford*, a sloop of war, was used as the flagship of Adm. David G. Farragut during the Civil War, while the *Olympia*, a protected cruiser, was used as the flagship of Adm. George Dewey during the Spanish-American War. The *Hartford* saw major action under Admiral Farragut in the Battle of Mobile Bay; and the *Olympia*, under Admiral Dewey, in the Battle of Manila Bay. Both were stationed at the Charleston Navy Yard for a time.

Seven

People at Work and Play

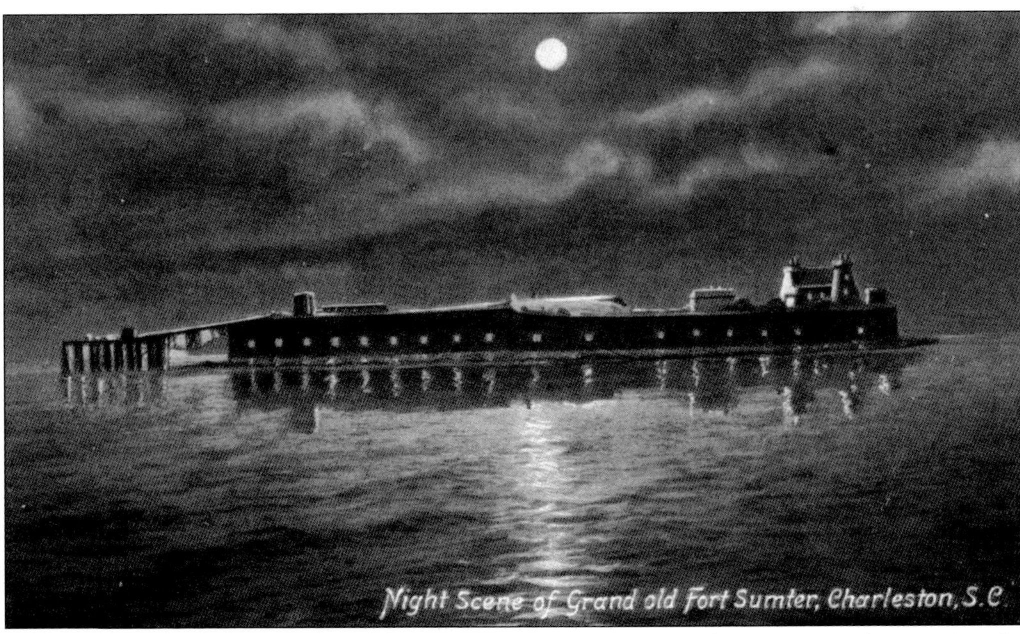

In the darkness, before the dawn of April 12, 1861, a blue flash from Mount Pleasant signaled Confederate forces surrounding Fort Sumter, which had been occupied by the Union forces from Fort Moultrie on December 26, 1860, to fire the shots that would begin the Civil War. Fort Sumter waited two hours before returning fire. The besieged fort had been begun in 1829 but was still unfinished. The bombardment lasted some 34 hours, before Major Anderson surrendered the fort to Gen. P.G.T. Beauregard, his Confederate counterpart and a former artillery student of his at West Point.

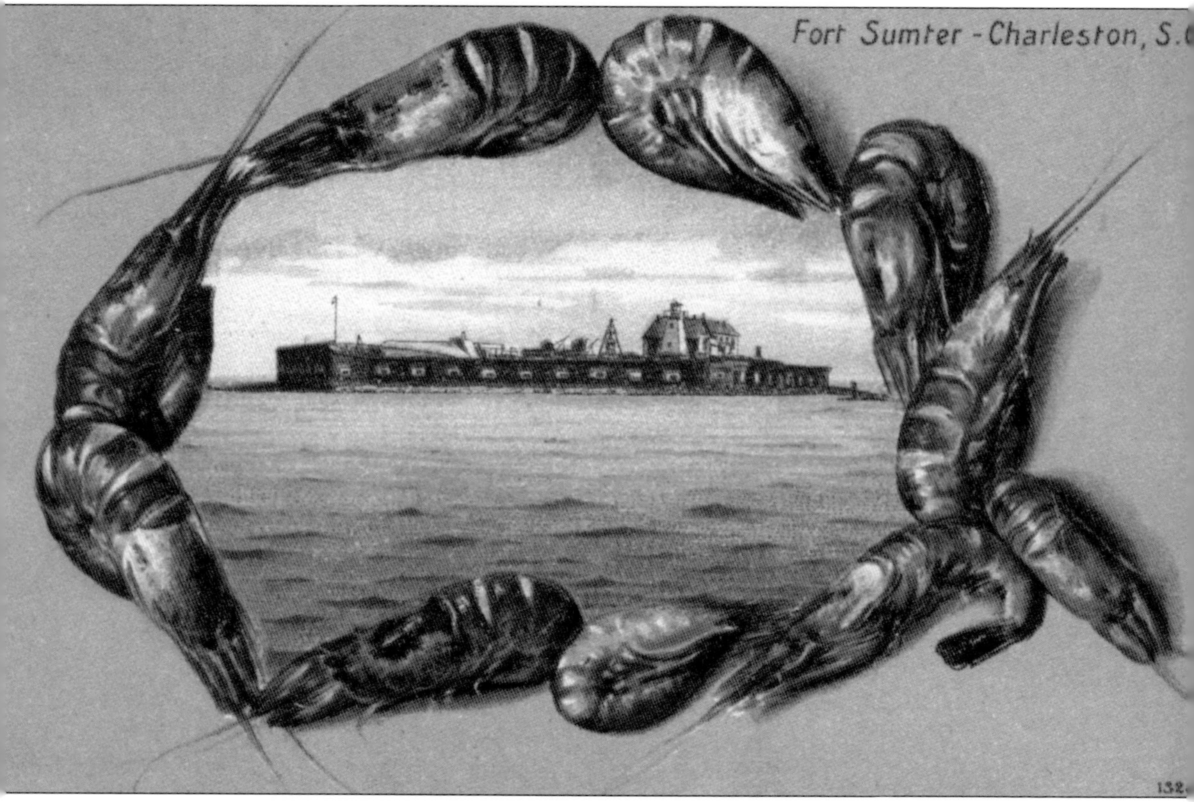

The *Evening Post* of April 9, 1902, reports that Theodore Roosevelt, the day before, became the first president of the United States to visit the fort in Charleston's harbor that Maj. Robert Anderson had commanded and surrendered to Confederate forces almost exactly 41 years earlier, beginning the Civil War. While there, Roosevelt toured all of the fort's magazines, watched its huge guns raised and lowered, and politicked with the fort's laborers. President Roosevelt's tour of Fort Sumter, which had been restored and garrisoned for the Spanish-American War, may have brought back memories of his own service in Cuba during that war, for which he would be posthumously awarded the Medal of Honor almost a century later, in 2001.

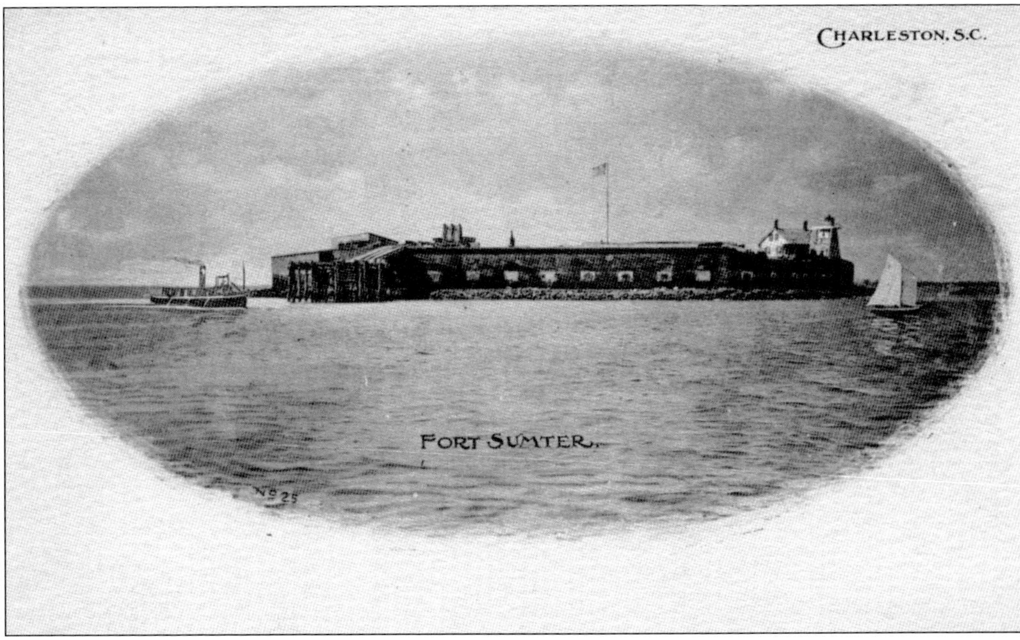

In 1833, the War Department approved naming the new fortification being built in Charleston's harbor after South Carolina Revolutionary War hero Thomas Sumter. The multitiered five-foot-thick walls were to protect not only Charleston but also the soldiers assigned to man its 135 guns. The first real test of the fort, walls, men, and guns was April 12, 1861.

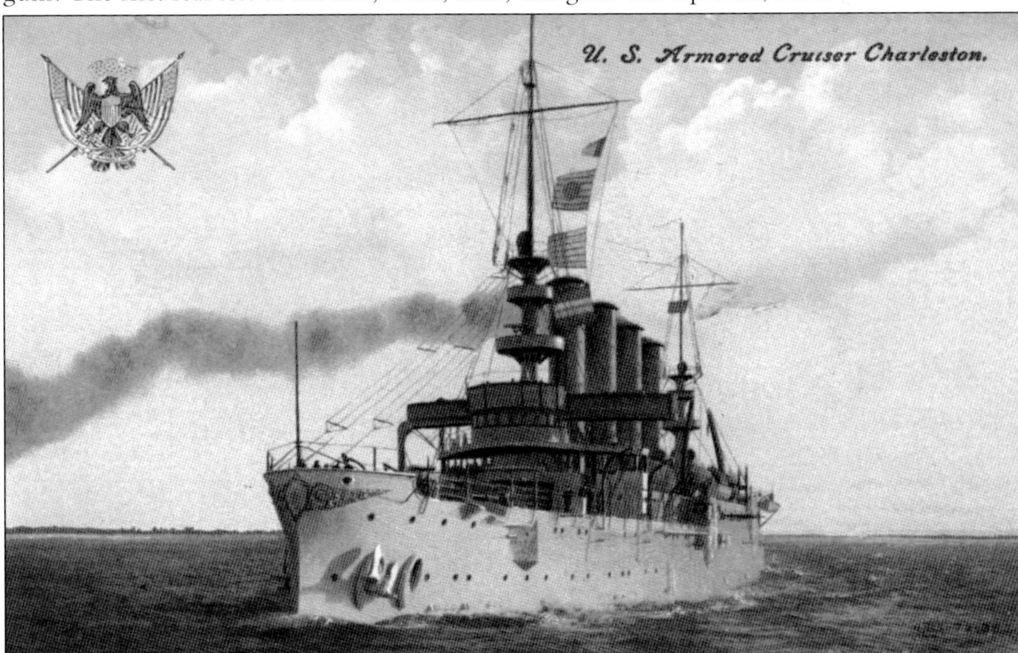

The *Evening Post* of March 12, 1906, carries a story of a sailor from the USS *Charleston* who had promised a cap ribbon in gold to one of those who had toured the ship, but he had lost the person's address. So, he mailed the ribbon in care of the newspaper with a description of the person, in hopes of the ribbon getting it to the recipient and keeping his word.

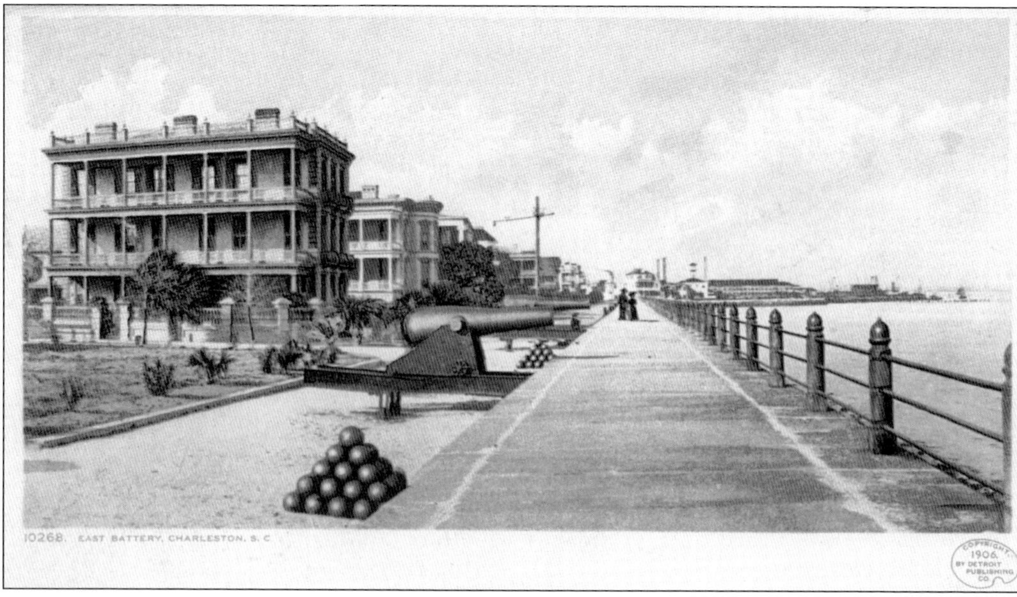

The area where the Ashley and Cooper Rivers meet, appropriately named the Battery, was originally the home of first British and, then, an American fortifications. Its battery of guns fired on Fort Sumter, beginning the Civil War, and its batteries (White Point, Ramsay, and King Street) defended the city. Between the defense of Charleston from the British in the War of 1812 and the Union in the Civil War, the Battery became a fashionable place for ladies to walk.

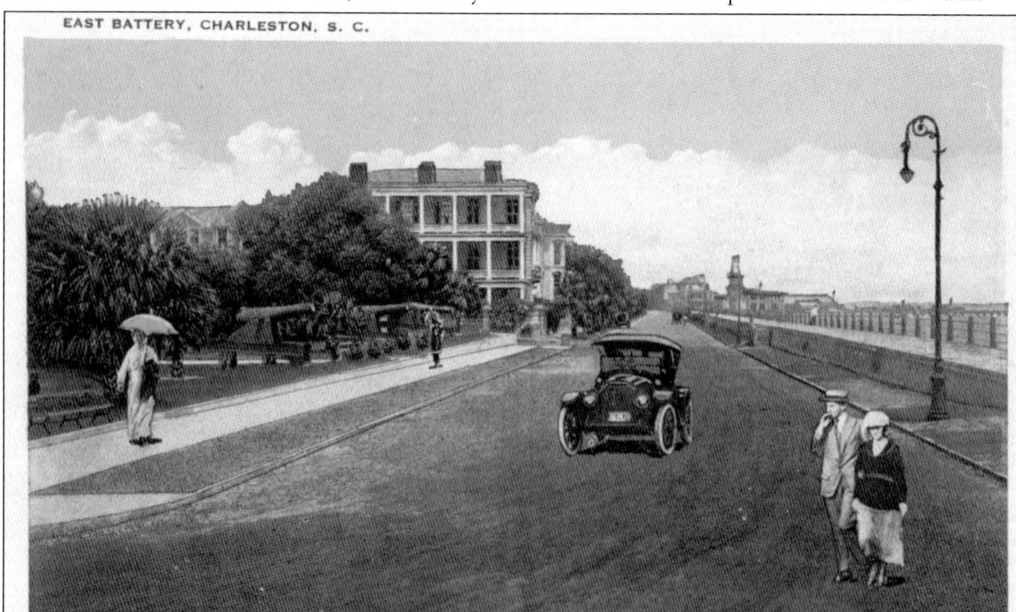

The *Evening Post* of July, 9, 1900, reports that the first horseless carriage to be seen on the streets of Charleston had been spotted on King Street that day. The horseless carriage, owned by Colgate and Company and a roving advertisement for Octagon soap, was not labeled an automobile, because they were powered by electricity, and this horseless carriage was powered by gasoline, and was therefore a locomobile. These new vehicles were light in weight and bounced driver and occupants about as they traversed the Belgian block and cobblestone streets of the city.

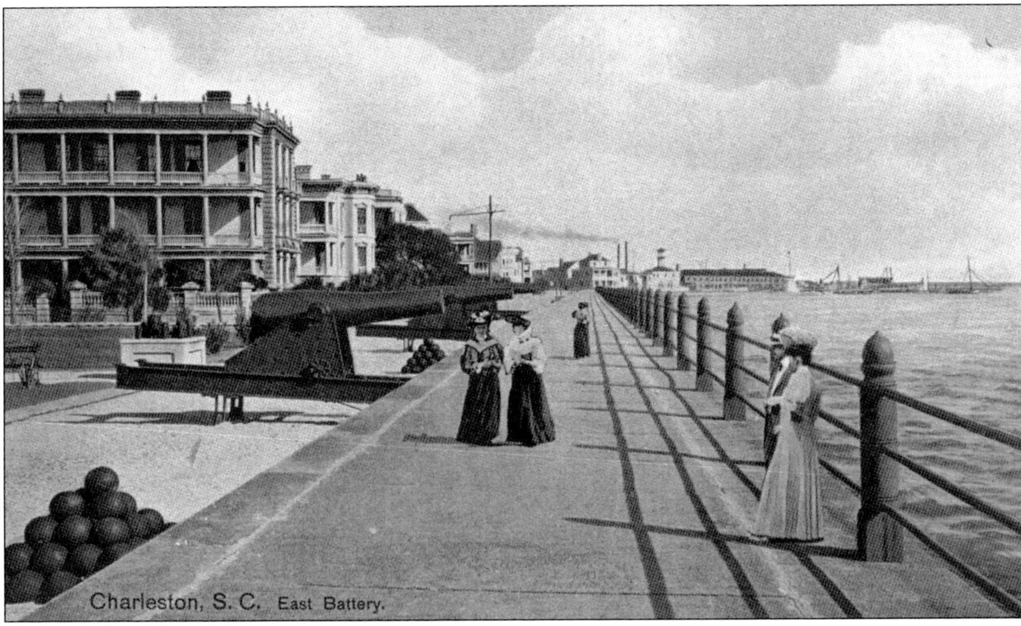

These ladies may be visitors in Charleston who came to marvel at the city's beautiful antebellum mansions, such as the Louis Desaussure House in the immediate background—built right before the Civil War began—within sight of its piazzas, or they may be local strollers who just like to walk the elevated slate walkways of the Battery and enjoy the ocean breezes as they pass both the cannons of that late war and time.

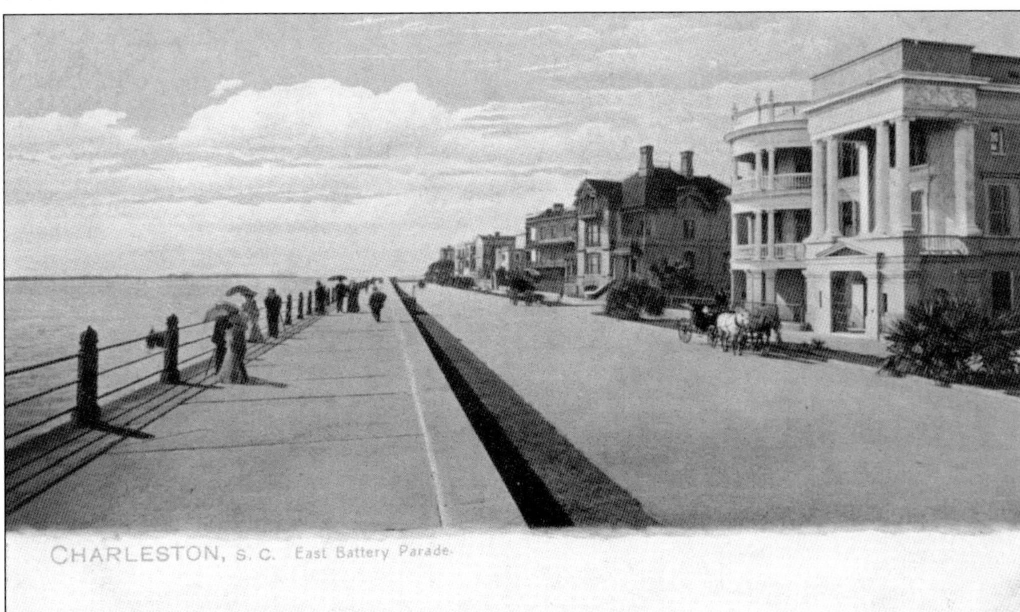

Perhaps these strollers are out to see the progress being made in the hauling of the reported 86-foot-long whale being hauled in April 1907 from Charleston's outer harbor past the High Battery and up the Cooper River for viewing. This whale was some 30 feet longer than the one captured in Charleston's harbor in December 1880, whose skeleton was destined to be hung from the ceiling of the city's new museum at Rutledge Avenue and Calhoun Street.

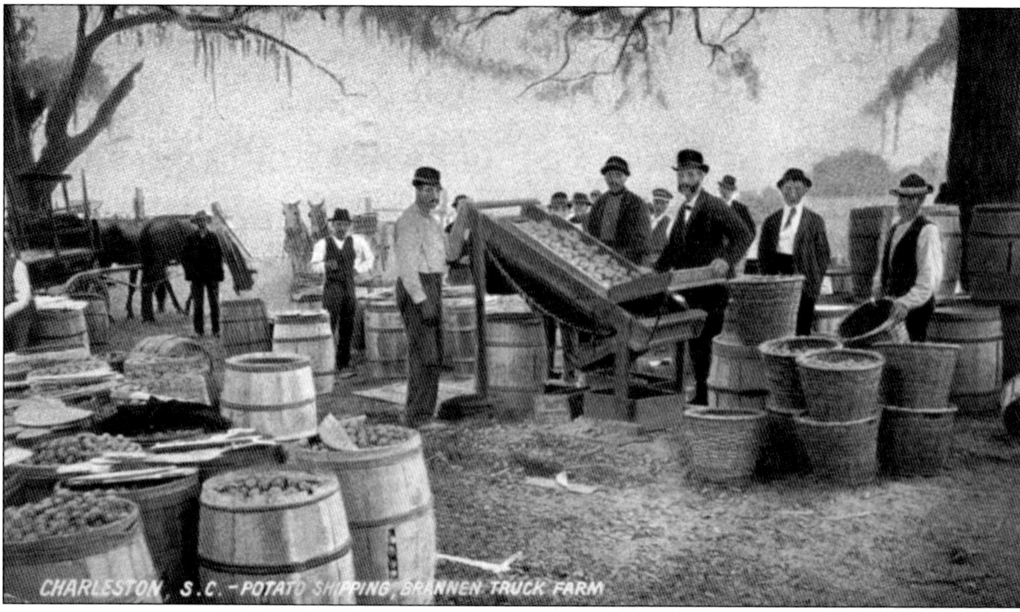

The Brannen Truck Farm was representative of a new post–Civil War industry. According to an October 27, 1904, article in Charleston's *News and Courier*, the rise of the truck-farming industry in the Lowcountry brought with it a rise in value of the land needed to support it. It notes that a 400-acre tract of land on "Young's [Yonges] Island, near Meggett's" that had sold for $925 in 1846, had recently sold for $14,700, even though only 213 acres had been cleared, and that a 45-acre tract two miles from Mount Pleasant to be used to raise asparagus sold for $1,650.

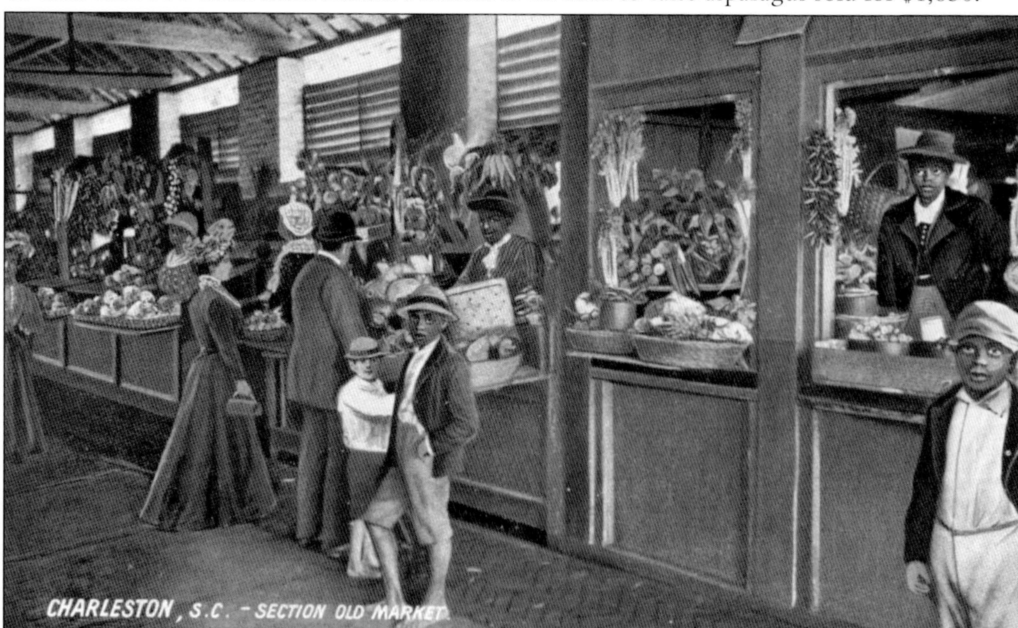

The vegetable section of the Old Market was the perfect place for sea island residents to sell their home-grown fresh produce to Charleston's housewives or professional men. The produce was brought in each morning on small boats from small island farms to be sold here or by street vendors.

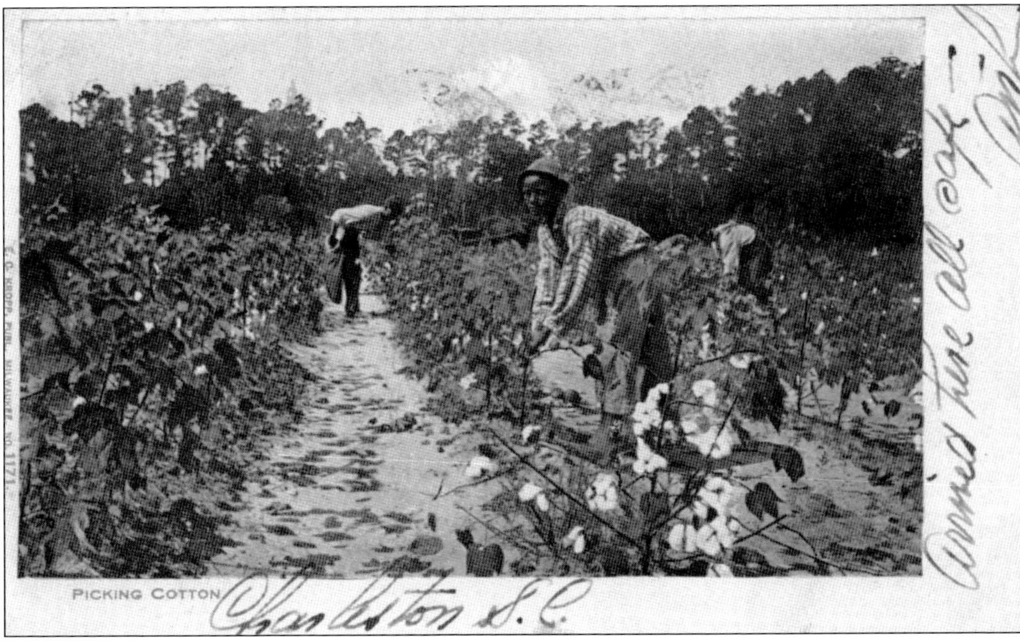

The September 20, 1906, *News and Courier*, quoting the *Charlotte Chronicle*, tells of picking cotton and wages. It states that cotton pickers being paid 60¢ per hundredweight could earn $9 picking a bale of cotton, while the pickers could earn $11.25 if paid 75¢ per hundredweight. To put in perspective: in 1913, it was reported in the *Anderson Intelligencer* that an almost-four-year-old picked 51 pounds in a day, while also keeping the cooking stove hot all day for his mother.

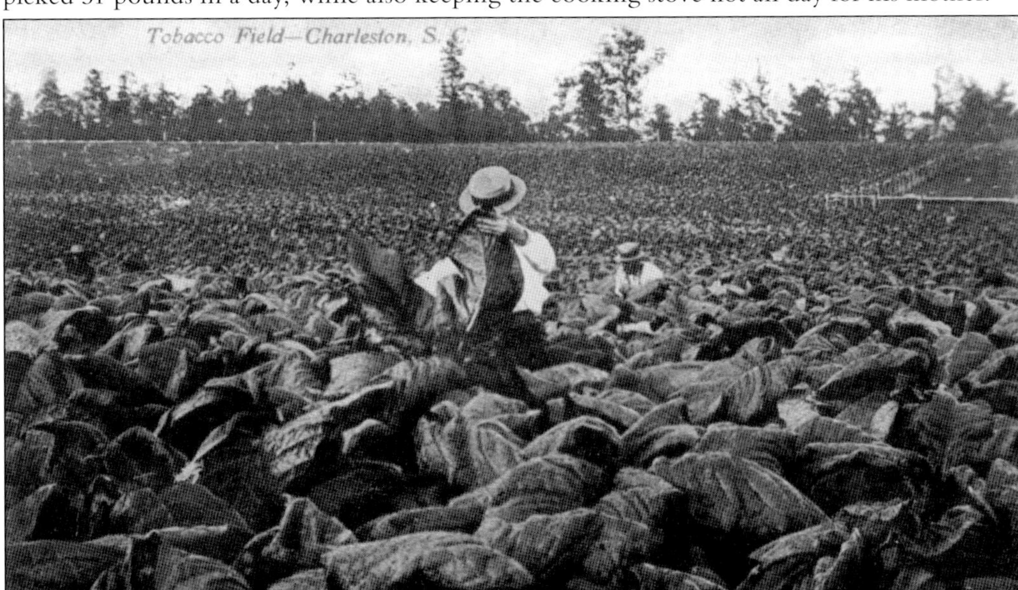

In 1902, twenty-five young women were the first to report to work for the American Cigar Company in the former Vesta Mill Building. The hours were from 7:00 a.m. to 6:00 p.m. with a 45-minute dinner break. They were to be paid $2 per week. As they became more proficient, the girls could expect to earn from $6 to $12 per week. Twelve years later, South Carolina brought its largest tobacco crop in history to market.

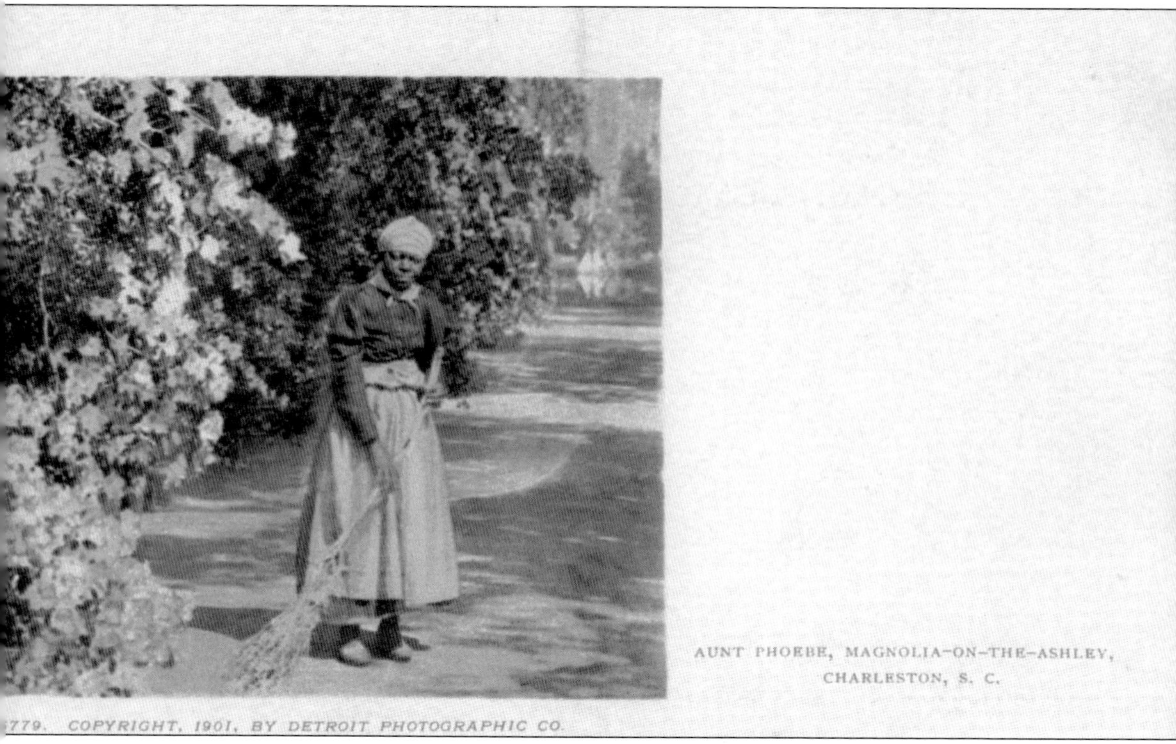

Magnolia-on-the-Ashley Garden's mauma Aunt Phoebe might be cleaning to get ready the gardens ready for the party of Helen "Nellie" Taft and her daughter, Helen. President Taft's family and their party were transported by the steamer *E.H. Jackson* on April 23, 1912, to the Magnolia dock. The boat ride and the gardens were closed to other visitors that afternoon.

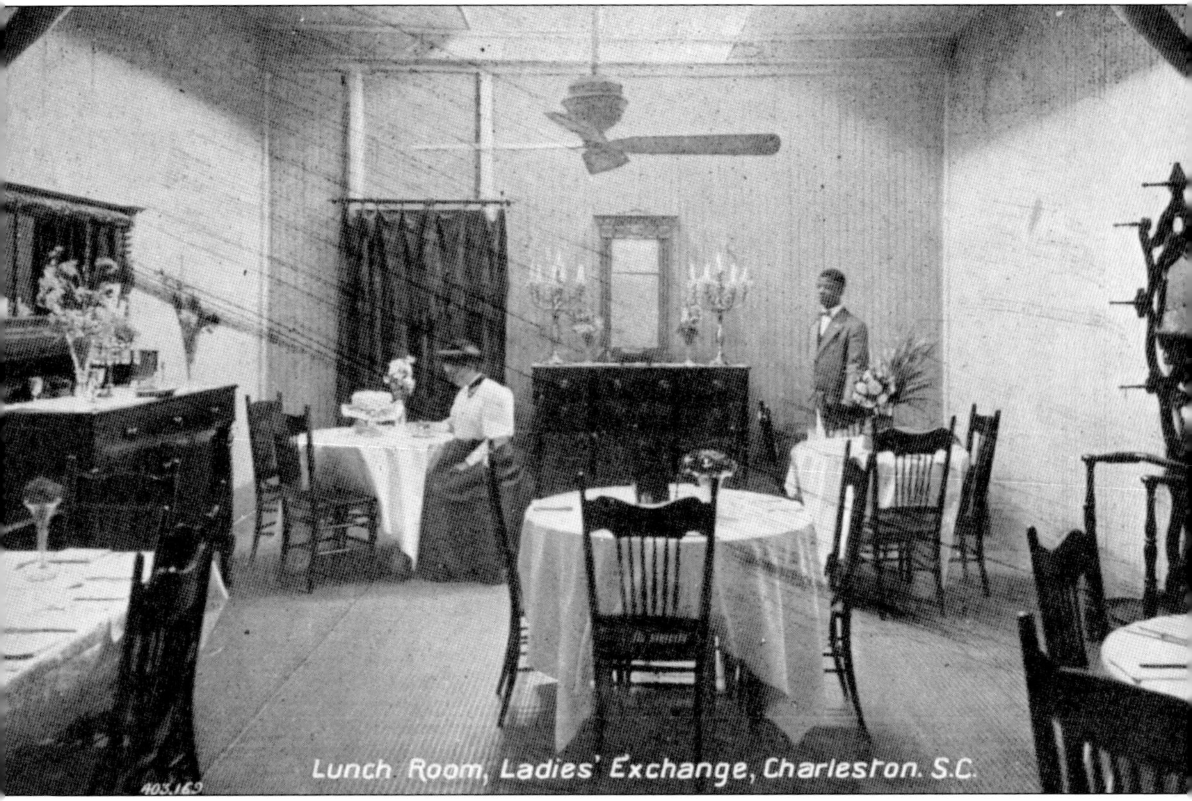

The Woman's Exchange for Woman's Work was organized in Charleston in December 1884. According to the *Constitution of By-Laws of the Charleston Exchange for Woman's Work, 1900*, "The object of the Corporation shall be to promote the efforts of gentle-women in reduced circumstances to support themselves and their families by the proceeds of the manufacture and sale of articles in their reach." A shop was opened on Hasell Street. Women could join the exchange for $1 and sell artwork, needlework, flowers, or whatever they could make of quality and receive 95 percent of the monies paid for it. The exchange opened a lunchroom on Hasell Street but moved everything to 215–217 King Street. The lunchroom's specialty was Lady Baltimore cake. It inspired Owen Wister, a customer and the author of *The Virginian* to write his *Lady Baltimore.* The book promoted not only the exchange but also Charleston. Tourism increased, and the cakes were shipped all over the country and beyond. The exchange began with $200 and 25 pieces of needlework. During its first 10 years, it paid out about $35,000.

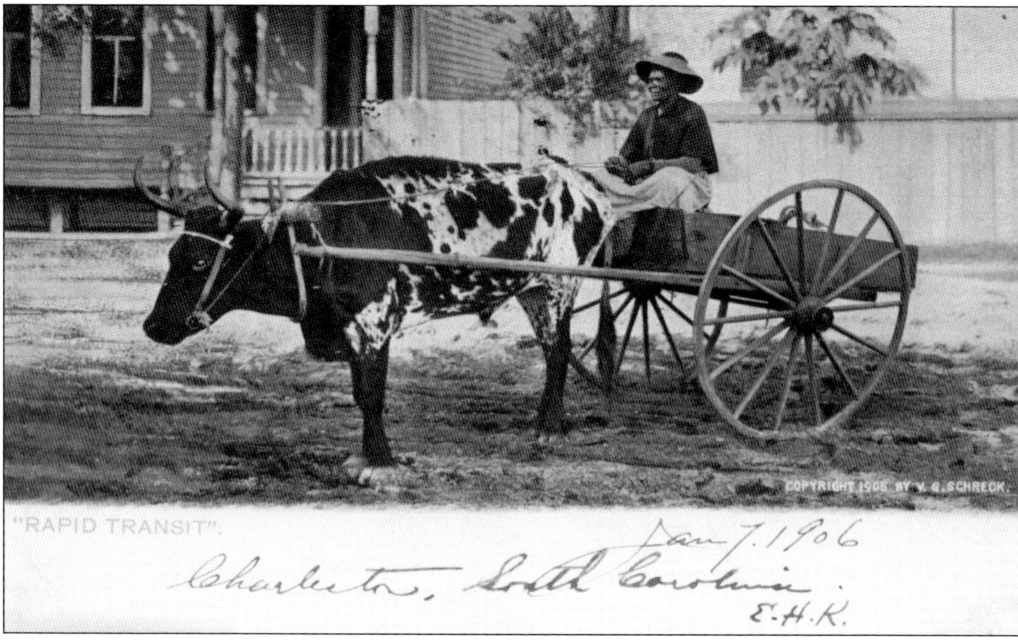

In 1907, Charleston had a little less than 620,000 square yards of paved or improved streets; San Antonio, Texas, had over three million. These paved streets were a mixture of cobblestone, granite, or Belgian block, brick, macadam, gravel, and asphalt or asphalt block, according to the 1910 census. This means of transportation may have made sense for some areas of the city.

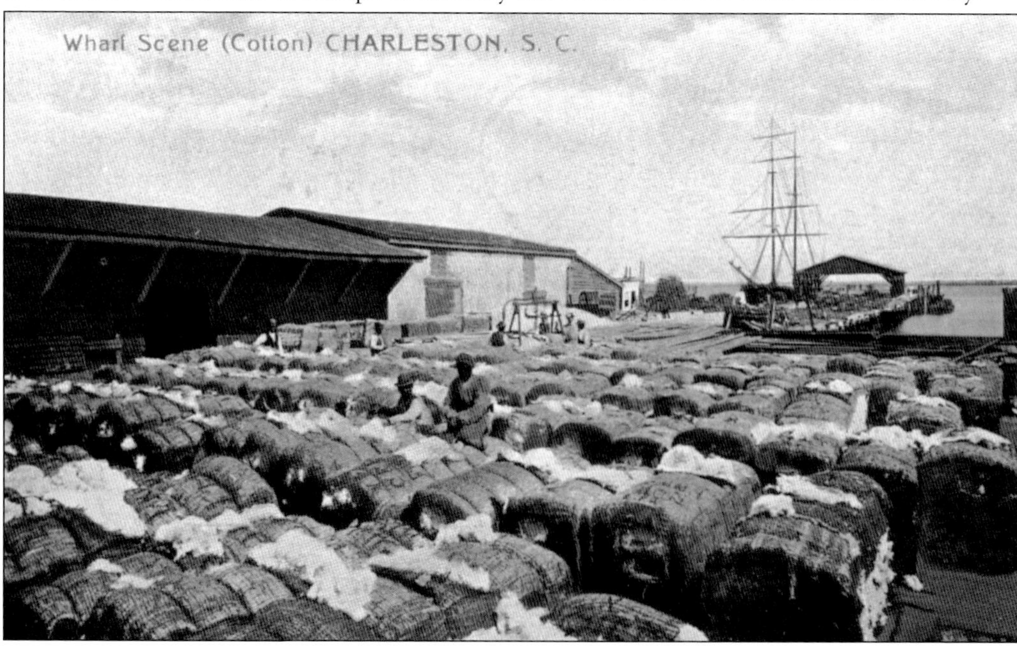

The September 23, 1910, *Charleston News and Courier* reports 125 colored wharf workers, about one-third of those employed, walked off their jobs when their demand for a raise from $1.25 to $1.75 a day was not met. Instead, they were given a raise to $1.50. This did not suit some; they threatened a permanent strike. For a 10-hour workday, the difference was 15¢ per hour, instead of 17.5¢. So, for a six-day workweek, the difference was between $9.00 per week and $10.50.

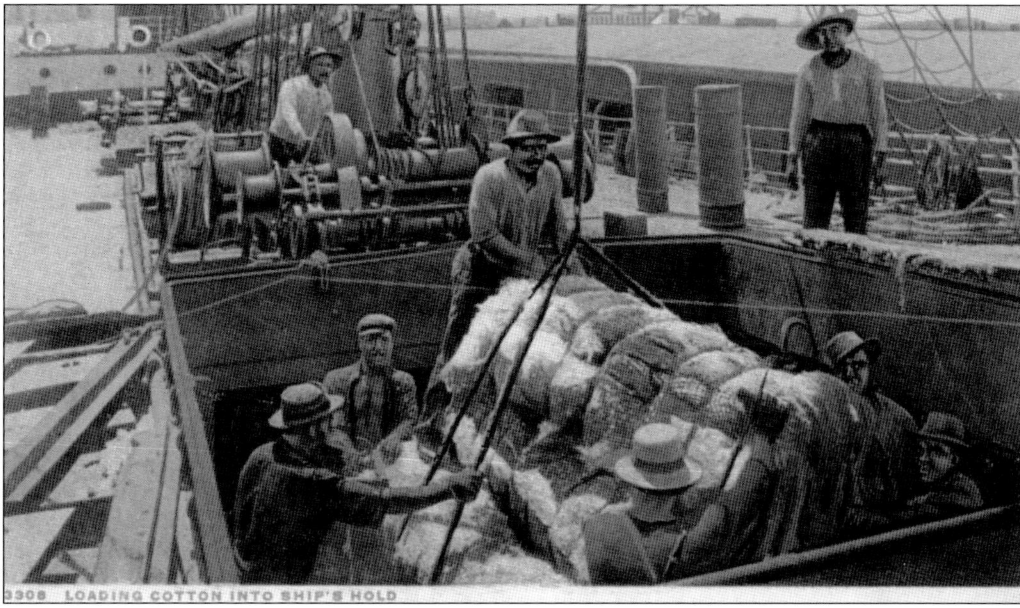

These men may have been among those who loaded the steamship *Californian* in September 1913. The ship took on some 9,300 bales of cotton. While in Charleston for the several days it took men like these to load her holes, she received more than her usual attention. While it was not her first visit to Charleston, it was her first visit since her encounter with the *Titanic* that fateful night in April 1912.

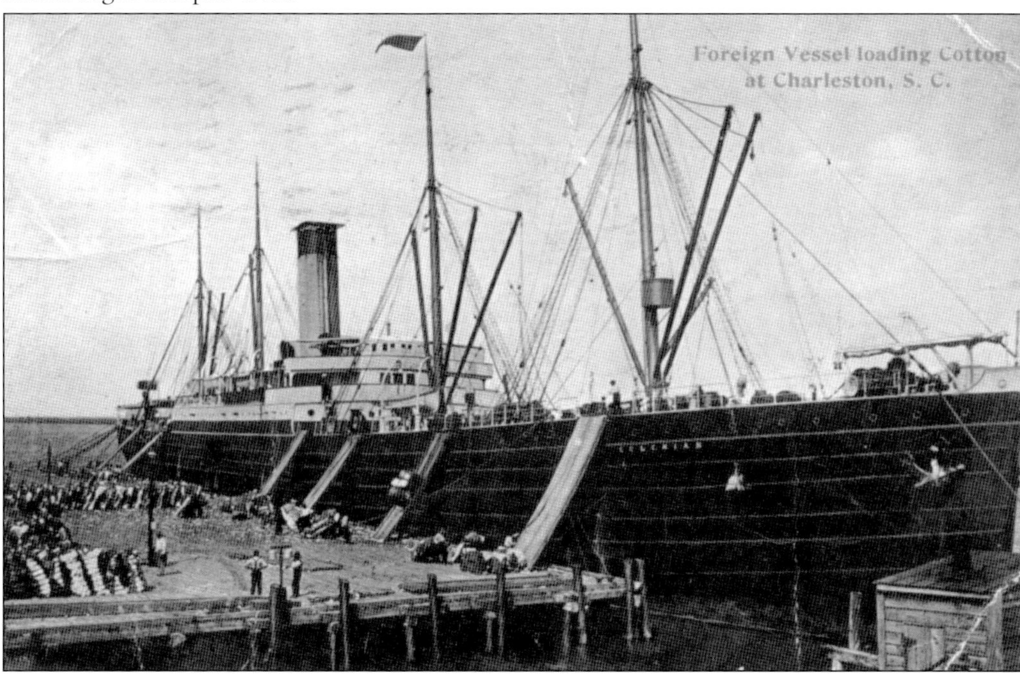

Shortly after the hurricane of 1911, it was reported in the *News and Courier* of September 12, 1911, that Freeman Owens, who had been in Charleston to film the city for advertising purposes, had been on the waterfront the day before and filmed a steamer, the *Washfield*, being loaded with thousands of bales of cotton. The scene must have looked much like this one.

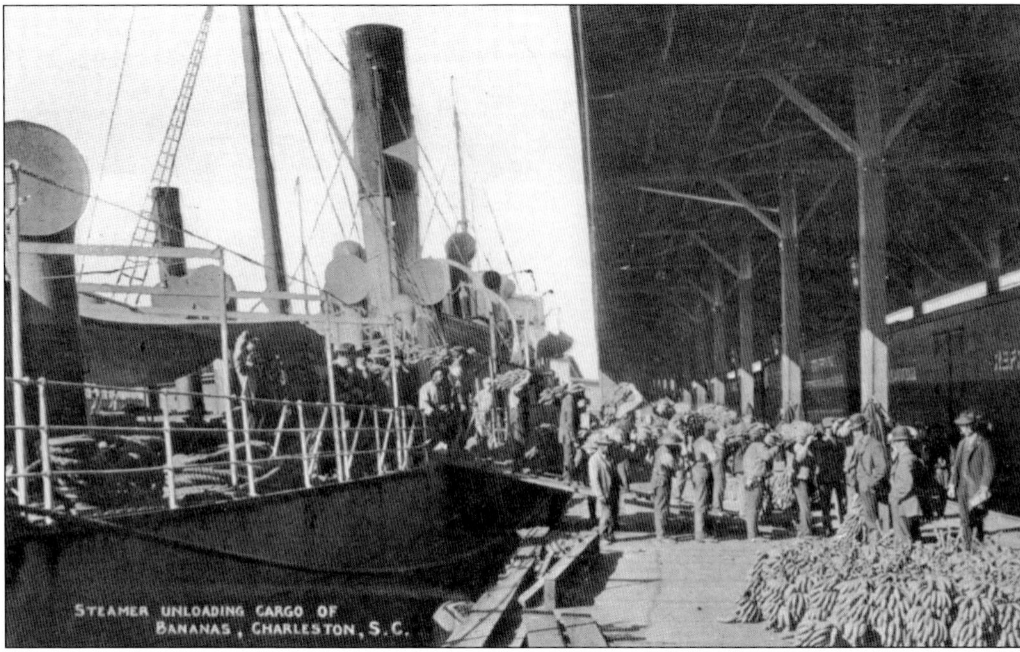

In 1908, the steamship *Lilly* docked in Charleston with some 18,000 bunches of bananas from Port Antonio, Jamaica, in her holes, to be unloaded and reloaded on waiting railway cars for quick distribution. The dock was filled with hundreds of men, both full-time and temporary workers, trying to expedite the process.

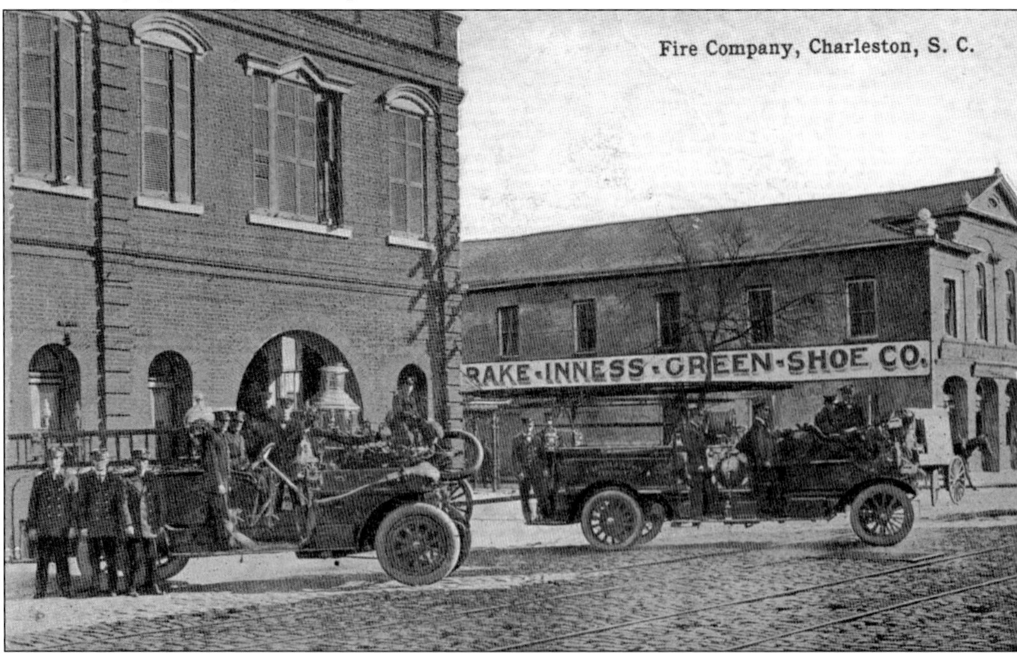

According to the September 20, 1910, *News and Courier*, Charleston's new $8,500 fire engine performed well during its test in the city. It had run through the unpaved streets of Charleston at 35 miles per hour, carrying 11 firemen and about 4,000 pounds of hoses and equipment. The new engine was assigned to Station No. 5, at Wentworth and Meeting Streets, pictured here.

The July 4, 1913, edition of the *News and Courier* explains the economics of vegetables, merchants, and hucksters. Early every morning, fresh island vegetables were brought into Charleston by boats docking at the wharf at the end of Tradd Street from about 5:00 a.m. There, if Charleston citizens were up and ready to shop, tomatoes could be bought for 50¢ a bushel, which is 32 quarts. The tomatoes are then retailed for between $2.50 and $4 a bushel, but the biggest profits came from selling them for between 10¢ to 12¢ a quart after purchasing them for about a 1.5¢ a quart. Profits for retail merchants or hucksters on tomatoes would, therefore, run from about 400 to 700 percent.

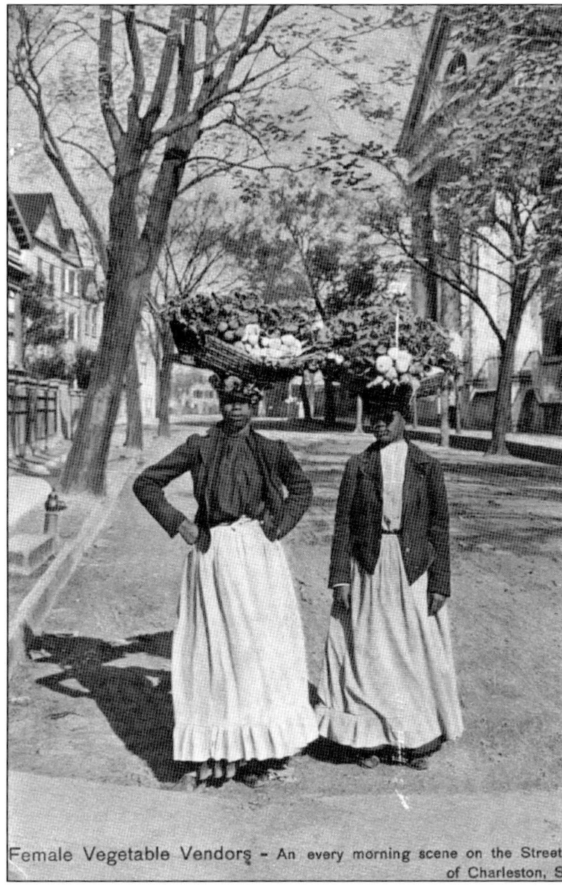

Female Vegetable Vendors - An every morning scene on the Streets of Charleston, S.

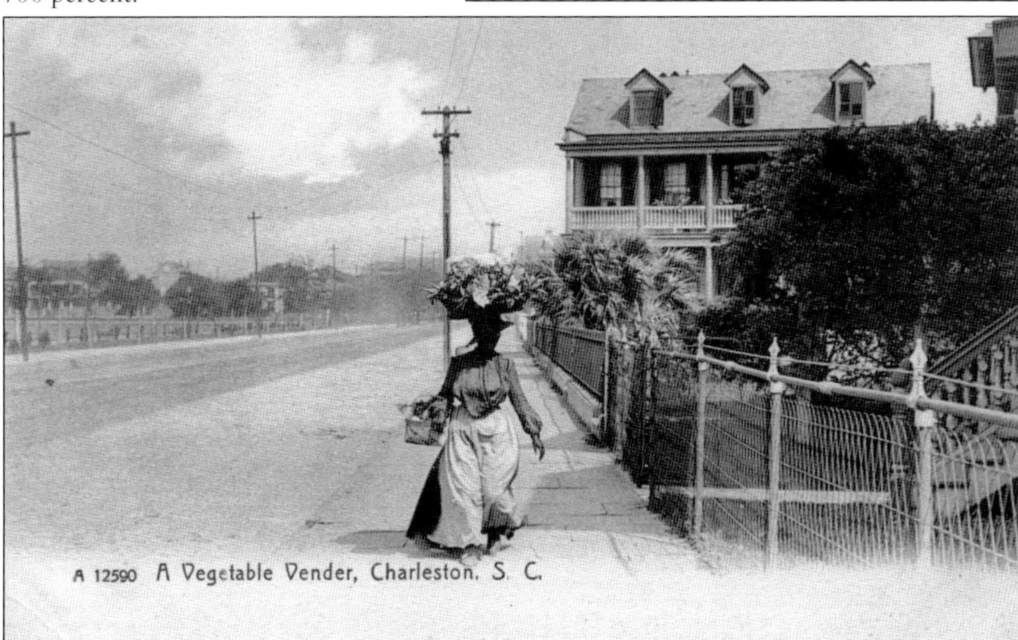

A 12590 A Vegetable Vender, Charleston. S. C.

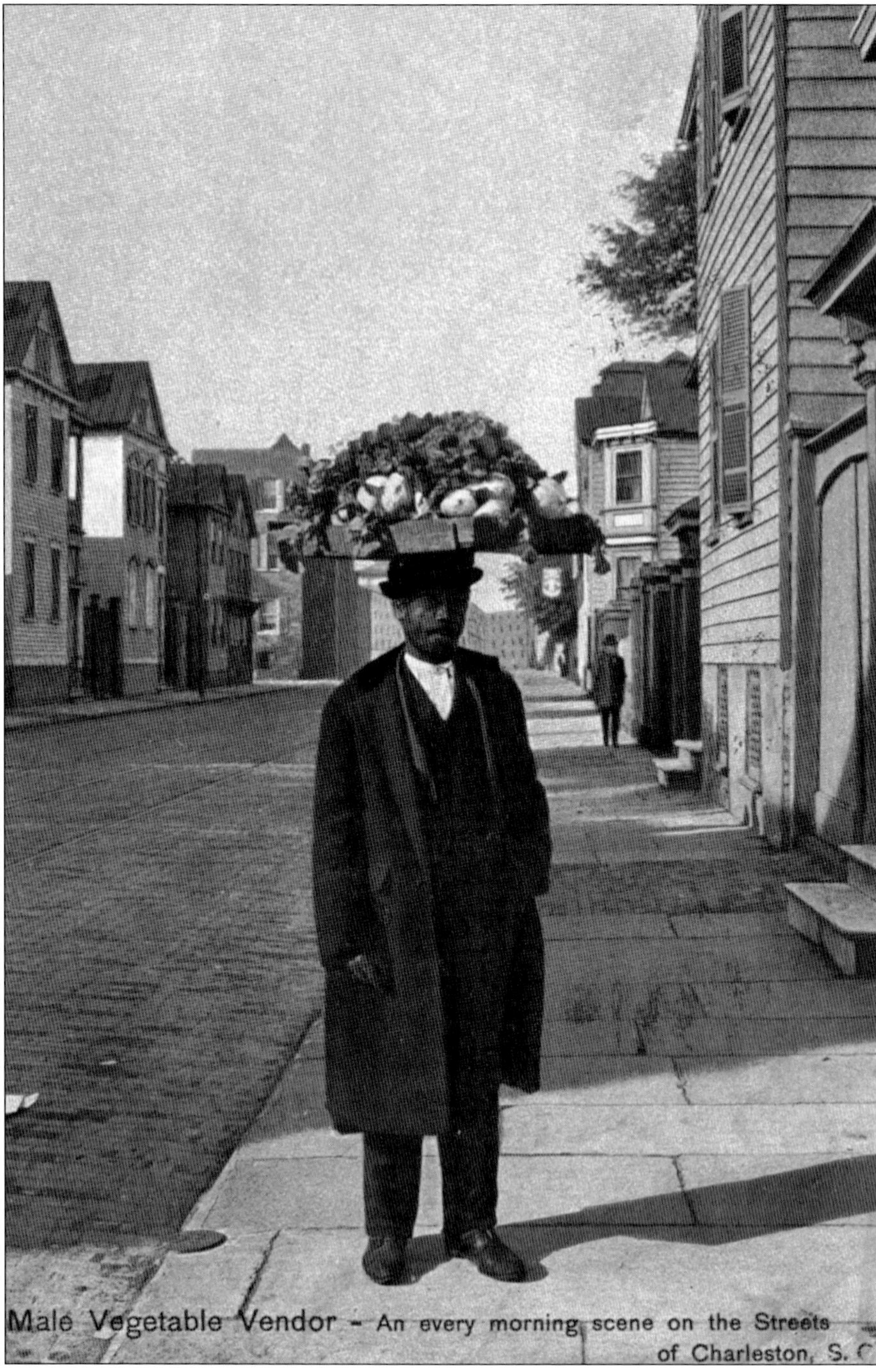

Street hucksters were required to be licensed, just like King Street merchants, to sell their wood, fruit, vegetables, shrimp, fish, or whatever and specifically governed by Section No. 742 of Charleston City Ordinances. Section No. 742 states that hucksters could not make their loud colorful cries for the sale of their goods before 6:00 a.m. or after 9:00 p.m. in the evening, except on Saturday nights. On Saturday night, they could continue to peddle their goods for an extra hour.

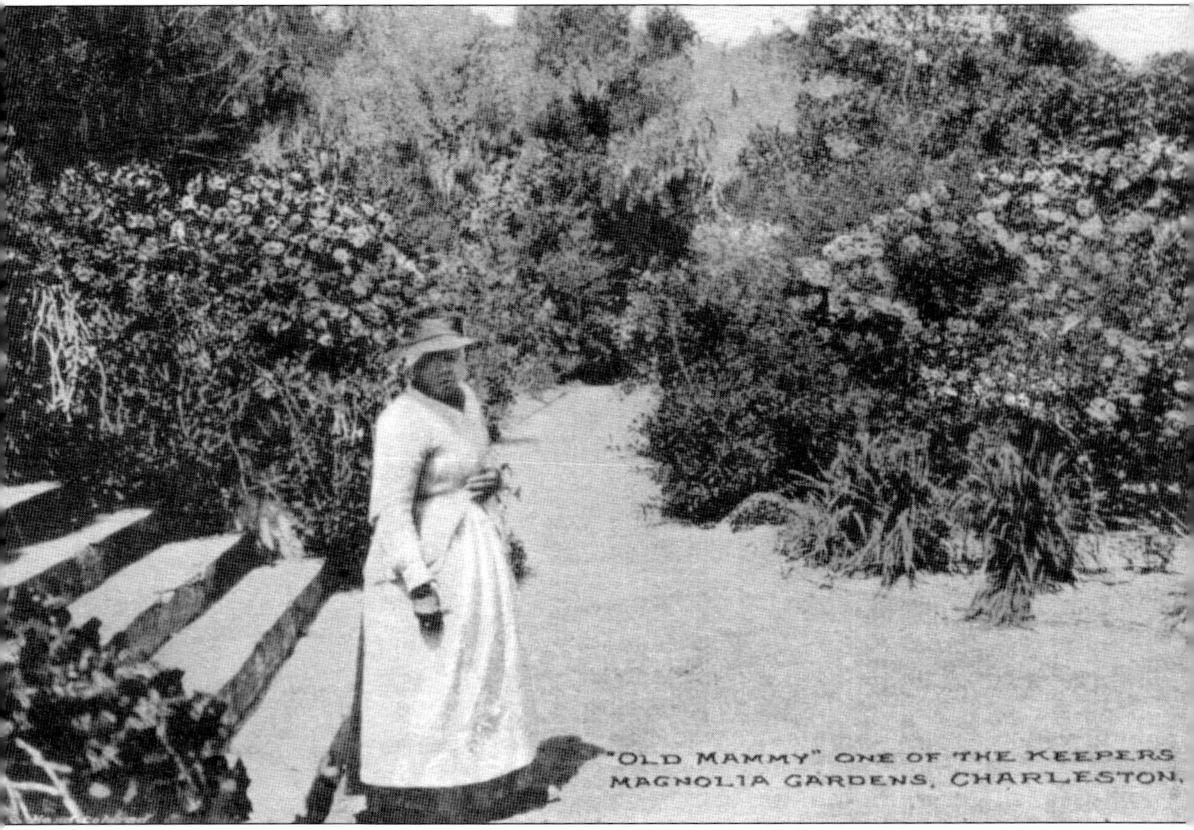

The maumas who worked Magnolia Gardens not only worked the house and its grounds, but when the boats from Charleston landed with tourists, they acted as tour guides and as the garden's protectors. They would both point out and name the types of flowers the visitors were seeing and make sure the guests did not disturb the gardens by taking samples with them for their own gardens.

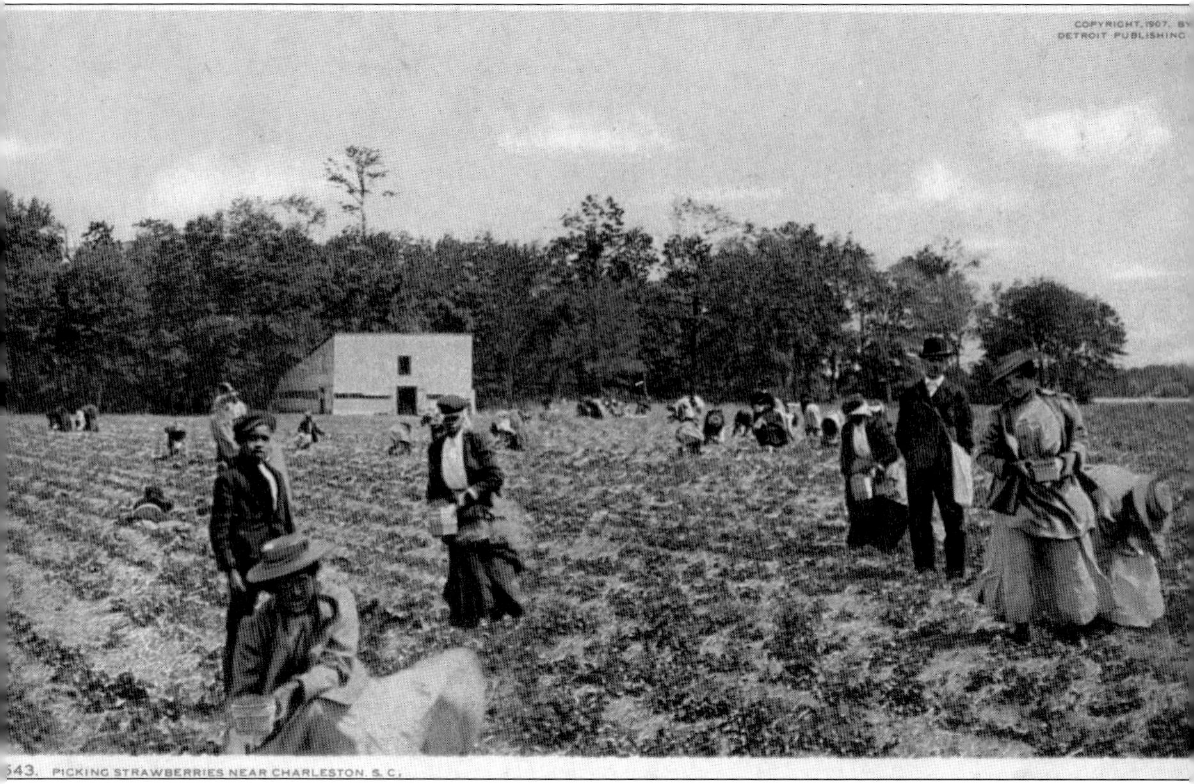

Growing strawberries could be profitable, according to an article that appears in the May 27, 1912, edition of the *News and Courier.* A farmer from Kershaw County said that with one-seventeenth of an acre, he had sold some $50 worth of strawberries in the past, and that at 10¢ a quart he had made a profit of some $140, after paying pickers $25, on a quarter of an acre of farmland. Compare this to a dock worker making 10¢ to 15¢ an hour loading cotton onto ships.

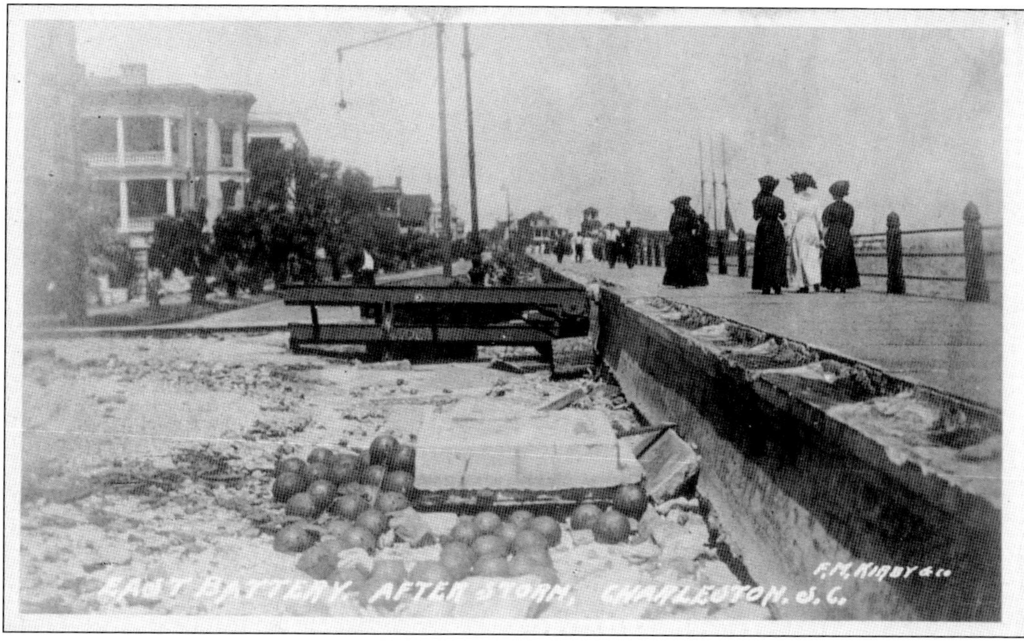

In 1903, Kodak introduced its No. 3A camera, which created postcard-sized images. These and similar subsequent cameras, coupled with Kodak's Velox photo paper, allowed amateurs to make their own real-photo postcards. As a result, would-be photojournalists could photograph subjects like post-hurricane Charleston, street scenes, or even informal portraits and have their best efforts printed as postcards to be mailed to concerned friends or distant relatives. While these did not fit the image of regular postcards sold in stores to visiting tourists, real-photo postcards became very popular in the early 1900s.

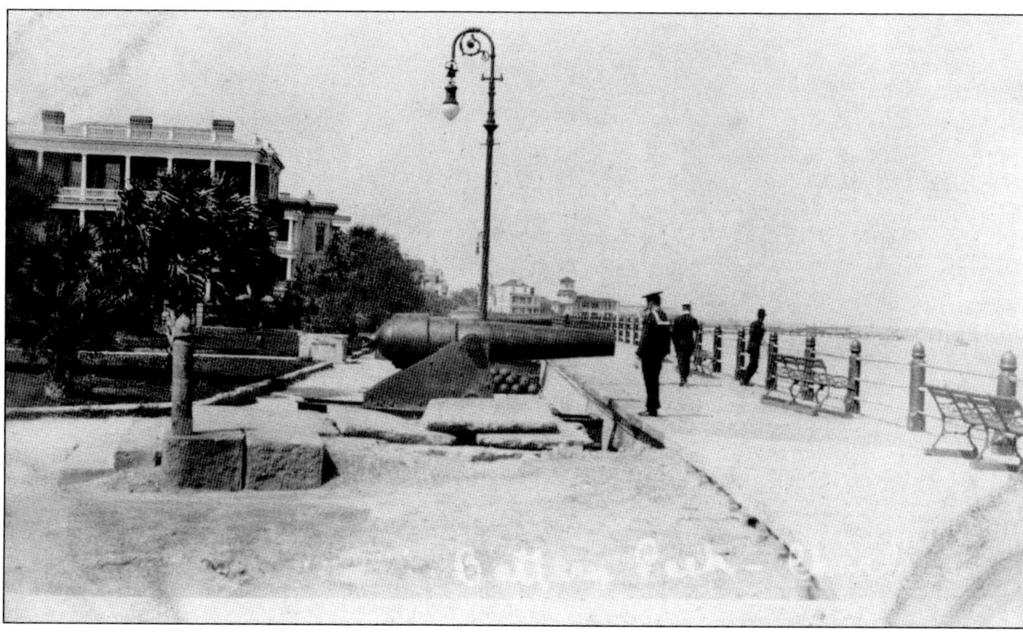

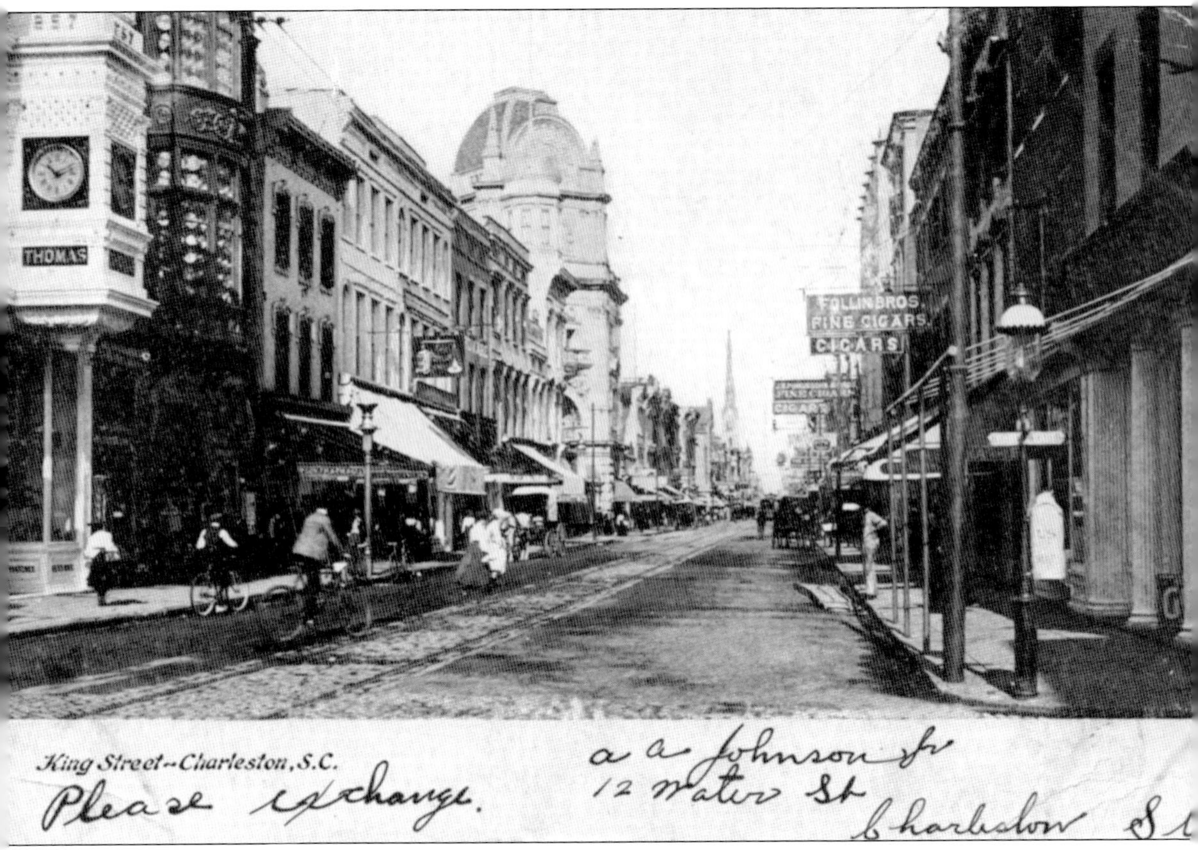

In this view looking down King Street, past the lady shoppers, the bicyclers, and the horse-drawn wagons and carriages is the domed Hirsh-Israel Company at 275 King Street, which, in 1906, offered boys school suits for $4 and quality men's suits from $16.50 to $35. Located on the corner of King and Wentwoth Streets, it was the scene of something more interesting than shopping on August 11, 1915. The *Evening Post* of the next afternoon reports the following about the event: "The crowd was so large on King street that traffic was congested for a block or more, and at the intersection with Wentwoth Street there was another closely packed assemblage. Satanet, the 'Virginia-dare-devil' started right from the street and climbed slowly upward, amid the attentive silence of the onlookers. Cheers from below greeted his accomplishment of the more stages of his trip. Satanet was arrayed in the color and cut of clothes alleged to be worn by satan and there were the usual horns growing out of the headpiece." Interestingly, in the same newspaper and on the same page as the story is a report that Carolina Carbonating Company has just acquired the exclusive rights to Satanet, "The Drink With a Wink," to be "sold at all soda founts and in bottles."

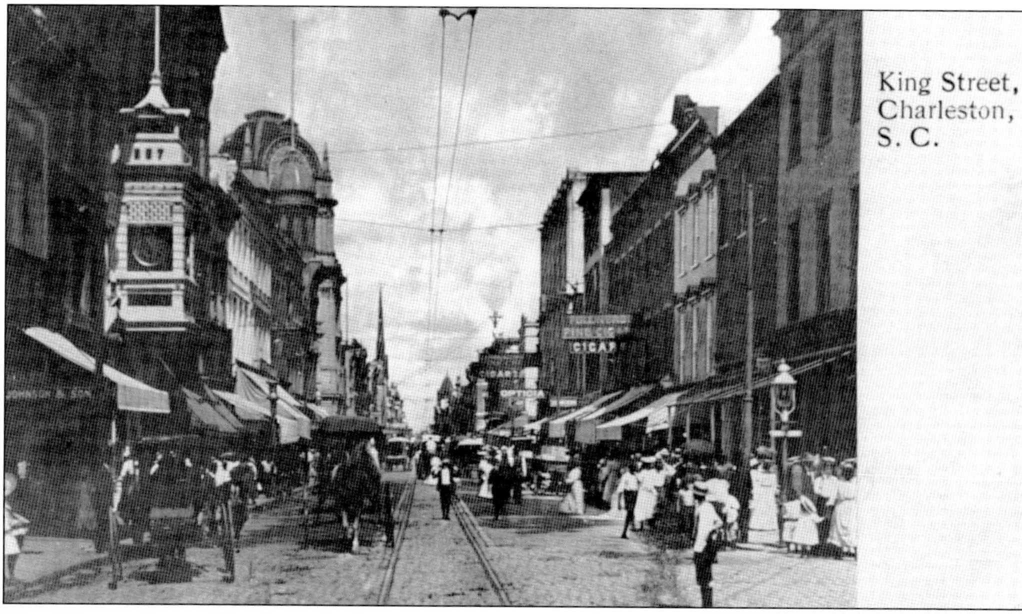

The Theatorium, Charleston's first moving-picture theater, opened at 321 King Street, near George Street, in early 1907. Admission was a nickel to see the films, which changed three times a week. One of the first moving pictures shown was titled *Arabian Nights*. At times, the theater used a professional singer and pianist to entertain during intermissions. On October 16, 1907, it was announced that the owners had sold the business, despite reportedly having some 3,100 patrons the previous Saturday, only to lease another building at 343 King Street, where they subsequently opened another theater they named the Majestic Theatre.

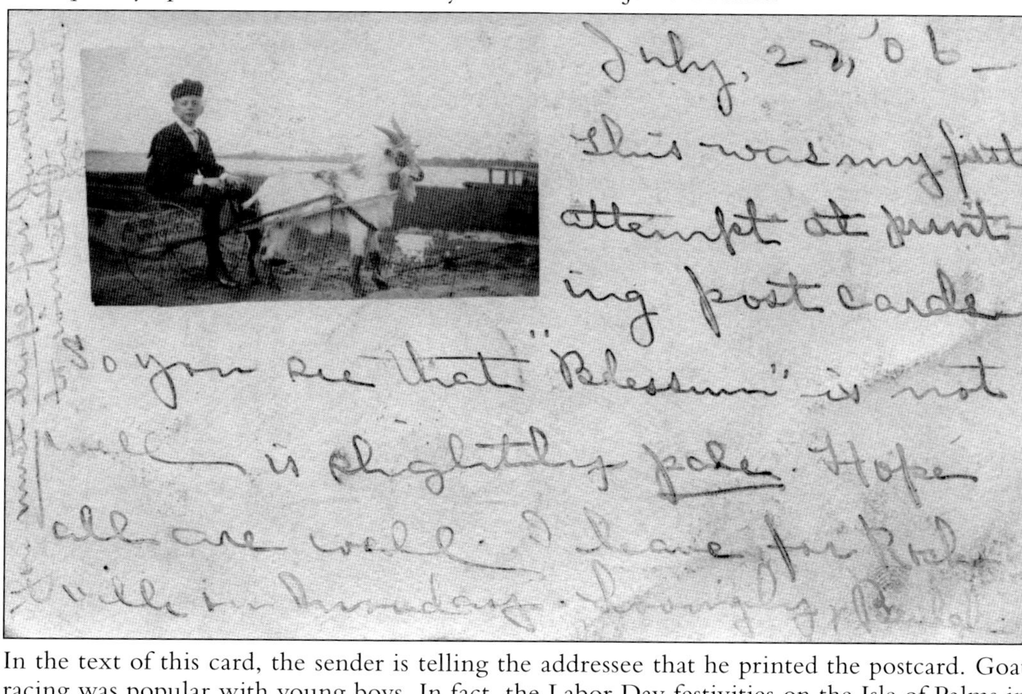

In the text of this card, the sender is telling the addressee that he printed the postcard. Goat racing was popular with young boys. In fact, the Labor Day festivities on the Isle of Palms in 1913 held goat-cart races that paid $5 and $2.50 in gold to the winners.

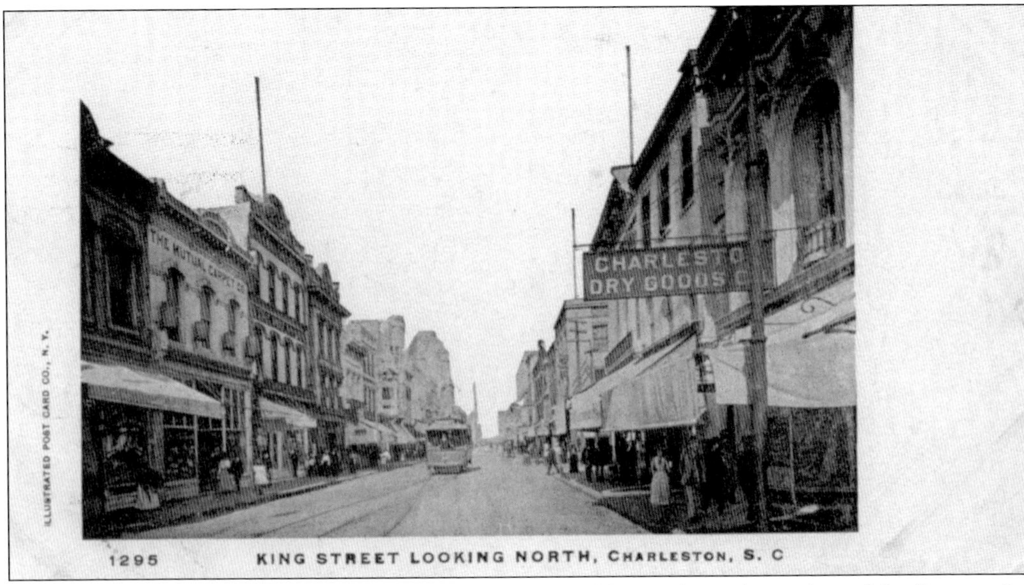

The June 26, 1897, *Evening Post* announces, "There will be no formal opening of the line to-day and the cars will run for a half hour today before passengers will be taken aboard . . . This will be the first time that the trolley has been run through the streets of the city proper and a large crowd will probably be out to see the cars run by. After a half hours test, if everything works smoothly, passengers will be taken aboard along the route regardless of street corner stations." By the time of this image, the trolley system had been in use for years.

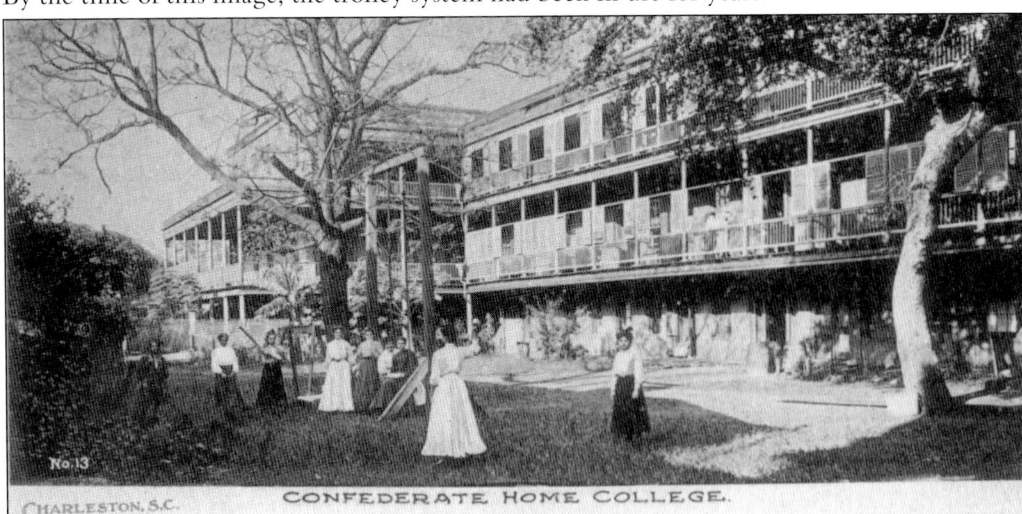

This building is located at 62 Broad Street. It has served as the home of the governor, a hotel, and a federal courthouse. But in 1867, the Snowden sisters Amarinthia and Isabella established the first home for Confederate mothers, widows, and orphans, which evolved into the Confederate Home and College for women, the only boarding school for women in Charleston. The *Meteor* of April 6, 1895, recalls that the Confederate Home was restored in 1887 after the earthquake of 1886 "by the people of the whole Union from the ruin. Its benefactors have been from many States whose sons were in deadly conflict with the sons of Carolina." The Confederate Home, as it is still called, sponsors college scholarships and affordable housing by hosting social events and operating as a popular wedding venue.

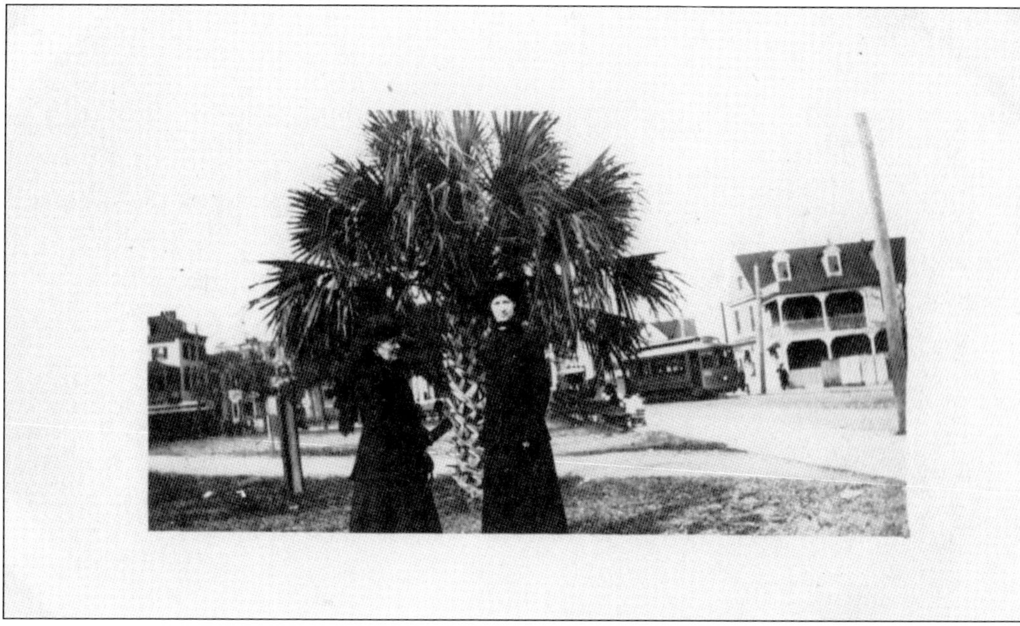

This is an example of a personal photograph taken and made into a postcard for mailing. This back of this portrait of two ladies in black is labeled "Charleston S.C. Xmas day, 1912." Note the trolley in the background.

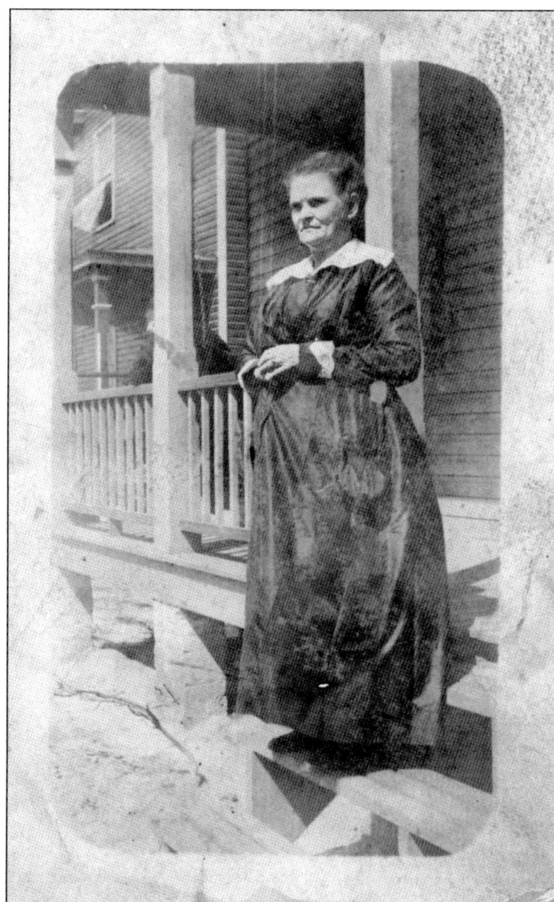

This lady appears to be standing on her front porch steps for what might have been a semiformal portrait or Easter Sunday photograph. The photograph was taken on Grove Street or in that area. Images like this one, printed as postcards, replaced cabinet card photographs in popularity, as people no longer had to depend on professional photographers for lasting images.

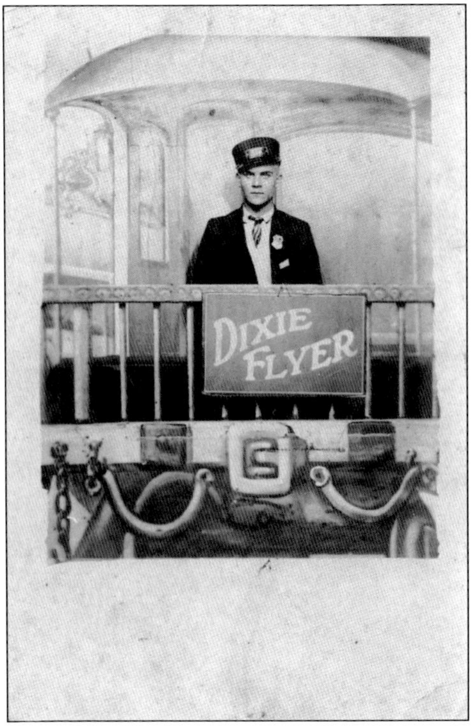

Interestingly, the Dixie Flyer was a train that began operating about 1892 and ran regular routes between Chicago and Florida, with no stops in South Carolina, but this card was likely shot and the postcard made either in Charleston or on the Isle of Palms. The man in the photograph may have been a real conductor on the Charleston trolley system or a local train.

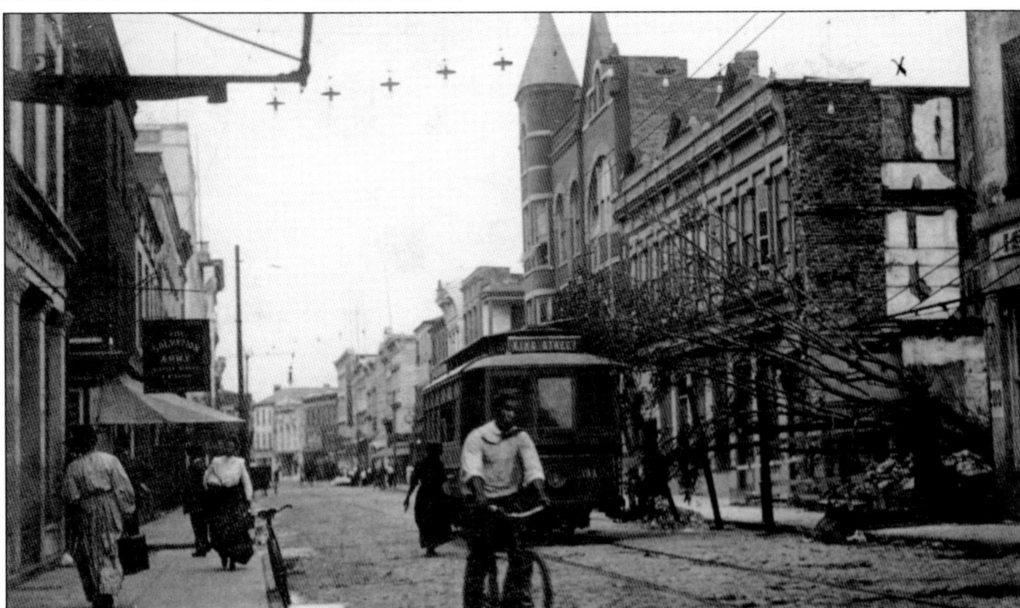

The August 29, 1911, *News and Courier* reports, "In Charleston the greatest of damage, of course, was done along the waterfront, but practically every house south of Calhoun Street testified to the fury of the gale. Along Broad Street, East Bay, King and Meeting streets scores of residences and places of business were unroofed and had the windows blown out. The rain, which fell heavily last night was in consequence most unwelcome, even though accompanied by but little wind. Hundreds of trees in all parts of the city were blown down or split to pieces."

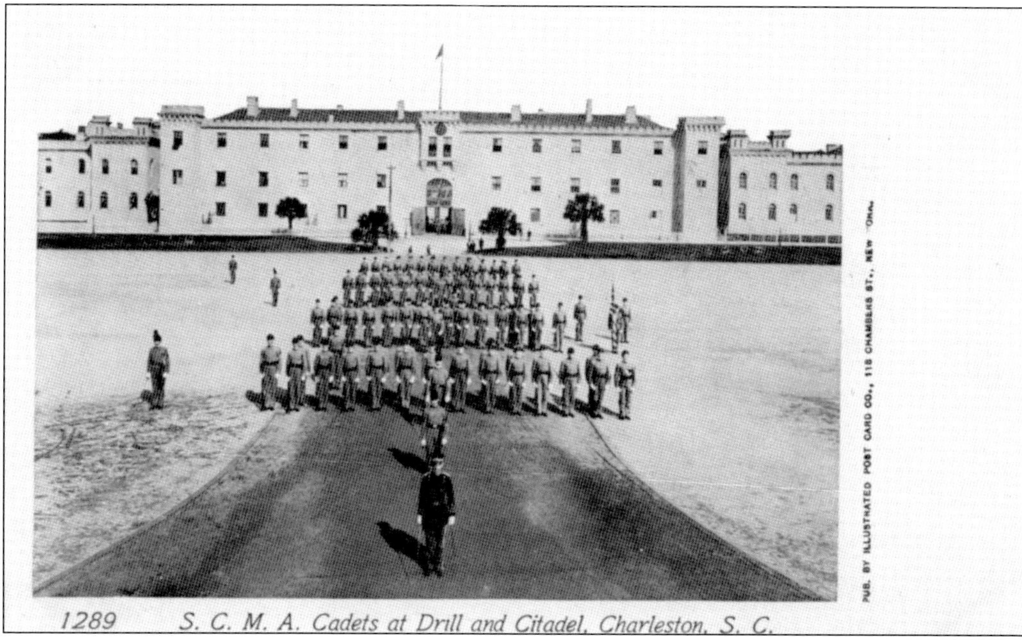

The South Carolina Military Academy began as an armory, facing Marion Square, in the early 1830s, in anticipation of coming resistance to the federal government. The armory became the state's military academy in 1842. Cadets from this armory-turned-school, similar to the ones pictured, were among those who fired the first shots of the Civil War in 1861.

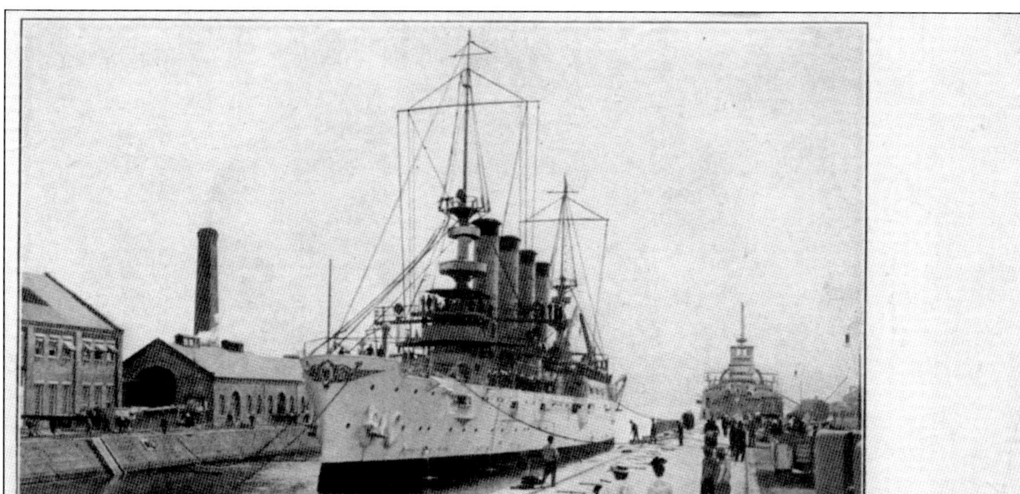

The *Evening Post* of January 13, 1906, announces that citizens of Charleston are welcomed to visit and tour the ship named for their city on Sunday, January 14, 1906, before she sets sail that afternoon to the bells of both St. Michael's and St. Philip's.